W9-AUO-610

ASSET ALLOCATION

THIRD EDITION

ASSET ALLOCATION

Balancing Financial Risk

ROGER C. GIBSON

McGraw-Hill

New York San Francisco Washington, D.C. Auckland Bogotá
Caracas Lisbon London Madrid Mexico City Milan
Montreal New Delhi San Juan Singapore
Sydney Tokyo Toronto

Library of Congress Cataloging-in-Publication Data

Gibson, Roger C.
    Asset allocation / by Roger C. Gibson—3rd ed.
        p.cm.
    ISBN 0-07-135724-6
    1. Portfolio management.   2. Asset allocation.   I. Title.
    HG4529.5.G53   1996
    332.6—dc21   00-029949

McGraw-Hill

A Division of The **McGraw·Hill** Companies

11 12 13 14 15 FGR/FGR 0 9 8 7 6

ISBN 0-07-135724-6

This book was set in New Century Schoolbook by McGraw-Hill's Professional Book Group composition unit, Hightstown, N.J.

Printed and bound by Quebecor/Martinsburg.

This publication is designed to provide accurate and authoritative information in regard to the subject matter covered. It is sold with the understanding that neither the author nor the publisher is engaged in rendering legal, accounting, investment, or other professional service. If legal advice or other expert assistance is required, the services of a competent professional person should be sought.

—From a Declaration of Principles jointly adopted by a committee of the American Bar Association and a Committee of Publishers

McGraw-Hill books are available at special quantity discounts to use as premiums and sales promotions, or for use in corporate training programs. For more information, please write to the Director of Special Sales, Professional Publishing, McGraw-Hill, Two Penn Plaza, New York, NY 10121-2298. Or contact your local bookstore.

 This book was printed on recycled, acid-free paper containing a minimum of 50% recycled, de-inked fiber.

This book is dedicated to
Sarah and Adam.
You are the best kids a dad ever had!

The royalties from this book will be donated to the Roger C. Gibson Family Foundation in memory of my father, Don B. Gibson, and in honor of my mother, Marianne A. Gibson. The Foundation grants financial assistance to various charities for the alleviation of human suffering and supports education and artistic endeavors.

CONTENTS

FOREWORD TO THE
FIRST EDITION

After 49 years of professional investment counseling world-wide, I believe that successful investing is mainly common sense. It is common sense to search for an asset where you can buy the greatest value for each dollar you pay. This means bargain hunting. For example, it is wise to compare a multitude of similar investments in order to select that one which can be bought for the lowest price in relation to other similar assets. If you buy a share of a company for a small fraction of its intrinsic value, then there is less risk of a major price decline and more opportunity for a major price increase.

To diversify your investments is clearly common sense so that those which produce more profits than expected will offset those which produce less. Even the best investment professional must expect that not more than two thirds of his decisions will prove to be above average in profits. Therefore, asset allocation and diversification are the foundation stones of successful long-term investing.

To diversify means that you do not put all of your assets in any one type of investment. Similarly, it is not wise to invest only in the shares of any one company, industry, or nation. If you search in all nations you are likely to find more good bargains and perhaps better bargains. Clearly you will reduce the risk because bear markets and business recessions occur at different times in different nations. Changing economic conditions also affect various types of investment assets differently. By diversifying among different types of assets, the value of your portfolio will not fluctuate as much.

To begin with modest assets and build a fortune obviously requires thrift. An investor seeking to become wealthy should adhere to an annual family expense budget that includes a large amount of savings. For example, during my first 15 years after college, I made a game of adhering to a budget that included saving 50 cents out of every dollar of earnings. Those who are thrifty will grow wealthy, and those who are spendthrifts will become poor.

Also, there is a magic formula called *dollar-cost averaging* in which you invest the same amount of money at regular intervals in an investment whose price fluctuates. At the end of the investment period, your average cost will be below the average price paid for the investment. In other words, your dollars will buy more shares when prices are low and fewer shares when prices are high, so that your average cost is low compared with the average for the market.

John D. Rockefeller said that to grow wealthy you must have your money work for you. In other words, be a lender and not a borrower. For example, If you have a big mortgage on your home, the interest paid will more than double the cost of the home. On the other hand, if you own a mortgage on a house, the annual interest on that mortgage will compound and make a fortune for you. If you never borrow money, interest will always work for you and not against you. You will also have peace of mind and be able to live through the bear markets and business recessions that occur in most nations about twice every 10 years.

It is only common sense to prepare for a bear market. Experts do not know when each bear market will begin, but you can be certain that there will be many bear markets during your lifetime. Commonsense investing means that you should prepare yourself both financially and psychologically. Financially you should be prepared to live through any bear market without having to sell at the wrong time. In fact, your financial planning should provide for additional investment funds so that you can buy when shares are unreasonably low in price. Preparing psychologically means to expect that there will be many bull markets and bear markets so that you will not sell at the wrong time or buy at the wrong time. To buy low and sell high is difficult for persons who are not psychologically prepared or who act on emotions rather than facts.

When my investment counsel company began in 1940, on the front page of our descriptive booklet were these words: "To buy when others are despondently selling and to sell when others are avidly buying requires the greatest fortitude and pays the greatest reward."

Probably no investment fact is more difficult to learn than the fact that the price of shares is never low except when most people are selling and never high except when most are buying. This makes investing totally different from other professions. For example, if you go to 10 doctors all of whom agree on the proper medicine, then clearly you should take that medicine. But if you go to 10 security analysts all of whom agree that you should buy a particular share or type of asset then quite clearly you must do the opposite. The reason is that if 100 percent are buying and then even one changes his mind and begins selling, then already you will have passed the peak price. Common sense is not common; but common sense and careful logic show that it is impossible to produce superior investment performance if you buy the same assets at the same time as others are buying.

When selecting shares for purchase there are many dozens of yardsticks for judging value. A most reliable yardstick is how high is the price in relation to earnings. However, it is even more important to ask how high is the price in relation to probable earnings 5 to 10 years in the future. A share is nothing more than a right to receive a share of future earnings. Growth in earnings usually results from superior management. Even the best professionals have great difficulty in judging the ability of management. For the part-time investor, the best way is to ask three questions. Is this company growing more rapidly than its competitors? Is the profit margin wider than its competitors? Are the annual earnings on invested assets larger than for competitors? These three simple indicators will tell you much about the ability of management.

History shows frequent and wide fluctuations in the prices of many types of assets. Proper asset allocation helps to dampen the impact that these price swings will have on your portfolio. Asset price fluctuations many be even greater and more frequent in the future because all human activity is speeding up. This is one reason why you should not select a professional advisor based on short-term performance. For example, an advisor who takes the most risk is likely to have top performance in a bull market and the opposite in a bear market. Individual investors as well as managers of pension funds and university endowments should judge the ability of investment advisors over at least one full market cycle and preferably several cycles. This helps to balance out the element of luck and reveal which advisor has received the blessing of common sense.

I hope that almost every adult will become an investor. When I became an investment counselor there were only 4 million shareholders in America, and now there are 48 million. The amount of money invested in American mutual funds is now 1000 times as great as it was 55 years ago. Thrift, common sense, and wise asset allocation can produce excellent results in the long run. For example, if you begin at age 25 to invest $2000 annually into your Individual Retirement Account where it can compound free of tax, and if you average a total return of 10 percent annually, you will have nearly a million dollars accumulated at age 65.

Investment management requires the broad consideration of all major investment alternatives. In this book, Roger Gibson develops the principles of asset allocation which make for good common sense investing in a rapidly changing world. In easily understood terms, he guides investment advisors and their clients step-by-step through a logical process for making the important asset allocation decisions. The broadly diversified investment approach Roger Gibson advocates should give investment advisors and their clients good investment results with increased peace of mind.

John M. Templeton
Chairman of the Templeton Foundations
April 11, 1989

ACKNOWLEDGMENTS

First, I want to express my appreciation to my editors, Catherine Schwent and Jane Palmieri, and to the staff of McGraw-Hill. Although this third edition took longer to complete than anticipated, their patience and encouragement kept the project moving to a successful conclusion.

A book such as this is impossible without the assistance of many companies who graciously provided research support and capital market performance data. Accordingly, I would like to thank Brinson Partners, Inc.; Goldman, Sachs & Co.; Ibbotson Associates; Morgan Stanley & Co., Inc.; National Association of Real Estate Investment Trusts, Inc.; Salomon Smith Barney; Standard & Poor's; Trinity Investment Management Corporation; and Vestek Systems, Inc.

I am very grateful to Darwin M. Bayston, Past President and Chief Executive Officer of the Association for Investment Management Research, who critiqued the draft of the first edition and made many helpful suggestions for improving the text. He also paved the way for the translation of the book into Japanese. I would also like to thank Nobel laureate Harry M. Markowitz, known as the "father of modern portfolio theory," for his kind endorsement of the third edition. His pioneering work is the foundation for the ideas discussed in this book.

I would like to thank the staff at Gibson Capital Management and the Center for Fiduciary Studies: Brenda Berczik, Keith R. Goldner, Mona Higgins, Debra Regec, and Michael Reinert. They always pitch in when I need help and continually rise to the challenge of coordinating the work of multiple businesses. Keith and Mike were particularly helpful in performing the computer and statistical work that produced many of the charts and graphs throughout the book that summarize investment performance relationships. Mona coordinated the logistical issues with McGraw-Hill and data providers as well as assisted in word processing and exhibit layout. My fiancé and partner, Brenda, made many helpful editorial suggestions that improved the readability of the manuscript and created the formats for many of the book's exhibits. My daughter Sarah, a creative writing major at John Hopkins University, gave the chapter proofs their final examination for accuracy. Thanks, Sarah. I also would like to thank my partner, Donald B. Trone, Co-Director of the Center for Fiduciary Studies, for his work in developing the sample Investment Policy Statement used in the book.

I wish to acknowledge several others who helped with the first and second editions of the book: Don "Spike" Phillips, Gary P. Brinson, Robert A. Levy, Ronald W. Kaiser, Amy Ost, Amy Gaber, Laraine Schmitt, Connie McKee, Philip M. Gallagher, Deborah J. Stahl, Michael D. Hirsch, A. Gregory Lintner, and Mary K. Ellison.

This is a book of concepts. Some are original, but many are borrowed. If you are intrigued by a certain idea, you may want to know the source. Where possible, I have acknowledged the author. Unfortunately, much of my material no longer has an identifiable origin. Thus, I ask forgiveness from those who have shaped my thinking but who are not directly given credit. I also want to deliver from possible blame those whose ideas I have borrowed and altered based on my own research and experience.

I especially want to thank Sir John M. Templeton, Chairman of the Templeton Foundations, which endeavor to build spiritual wealth for the world. Mr. Templeton has been an inspiration to me both spiritually and professionally. I am very honored that a person who produced one of the world's best long-term investment track records wrote the Foreword to this book. Such investment genius is exceedingly rare.

My thanks to the many investment and financial professionals from across the country who have attended the courses offered at the Center for Fiduciary Studies and the presentations on asset allocation and modern portfolio theory that I have been privileged to make at numerous conferences. The quality of dialogue at these lectures has been of great value in refining the ideas in this book.

Finally, I would like to acknowledge and thank all of my clients, present and future, who make my profession as an investment advisor a challenging and rewarding experience.

Roger C. Gibson, CFA, CFP

Introduction

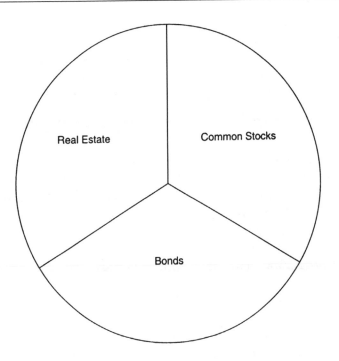

Let every man divide his money into three parts, and invest a
third in land, a third in business, and a third let him keep in
reserve.

—Talmud
Circa 1200 B.C.–500 A.D.

Asset allocation is not a new idea. The Talmud quote above is
approximately 2000 years old. Whoever said it knew something
about risk. He also knew something about return. He may have
been the world's first proponent of asset allocation. Today we
talk about asset allocation rather than diversification, but it is
really just a new name for a very old and time-tested investment strategy. A more contemporary translation of the advice
might read: "Let every investor create a diversified portfolio

that allocates one third to real estate investments, one third to common stocks, with the remaining one third allocated to cash equivalents and bonds."

Is it still good advice today? Let's examine the recommendation in more detail. The overall portfolio balance is one-third fixed-income investments and two-thirds equity investments. The one-third allocated to fixed-income investments mitigates the volatility risk inherent in the two-thirds allocated to equity investments. Diversification across two major forms of equity investing with dissimilar patterns of returns further reduces the equity risk. The result is a balanced portfolio that is tilted toward equities, appropriate for an investor with a longer investment time horizon who is simultaneously concerned about both risk and return. It is a remarkably elegant and powerful asset allocation strategy. Imagine trying to develop a one-sentence investment strategy, knowing that a wide variety of investors, most of whom are not yet born, will follow the advice for the next 2000 years! You would be hard-pressed to come up with something better.

The unknown author of the Talmud quote could not possibly have envisioned today's investment world. Over the past decade, democracies and free enterprise systems have replaced many of the world's dictatorships and centrally directed economies. New capital markets are forming, and investment alternatives have proliferated. People from around the world can exchange volumes of information instantaneously via the Internet, virtually without cost. The world has truly gotten smaller and increasingly interconnected as economic events in one part of the world impact markets on the other side of the globe.

In spite of all of this change, investors are not that different today from the way they were a hundred years ago. They want high returns, and they do not want to incur risk in securing those returns. Unfortunately, when it comes to investments, everyone has an opinion and misconceptions abound. These misconceptions are most prevalent and dangerous in the area of asset allocation decision making. For example, an investor may inappropriately reject a major investment asset class, perhaps bonds or common stocks, even though that asset class may play an important role in developing the best strategy to reach his or her objectives. It is not surprising, therefore, that many investors have portfolio structures that accurately reflect their comfort levels and investment preferences yet are not the best asset allocations for realizing their financial goals. In these situations it is not enough for an investment advisor to clearly evaluate a client's circumstances and develop an appropriate strategy if the client does not have the conceptual knowledge and frame of reference to understand that the recommendations are in his or her best interest.

Often an advisor and a client agree to sidestep the problem by having the client abandon all aspects of the investment management process to the investment advisor's discretion. In essence, the client says to the investment advisor: "Investment management is your job, not mine. That's why I hired you. I trust you. Just tell me this time next year how we're doing." While trust is essential in a client-advisor relationship, it is generally not sufficient to carry the client through extreme market conditions, when emotions are most likely to override reason.

The good news is that the problem has a solution. It involves educating the investor regarding capital market behavior and the principles of investment portfolio management. With the proper frame of reference, an informed investor can confidently develop an appropriate asset allocation strategy with the guidance of his or her investment advisor. Over time, the asset allocation decisions will be the primary determinant of a portfolio's volatility/return characteristics. It is therefore essential that the investor be actively involved.

This book presents a disciplined framework within which investment professionals and their clients can make the most important decisions impacting portfolio performance. A major theme is that successful money management requires successful management of the investor's expectations. At the outset, it is acknowledged that for this decision-making framework to be successful in practice it must:

- Be conceptually sound.

- Be comprehensible to investors without requiring an inordinate time commitment on their part.

- Facilitate the development of appropriate individually tailored solutions based on the investor's unique needs and circumstances.
- Be standardized with respect to the steps to be followed.
- Continue to have relevance and effectiveness in the future throughout changes in investment markets.

I will draw on and explore the concepts of modern portfolio theory for the purpose of enhancing the conceptual understanding of the subject matter, but my emphasis will be on the practical implications of these theories. As the gap between theory and practice narrows, the money management process becomes more effective. It is my hope that this book will contribute to the design of better portfolios for investors and that those investors will have the confidence to remain committed to the path that moves them toward the realization of their financial goals.

CHAPTER 1

The Importance
of Asset Allocation

Not only is there but one way of *doing* things rightly, there is but one way of *seeing* them, and that is seeing the whole of them.

—John Ruskin (1819–1900)
The Two Paths, 1885

The capital markets have changed dramatically over the last few decades. Money management has undergone a concurrent evolution. In the early 1960s the term *asset allocation* did not exist. The traditional view of diversification was simply to "avoid putting all of your eggs in one basket." The argument was that if all of your money was placed in one investment, your range of possible outcomes was very wide—you might win very big, but you also had the possibility of losing very big. Alternatively, if you spread your money among a number of different investments, the likelihood was that you would not be either right on all of them or wrong on all of them at the same time. There was an advantage, therefore, in having a narrower range of outcomes.

For the individual investor those were the days when broad diversification meant owning several dozen stocks and bonds along with some cash equivalents. For pension plans and other institutional portfolios, the same asset classes were often used in a balanced fund with a single manager. Because the U.S. stock and bond markets constituted the major portion of the world capital markets, most investors did not even consider international investing. Bonds traded in a very narrow price range. Security analysis focused more on common stocks, where the payoff seemed greatest for superior investment skill. The majority of transactions on capital market exchanges were non-institutional, and so it was commonly believed that a full-time, skilled professional should be able to consistently "beat the market." The investment manager's job was to add value through successful market timing and/or superior security selection. The focus was much more on individual securities than on the total portfolio. The "prudent man rule," with its emphasis on individual assets, reinforced this type of thinking in the fiduciary community.

Time passed, and bonds moved out of their narrow trading ranges as price volatility increased dramatically due to large swings in interest rates. Multiple managers on both the fixed-income and equity portions of institutional portfolios replaced the single balanced manager approach. Institutional trading on the exchanges increased to more than 80 percent of all activity. The full-time professionals were no longer competing against amateurs. They were now competing against each other.

Imagine for a moment the floor of the New York Stock Exchange. Millions of transactions are occurring between willing buyers and sellers. Around any single transaction, the buyer has concluded that the security is worth more than the money, while the seller has concluded that the money is worth more than the security. Both parties to the transactions are likely to be institutions that have nearly instantaneous access to all publicly available relevant information concerning the value of the security. Each has very talented, well-educated investment analysts who have carefully evaluated this information and have interestingly reached opposite conclusions. At the moment of the trade, both parties are acting from a position of informed conviction, even though time will prove one of them right and the other one wrong. Because of the dynamics of a free market, their transaction price equates supply with demand for the security and thereby clears the market. A free market price is therefore a consensus of a security's intrinsic value.

In the money management business, the stakes are high and the rewards are correspondingly great for successful money managers who are able to produce a consistently superior return. It is no wonder that so many bright, talented people are drawn to the profession. In such a marketplace, however, it is difficult to imagine that the market price for any widely followed security will depart meaningfully from its true underlying value. Such is the nature of an efficient market.

In both the money management and the academic communities there has been much ongoing controversy regarding the degree of efficiency of the capital markets. The debate has far-reaching implications. To the extent that a market is inefficient, opportunities exist for individuals to exercise superior skill to produce an above-average return. There do seem to be various "market anomalies" which indicate that the capital markets are not perfectly efficient. Most research evidence, however, supports the notion that these markets are reasonably efficient. The accelerating advances being made in information processing technologies will undoubtedly drive the markets to become even more efficient in the future. It thus will become increasingly unlikely that anyone will be able to consistently beat the market.

The tremendous growth in the use of index funds serves as tangible evidence that the issue is not of only academic curiosity. In an efficient capital market, the expectation is that active management, with its associated transaction costs, will result in below-average performance over time. If that is true, one way to win the game is never to play it at all. Those who have invested in index funds have chosen not to play the security selection game. It is ironic (yet logical) that the same high-powered money management talent that creates the efficiency of the marketplace makes the achievement of an above-average return so exceedingly difficult. Even in those rare situations where a money management organization has a unique proprietary insight that enables it to produce a superior result, the expectation is that the advantage will be eroded over time as other money management organizations discover and exploit the process.

In 1952, Harry M. Markowitz published an article entitled "Portfolio Selection."[1] In this article, he developed the first math-

---

1. Harry M. Markowitz, "Portfolio Selection," *Journal of Finance,* vol. 7, no. 1 (March 1952).

ematical model that specified the volatility reduction that occurs in a portfolio as a result of combining investments with different patterns of return. The amazing thing about his accomplishment is that he developed his thesis nearly a half century ago, long before the advent of the modern computer. His influence on the world of modern finance and investment management has been so profound that he became known as the "father of modern portfolio theory" and was awarded the Nobel Prize for Economics in 1990.

Before modern portfolio theory, investment management was a two-dimensional process focusing primarily on the volatility and return characteristics of individual securities. As a result of Harry Markowitz's work, recognition grew regarding the importance of the interrelationships among securities within portfolios. Modern portfolio theory added a third dimension to portfolio management that evaluates a security's *diversification effect* on a portfolio. This term refers to the impact that the inclusion of a particular asset class or security will have on the volatility and return characteristics of the overall portfolio.

Modern portfolio theory thus shifted the focus of attention away from individual securities and toward a consideration of the portfolio as a whole. The notion of diversification had to be simultaneously reconsidered. Optimal diversification goes beyond the idea of simply using a number of baskets in which to carry one's eggs. Major emphasis must also be placed on finding baskets that are distinctly different from one another. That is important because each basket's unique pattern of returns partially offsets the others, with the effect of smoothing overall portfolio volatility.

In an efficient capital market, security prices are always fair. Given this, modern portfolio theory stresses that it is wise to invest in a broad array of diverse investments. These concepts were later given legislative endorsement in the Employee Retirement Income Security Act of 1974, which stressed the importance of diversification within a broad portfolio context. More recently, the basic rule governing the investment of trust assets, known as the prudent investor rule, has been restated to "focus on the trust's portfolio as a whole and the investment strategy on which it is based rather than viewing a specific investment in isolation."[2]

---

2. *Restatement of the Law / Trusts / Prudent Investor Rule* (St. Paul, MN: American Law Institute Publishers, 1992), p. ix.

The investment world of today is indeed very different from that of the past. The number and variety of investment alternatives have increased dramatically, and the once well-defined boundaries between asset classes often overlap one another. We now deal in a global marketplace. Figure 1–1 shows that the non-U.S. capital markets are as large, and therefore as important, as the U.S. capital markets. Computer technology delivers relevant new information regarding a multitude of investment alternatives almost instantaneously to a marketplace now dominated by institutional investors. The traditionally diversified domestic stock and bond portfolio will become increasingly inadequate in the investment world of the future.

Designing an investment portfolio consists of several steps:

1. Deciding which asset classes will be represented in the portfolio.

2. Determining the long-term "target" percentage of the portfolio to allocate to each of these asset classes.

3. Specifying for each asset class the range within which the allocation can be altered in an attempt to exploit

FIGURE 1-1

Total Investable Capital Market
December 31, 1998 (Preliminary)

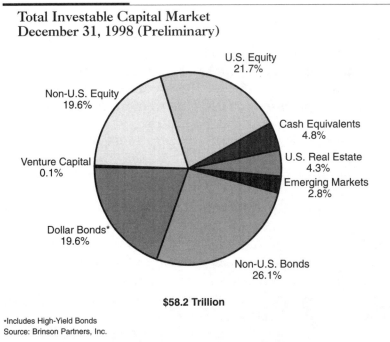

$58.2 Trillion

*Includes High-Yield Bonds
Source: Brinson Partners, Inc.

better performance possibilities from one asset class versus another.

4. Selection of securities within each of the asset classes.

The first two steps form the foundation for the portfolio's volatility/return characteristics and are often referred to as *investment policy decisions.* Traditionally, a diversified portfolio was built with three asset classes: cash equivalents, bonds, and stocks. Other asset classes, however, should be explicitly considered. Among them, for example, are international bonds, international stocks, real estate, and commodities. To the extent to which these various asset classes are affected differently by changing economic events, each will have its own unique pattern of returns. It is the ability of one asset class's pattern of returns to partially offset another asset class's pattern that drives the power of diversification in reducing portfolio volatility. When considering which asset classes to include in the portfolio, one should begin with the position that all major asset classes will be represented unless specific, sound reasons can be established for the exclusion of a particular class or classes.

A variety of methods can be used to determine the target weights assigned to each of the various asset classes. Modern portfolio theory suggests that in an efficient market, an investor with average volatility tolerance should hold a portfolio that mirrors the proportions in which the world's wealth is allocated among the various asset classes. This would give an asset allocation similar to that shown in Figure 1–1.

In practice, however, investors vary considerably in their unique needs and circumstances. Thus, the use of one target allocation for all investors is an example of "cutting the person to fit the cloth." The investor's investment objectives, relevant time horizon, and volatility tolerance combine to determine whether his or her portfolio should be structured for greater principal stability with correspondingly lower returns or, alternatively, for higher growth at the price of more volatility. In either case, the goal is to use the best allocation across the various asset classes in order to achieve the highest expected return relative to the volatility assumed.

For step 3, minimum and maximum limits are often set for each asset class's portfolio commitment. If, for example, stocks are judged to be unusually attractive relative to other asset classes, the proportion of stocks is moved to its upper limit. At other times, when stocks appear to be overvalued, the commitment is moved down to its minimum allocation. This represents the "market timing" dimension of the investment management process. The success of market timing activities presumes the existence of inefficiencies in the pricing mechanism among asset classes, coupled with the superior skill needed to identify and act on that mispricing. In its most extreme form, market timing takes the form of allocating 100 percent of the portfolio to either cash equivalents or stocks in an attempt to participate fully in common stock bull markets while resting safely in cash equivalents during bear markets. The obvious danger of such an approach lies in being in the wrong place at the wrong time with 100 percent of one's capital. The minimum and maximum limits set for each asset class in step 3 act to minimize this risk by requiring that the portfolio avoid extreme allocations.

Various strategies are used to attempt to identify and exploit asset class mispricing. Technical analysis, for example, attempts to predict future price movements on the basis of the patterns of past price movements and the volume of security transactions. The overwhelming body of research evidence indicates that such approaches do not beat a naive "buy and hold" strategy. Other approaches rely on sophisticated forecasting procedures to determine the relative attractiveness of one asset class versus another. The same caveat exists with respect to the difficulty of seeing something everyone else is missing and being able to act confidently on that foresight. A review of both the empirical evidence and the research work done on the subject suggests that attempts to improve investment performance through market timing will most likely fail.

For step 4, security selection can be accomplished either actively or passively. If it is done passively, index funds can be used for the various asset classes in order to obtain the desired breadth of diversification while minimizing transaction costs and management fees. Active security selection is predicated on the belief that exploitable inefficiencies exist at the individual security level and can be identified through skilled analysis. To add value, an active manager must produce an incremental return in excess of the transaction costs and associated fees—a very difficult though not necessarily impossible achievement.

Traditionally, money management has been equated with the third and fourth steps of the process: market timing and security selection. Ironically, it is because of the tremendous intelligence and skill of the investment professionals engaging in these activities that the probability for success in these areas is so low. Yet the choice of asset classes and their respective weights in a portfolio has had, and will continue to have, a large impact on future performance. To many it is surprising that, over time, the investment policy decisions regarding the choice of asset classes and their relative long-term weightings within the portfolio likely will have a greater impact on their future investment performance than do the shifting of money among asset classes and the selection of securities within asset classes.

The focus of "value added" is shifting decidedly in favor of a fuller involvement by both investment advisors and investors with the issue of proper asset allocation. By definitively exploring these issues and committing the decisions to writing in the form of an investment policy statement, both investment advisors and investors have the advantage of a common, shared frame of reference for evaluating investment performance and monitoring the progress being made relative to the achievement of financial goals. Investment management is also demystified, and the likelihood is increased that a properly conceived, sound investment strategy will be adhered to during those phases of the market cycle when the temptation to depart from established policy is at its height.

Dramatic support for the importance of asset allocation is provided by a study of 91 large pension plans covering the period 1974 through 1983.[3] The study sought to attribute the variation in quarterly total returns among the plans to three factors: asset allocation policy, market timing, and security selection. The study dramatically supports the notion that asset allocation policy is the

3. Gary P. Brinson, L. Randolph Hood, and Gilbert L. Beebower, "Determinants of Portfolio Performance," *Financial Analysts Journal,* July–August 1986, pp. 39–44.

primary determinant of portfolio performance, with market timing and security selection both playing lesser roles. The study was subsequently updated with additional data and again arrived at the same conclusion.[4] Figure 1–2 shows the startling results: Asset allocation policy explained 91.5 percent of the variation in quarterly total returns among the pension plans. The security selection and market timing factors, by contrast, explained only 4.6 percent and 1.8 percent of the variation, respectively!

If asset allocation is the primary determinant of portfolio performance, why is so much attention obstinately focused on security selection and market timing? Part of the reason is historical.

FIGURE 1–2

Determinants of Portfolio Performance

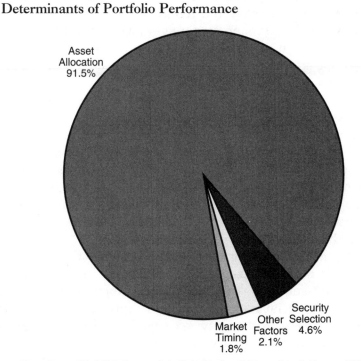

Source: "Determinants of Portfolio Performance II: An Update" by Gary P. Brinson, Brian D. Singer, and Gilbert L. Beebower, *Financial Analysts Journal,* May–June 1991.

4. Gary P. Brinson, Brian D. Singer, and Gilbert L. Beebower, "Determinants of Portfolio Performance II: An Update," *Financial Analysts Journal,* May–June 1991, pp. 40–48.

The money management profession is rooted in the notion that superior skill can beat the market. Traditionally, investment management has been synonymous with market timing and security selection. Many investment professionals wrongly conclude that were it not for the expectation of superior results from these tasks, the profession would not exist.

The realities of the marketplace, however, stubbornly persist. Research studies repeatedly show that most money managers underperform the market on average over time, and those who do outperform the market in one time period do not have a better than even chance of outperforming the market in the next time period. This is not a surprising conclusion. Professionals populate the marketplace, and by definition, the majority cannot outperform the average. Given the transaction costs and management fees incurred in attempting to do so, it is expected that in the future most money managers will continue to underperform the market as a whole.

The hope offered through market timing and security selection has tremendous, seductive appeal. All investors want to enjoy the pleasures of a good market and avoid the pain of a bad market. As a result, the hypothesis that most professional money managers can add value through successful market timing and security selection has never been challenged in the minds of many. As data emerge to refute the hypothesis, the tendency is often to attempt to revise the data to fit the hypothesis. Investors' misconceptions and wishful thinking often support the process, given their desire to find money managers willing to assure them of superior results.

An example of revising the data to fit the hypothesis involves screening the performance of money managers in an attempt to find those with superior skills. In an article appearing in an issue of a popular financial magazine, several hundred mutual funds were reviewed. The author advised against making a judgment based on one year's superior results. Instead, he suggested finding managers who maintained above-average performance results in each of the last five years. The investor could then choose from among these "better" money managers. However, this approach does not adequately differentiate between above-average results produced by luck and those produced by skill.

Consider, for example, a group of 1000 money managers, each of whom makes security decisions on the basis of a random process, like rolling dice. At the end of the first year we can rank these 1000 money managers on the basis of their returns. By definition, 500 will be above average and 500 will be below average. Eliminating those with below-average performance in the first year, the remaining above-average managers continue rolling dice and making security selections through the second year. Half of these will be above average, and half will be below average. Those who underperform will again be eliminated from consideration. Continuing in this manner, by the end of the fifth year, we will have a group of slightly more than 30 who had above-average performance in each of the five years. Our knowledge of the random process used by these managers to make security selections prevents us from crediting superior selection for the results achieved. In the real world of money management, however, where the promise of superior results is often made, identifying 30 managers out of a universe of 1000 who have outperformed the market in each of the preceding five years can lead one to be too quick to assume that the performance is due to superior skill rather than luck.

Given the complexity of the investment management process, there will always be a wide dispersion of returns produced by various money managers during any particular time frame. This dispersion produces an illusion that the skill levels of these managers vary as much as their results do. In reality, short-run variations in performance are heavily influenced by chance. Without realizing this, many investors continue to compare their performance against the results achieved by the latest investment "guru." In the end, investors often chase those performance numbers by constantly reallocating money from one manager to another as the search goes on for the elusive money manager who will produce the same superior performance tomorrow that was produced for someone else yesterday.

This does not imply that managers with superior skill do not exist but rather that they are rare and extraordinarily difficult to conclusively identify. Professor Barr Rosenberg developed a statistical approach to determine the length of time during which above-average performance must continue in order for the appraiser to be confident that the incremental return is attributable to superior skill rather than to luck. This calculation indicates that very long periods of time are usually required—often several decades. By this yardstick, the impressive long-term track records of rare investment managers such as John M. Templeton and a handful of others attest to the impact that truly superior skill can have on investment results.

The expected payoff from superior skill will vary depending on where the skill is directed. Not all sectors of the capital markets may be equally efficient. For example, small company stocks do not command as much institutional research as do large company stocks. Similarly, various international capital markets may not be as efficient as the U.S. capital market. Where inefficiencies exist, there may be exploitable opportunities for superior investment analysis to produce value added. These opportunities should not be overlooked, but it should also be expected that over time, the increasing efficiency of the market will continue to narrow the possible incremental rewards from superior skill as more investors act to exploit these opportunities.

For centuries, Sir Isaac Newton's conception of the laws of nature was accepted without question. The universe followed deterministic, billiard-ball-like laws of cause and effect. The work of Albert Einstein ended this worldview. Modern physics has changed the notions of time and space. Now the universe is viewed in a context in which everything is relative to everything else. Einstein's work did not invalidate Newton's laws of physics; it merely defined the limited context within which Newton's mechanistic laws are true. Likewise, traditional money management, with its emphasis on individual security selection, has been eclipsed by modern portfolio theory, which, in the spirit of Einstein, considers each asset class not as an end in itself but rather as it stands in relationship to all others. Modern portfolio theory does not invalidate traditional money management approaches so much as it prescribes the limits within which they are valid and can add value. (Indeed, without financial analysis and the buying and selling activities of intelligent investors, the marketplace would not be as efficient as it is!)

Money management today is being transformed within the wider and more important context of asset allocation and investment policy. The goal is no longer to beat the market but rather to devise appropriate long-term strategies that will move investors to their financial goals with the least amount of risk. These strategies do not fight the capital markets so much as they intelligently ride with them. Money management today requires a holistic approach in its view of both the investment world and the investor's situation. Investment advisors can be very valuable to their clients by helping them devise appropriate asset allocation strategies designed to realize their objectives and then encouraging them to adhere to their strategies with discipline. Investors have been trained to look over their advisors' shoulders and evaluate the results. If an investor *perceives* that a strategy is not working, he or she will look for a new advisor. In investment management, perceptions often differ from reality. That is why it is so important that both the investor and his or her advisor share a common frame of reference regarding the capital markets and the investment management process.

It is easy to fall into the trap of assuming that investors have a grasp of basic investment concepts when in reality their understanding may be quite limited. At the risk of being rudimentary, it is advisable to avoid this danger by taking the time to define terms and explain concepts at the outset. In the next chapter we will discuss the historical performance of the capital markets. Keep in mind that although the information may be familiar to you, it is unknown territory to many investors. For this reason, we shall engage in this review of the basics, in order to give investment professionals a methodology for developing a common frame of reference with their clients. Armed with knowledge, investors will be more comfortable with the investment policies most appropriate for them.

Historical Review
of Capital Market
Investment Performance

Hindsight is always 20-20.

—Billy Wilder (1906–)
Columbo's Hollywood

Extensive questionnaires are often compiled during the initial meeting between a prospective client and a money manager. The client is asked to describe the facts of his financial situation, state his investment objective, and specify his risk tolerance. With this information, the money manager designs a suitable investment strategy. There are problems, however. What assurance does a money manager have that a client has realistic expectations regarding investment performance? Can the money manager be confident that the client clearly perceives all the risks involved in the money management process and the relative danger posed by those risks?

Often, such problems are easily identified. An example is a client who states, "I want to earn a compound annual return of between 15 and 25 percent, but I don't want to take any chances with my principal. I'm basically a conservative person." It is generally agreed that a successful investment strategy must be consistent with a client's volatility tolerance. It is less obvious, however, that a client's stated tolerance for volatility may be inordinately influenced by fears triggered by a lack of investment knowledge. Here the problem lies not within the capital markets but rather within the client.

An investment-advisory relationship will inevitably encounter difficulties if the client has an "investment worldview" different from that of the advisor. This situation is a time bomb waiting to explode. In October 1987 the U.S. stock market experienced the largest single-day decline in history. Following the crash, an advisory relationship would have been in trouble if the money manager's investment strategy had been predicated on the notion that market timing is not possible but the client believed that it was the money manager's job to protect her from stock market declines.

Clients' expectations tend to err in optimistic directions. Generally, people believe that higher returns are possible with less volatility than is actually the case. An important rule in investment management is therefore to first manage the client's expectations and then manage his or her money. It is crucial that the client and the money manager share a common investment worldview before the investment strategy is implemented. Realistic expectations are needed for the development of realistic objectives. Clients must understand *all* types of risks and must accurately assess the relative importance of each type in their particular situations. The myth of the "ideal investment" must be destroyed. There are no liquid investment alternatives with stable guaranteed principal values which can provide real returns by consistently beating the combined impact of inflation and income taxes. Any misconceptions that go uncorrected will have a tendency to surface later, often to the detriment of the investment management process.

Clients also need to be educated about the importance of their *time horizons* in establishing appropriate investment strategies. These educational tasks can be accomplished with a thorough review of the historical performance of the capital markets. The investment worldview that emerges from this process serves as a foundation for the investment philosophy and money management approach used in helping clients reach their financial goals.

One of the best sources of up-to-date information regarding the investment performance of various investment alternatives is Ibbotson Associates' Yearbook, *Stocks, Bonds, Bills and Inflation*. The data cover the time period 1926 to the present. During these decades, the capital markets experienced periods of both war and peace, inflation and deflation, and several cycles of economic expansion and contraction. Figure 2–1 traces the cumulative effect of compounded total returns on $1 invested at the end of 1925 for various investment alternatives. These performance figures are not adjusted for the impact of income taxes and generally do not take into consideration transaction costs. The vertical axis on the graph is a logarithmic scale where a

FIGURE 2–1

Wealth Indices of Investments in the U.S. Capital Markets, December 31, 1925, to December 31, 1998 (Year-End 1925 = $1)

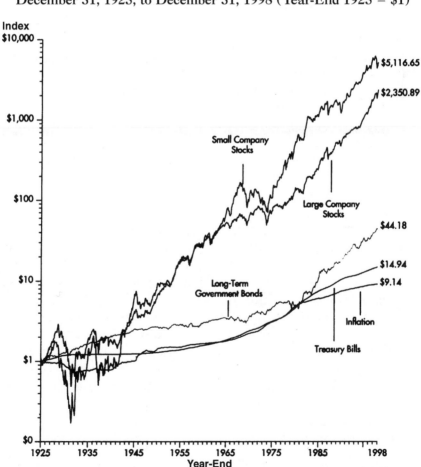

given vertical distance represents a specific percentage change, regardless of where it is measured. A logarithmic scale is often used to facilitate the comparison on the same graph of alternatives with widely varying results.

INFLATION

The measure of inflation used in Figure 2–2 is the Consumer Price Index for All Urban Consumers (CPI-U), as compiled by the Bureau of Labor Statistics.[1] Many experts prefer the Gross National Product Deflator as a better measurement of inflation, but the CPI-U is widely publicized and more commonly used. As a proxy for the cost of living, let us assume that at the end of 1925 a breakfast of bacon and eggs, toast, and coffee costs $1. During the following 73 years, inflation increased the cost of living over nine times, pushing the price of this same breakfast to $9.14 by the end of 1998.

The first seven years of this period, however, were deflationary, averaging a compound decline in the cost of living of 4.4 percent per year, reducing the price of our hypothetical breakfast to $.73 by the end of 1932. It was not until the end of 1945 that inflation had pushed the cost of our breakfast back to $1. The over ninefold increase in the cost of living shown in Figure 2–2 is therefore primarily a story of the inflation following World War II.

Historically, wars often have been accompanied by periods of high inflation, but usually a postwar deflation would bring price levels back down again. This did not occur, however, following World War II. Inflation continued, although at a modest compound annual rate of 2.8 percent over the next two decades. From the mid-1960s through 1981, inflation became much more serious, compounding at an average rate of 7 percent annually. At this pace, the cost of living doubles approximately every decade. From 1982 through 1998, inflation returned to a more modest 3.3 percent compound annual rate.

The persistent inflation following World War II was not confined to the United States alone. It has been a worldwide

---

1. Before 1978, the CPI (as opposed to the CPI-U) was used.

FIGURE 2-2

Inflation: Cumulative Index and Rates of Change

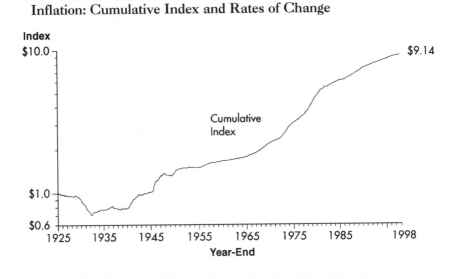

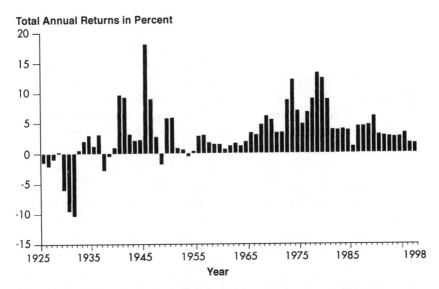

phenomenon, to varying degrees, in different countries at different times. Governments are the primary beneficiaries of inflation. This is in part due to tax structures that tax nominal rather than real income, with an accompanying shift of wealth from the private sector to the public sector. Our country's past budget deficits provide evidence that our government's revenues often fail to cover expenditures, with the difference funded predominantly by issuing government bonds. For the entire 73-year period, inflation had a compound annual rate of 3.1 percent, ranging from a low of −10.3 percent in 1932 to a high of 18.2 percent in 1946.

TREASURY BILLS

Treasury bills are short-term loans to the U.S. Treasury Department. They are sold at a discount from their maturity value, pay no coupons, and have maturities up to one year. Because they are a direct obligation of the federal government, they are free of default risk. The lender is assured that his or her money will be returned with interest upon maturity. Even though the rate of return on Treasury bills varies from period to period, at the time of purchase the return is known with certainty. Figure 2–3 shows that $1 invested in Treasury bills at the end of 1925 with reinvestment of interest grew to be worth $14.94 by the end of 1998. The average compound rate of return over this 73-year period was 3.8 percent, compared with an average inflation rate of 3.1 percent over the same time period.

Figure 2–3 also shows the year-by-year pattern of returns on Treasury bills. Despite the modest nominal returns from Treasury bills during the late 1920s and early 1930s, the real returns were quite high because of the deflationary environment. During the 1940s, the federal government pegged Treasury bill yields at low levels during a period of higher inflation, with the result that real interest rates were negative. Treasury bill yields were deregulated in 1951, and since then yields have followed inflation rates more closely. Over the entire 73-year period, returns ranged from a low of 0 percent to high of 14.7 percent.

The Treasury bill's stability of principal value is its great virtue. The price paid for this advantage is a rate of return only

FIGURE 2-3

U.S. Treasury Bills: Return Index and Returns

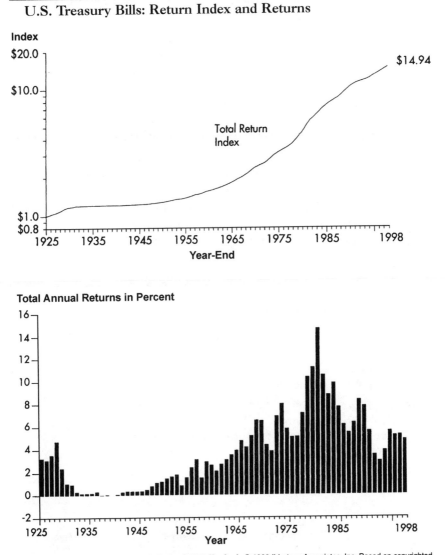

marginally ahead of inflation. It should be noted that these are pre-tax performance numbers. Had the Treasury bill returns been adjusted downward for payment of income taxes, the performance would have lagged considerably behind inflation. The investment implication is clear. For a Treasury bill investor to stay whole in real terms, she would have to live in a tax-free world and never draw on the interest earned for meeting her living expenses.

When the combined effects of inflation and taxation are considered, Treasury bills and other forms of short-term, interest-bearing securities are not riskless investments. Consider the situation of a 50-year-old widow, as summarized in Table 2–1. If she is of average health, she has a life expectancy of approximately 30 more years. Let us assume that certificate of deposit (CD) interest rates are at 5 percent, with an underlying average inflation rate of 4 percent. With $1,000,000 available for investment, CDs could provide her with $50,000 of annual income.

Assume that she never touches a penny's worth of principal but fully uses the interest income for her living expenses. Over the next decade the cost of living will advance nearly 50 percent,

TABLE 2 – 1

The Impact of Inflation

Widow, Age 50
30-Year Life Expectancy
5% Certificate of Deposit Interest Rate
4% Average Inflation Rate
$1,000,000 Available for Investment

Year	(A) Capital Purchasing Power	(B) CD Interest Rate	(C) = (A) × (B) Real Yield
Now	$1,000,000	5%	$50,000
10	675,564	5%	33,778
20	456,387	5%	22,819
30	308,319	5%	15,416

reducing the purchasing power of her $1,000,000 by almost one-third, to $675,564. Her $50,000 income stream likewise loses nearly one-third of its value and can purchase only $33,778 worth of goods and services. Continuing in this same manner over the remaining two decades of her life expectancy, the purchasing power of her initial $1,000,000 drops to only $308,319, with an annual income stream capable of purchasing only $15,416 worth of goods and services!

Many investors who fear the risks associated with equity investments seek what they perceive to be a safe haven in short-term, interest-generating investments. This illustration can be effectively used to underscore the purchasing-power risk inherent in such investments. Often investors are not sufficiently sensitive to the issue of inflation because of the insidious way that inflation takes its toll. Although investors should be concerned primarily with their real returns (i.e., returns adjusted for inflation), often they seem more interested in their nominal results.

For example, during the high interest rate environment 1979 through 1981, Treasury bill returns averaged 12.1 percent, which produced an 8.5 percent after-tax return for a 30 percent marginal-tax-bracket investor. Inflation over the same time period averaged 11.5 percent, producing a Treasury bill after-tax real *loss* of 3 percent per year. Three years later, many of these same investors were complaining as they saw the average Treasury bill returns from 1982 through 1984 decline to 9.7 percent, which equated to a 6.8 percent after-tax return for the same 30 percent marginal-tax-bracket investor. These returns were achieved, however, during a period when inflation averaged 3.9 percent, thus providing investors with a positive real return after taxes of nearly 3 percent per year. Investors need to clearly understand the money illusion of wealth accumulating when in fact it may be eroding.

Of course, there are other ways to lend money at interest for short periods of time. Commercial paper is unsecured, short-term promissory notes issued by corporations. Historically, commercial paper has produced yields of .5 percent to 1 percent more than U.S. Treasury bills. In general, cash equivalents— defined as any short-term, interest-bearing security—share many of the same advantages and disadvantages possessed by

Treasury bills. Although the real return from cash equivalents
will fluctuate from positive to negative, on average it is expected
that they will produce pre-tax returns of approximately 1 percent
above the inflation rate.

BONDS

Bonds are negotiable promissory notes of a corporation or government entity. They usually pay a series of interest payments
followed by a return of principal at maturity. The par value (face
value) of a bond appears on the front of the bond certificate and
is ordinarily the amount the issuing company initially borrowed
and promises to repay at maturity. The coupon rate is the stated
rate of interest on a bond, which when multiplied by the par
value determines the annual interest payments to be paid. The
market price of a bond is usually different from its face value. A
variety of factors determines the market price of a bond, including the current interest rate environment and the bond's coupon
rate, creditworthiness, maturity date, call provisions, and tax
status. Bonds are often referred to as *fixed-income securities*. The
term is somewhat misleading. Only the maximum payment is
fixed, not the income paid. In the case of some corporate bonds,
for example, interest payments are not always paid as promised.

Bond prices depend in large measure on the prevailing
interest rate environment. The fluctuation in bond prices, due to
changes in interest rates, is referred to as *interest rate risk*.
When first exposed to the concept, many clients may be puzzled
by the inverse relationship between interest rate movements
and bond prices. A simple illustration can clarify the concept.
Suppose an investor purchases a newly issued 20-year corporate
bond at its $10,000 par value. The bond has a 7 percent coupon
rate, providing the investor with $700 of interest payments
annually. Over the following year the interest rate environment
increases such that similar newly issued 20-year corporate
bonds must provide an 8 percent coupon bond payment in order
to entice investors to purchase them. If the holder of the 7 percent coupon bond wants to sell it in this higher interest rate
environment, he will find that no one is willing to pay him the
original $10,000 purchase price. There is no incentive to buy a

$700 per year stream of interest payments when the same $10,000 will now buy an $800 per year stream of interest payments, given the higher interest rates prevailing. The 7 percent coupon bond clearly has value, however, and its price in the marketplace would have declined until it reached a level where the $700 payments on the lower market value coupled with the return of face value at maturity is as attractive as the $800 annual interest payments on the newly issued $10,000 bond.

The discount rate that equates the present value of the bond's stream of future cash flows (interest payments plus return of principal) to the bond's current market value is the bond's *yield to maturity*. (Mathematically, it is the bond's internal rate of return.) The yield to maturity is often simply referred to as the *yield* and takes into consideration the annual interest payments, the number of years to maturity, and the difference between the bond's purchase price and its redemption value at maturity. The yield to maturity must be differentiated from the *current yield* of a bond, which is simply the annual interest payments divided by the current market price of the bond. The yield to maturity on a bond will be greater than the current yield when the market value of the bond is less than its par value. This is because the yield to maturity takes into consideration the average annual increase in the bond's value as it approaches full par value at maturity. Conversely, the yield to maturity on a bond will be less than the current yield when the market value of the bond is greater than its par value.

Bond investors can choose from a wide variety of alternatives. The characteristics of bonds can most easily be described along three dimensions: interest-rate-risk sensitivity, creditworthiness, and tax status. Interest-rate-risk sensitivity refers to the magnitude of price changes induced by movements in interest rates. As a first approximation, the maturity of a bond is a rough indicator of how sensitive its price will be to interest rate changes. All other things being equal, the longer the maturity is, the more the bond price will fluctuate for a given interest rate movement. The marketplace normally prices bonds with various maturities such that longer-maturity bonds with more price sensitivity have higher yields than do shorter-maturity securities with more stable principal values. This gives rise to the normal upward-sloping yield curve, as shown in Figure 2–4. The yield curve plots the relationship between bond yields and corresponding maturities.[2]

When we discussed the historical performance of Treasury bills, we commented that their returns tend to follow short-term movements in the inflation rate. Longer-term yields, however, are not as sensitive to changes in annual inflation rates because the yield on a long-term bond reflects consensus expectations regarding inflation over the entire life of the bond. This results in less movement in the long-maturity portion of the yield curve. For example, historically a 1 percent change in the yield to maturity for one-year bonds has been associated with .6 percent and .3 percent changes in yield to maturity, respectively, for three- and six-year-maturity bonds. Interest-rate-risk sensitivity

FIGURE 2–4

Normal Yield Curve

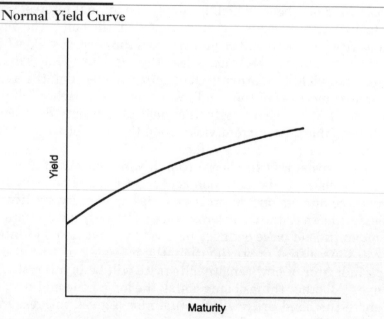

2. Duration is a better measure of interest-rate-risk sensitivity than is maturity. A discussion of duration and an example of how it is calculated are contained in the Appendix to this chapter.

is an extremely important concept for a client to understand. It makes even U.S. government bonds risky and is therefore as important to consider as the creditworthiness of a bond.

The creditworthiness of a bond concerns the likelihood that payments of interest and return of principal will be made as promised. Direct government obligations, such as Treasury bills and Treasury bonds, are backed by the full faith and credit of the federal government and are considered to be free of default risk. Corporate bonds, however, have varying degrees of creditworthiness, and their yields to maturity vary accordingly, with the highest yields associated with those bonds that have the highest possibility of default.

The last dimension concerns the tax status of the bond. Certain kinds of municipal bonds issued by local and state governments are free from federal income taxes and can be issued at lower yields. Corporate and federal government bonds, however, generate interest income fully subject to federal income taxes. For high-tax-bracket investors, municipal securities should always be considered in addition to taxable obligations. Let us now review the historical performance of long-term government bonds, intermediate-term government bonds, and long-term corporate bonds.

LONG-TERM GOVERNMENT BONDS

Long-term government bonds are direct obligations of the U.S. government and are regarded as the most creditworthy issues obtainable. The following performance numbers are based on the construction of a portfolio containing one bond with a reasonably current coupon and a remaining term to maturity of approximately 20 years. Figure 2–1 traces the cumulative performance of a $1 investment in long-term government bonds in comparison with other investment alternatives. Figure 2–5 shows the long-term government bonds' return indices for total returns versus capital appreciation only. The total return index shows the combined effect of bond price movements coupled with reinvestment of income. In measuring the total annual return from a government bond, the income earned from the bond is added to the change in the price of the bond before the resulting sum is divided

FIGURE 2-5

Long-Term Government Bonds: Return Indices, Returns, and Yields

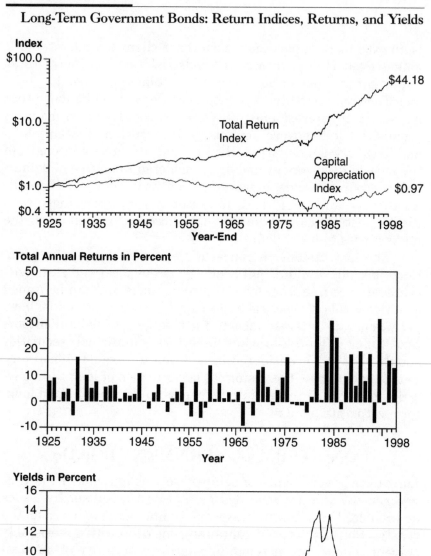

by the value of the bond at the beginning of the time period. The capital appreciation return is defined to be the total return minus the bond's yield to maturity. The capital appreciation index accordingly reflects only bond price changes caused by interest rate movements. The only way an investor can be assured of receiving the current yield to maturity on a long-term government bond is by holding the bond until maturity. If it is sold prior to maturity, an intervening interest rate movement will produce a corresponding capital gain or capital loss, making the investor's actual return vary.

As we lengthen the time horizon over which we lend money to the government through the purchase of a long-term government bond, we leave behind the stable principal value characteristic of short-term Treasury bills. Interest rate risk now enters the equation. Given that risk, we expect to be compensated for bearing it in the form of a higher yield on our invested dollar. In Figure 2–5, we see that $1 invested in long-term government bonds at the end of 1925 grew to be worth $44.18, with full reinvestment of income, by the end of 1998. This is a compound annual return of 5.3 percent. This surpasses the Treasury bills' corresponding 1998 ending value of $14.94, produced by a compound return of 3.8 percent. As a result of the interest rate risk of long-term government bonds, the returns were much more volatile than those of Treasury bills, ranging from a low of −9.2 percent in 1967 to a high of 40.4 percent in 1982.

In working with clients, there is a danger in focusing too much attention on the relationships among long-term average returns without discussing the variations in performance which occur over shorter time periods. To facilitate this historical review, let us consider three decidedly different periods. The first is 1926 through the conclusion of World War II in 1945. The second is 1946 through the interest rate cycle peak of 1981. The third is the disinflationary period 1982 through the end of 1998.

From 1926 through 1945, the average compound inflation rate was less than .1 percent because of the deflation that existed for the first several years of this period. This can be seen clearly in Figure 2–2, which traces the CPI from its initial $1 value in 1926 down to a low of $.73 in 1932 before rising again to just over $1 by the end of 1945. The superior performance of bonds is evident in the steady rise in value shown in Figure 2–5. Government bonds performed exceedingly well and provided investors with a compound annual growth rate of 4.7 percent. Because the average inflation rate was close to zero, bonds had a real compound return almost identical to their nominal compound return. By comparison, Treasury bills had a compound return of 1.1 percent. By the end of 1945, $1 invested in government bonds with full reinvestment of income had grown to be worth $2.51— more than twice as much as a $1 investment in Treasury bills, which grew to be worth $1.24.

An examination of the bottom graph in Figure 2–5 shows that yields were relatively stable during this period and trended downward within a relatively narrow range of 2 to 4 percent. The downward trend produced a corresponding appreciation in bond prices. This can be clearly identified on the top graph in Figure 2–5, which shows the capital appreciation index reaching a maximum for the entire 73-year period of $1.42 by the end of this period. The middle chart in Figure 2–5 shows the pattern of total annual returns. This confirms the positive performance achieved during this time period. With the notable exception of 1931, when government bonds had a total return of −5.3 percent, total annual returns during this two-decade time period were positive.

During the second period, which extends from the beginning of 1946 through the end of 1981, government bonds experienced a prolonged bear market. Figure 2–2 shows a brief period following World War II during which inflation increased sharply and then leveled off for two decades before beginning its prolonged acceleration from the 1970s through the end of 1981. Over the entire period, the compound annual inflation rate was 4.7 percent. Short-term interest rates and Treasury bill returns lagged inflation during the first portion of this period as a result of the federal government's action in pegging interest rates at artificially low levels. Following deregulation of Treasury bill rates, however, Treasury bill returns closely mirrored the accelerating inflation and interest rate environments that characterized this period.

The bottom graph in Figure 2–5 shows a pattern of increasing yields pushed by an accelerating inflationary environment.

The middle graph shows frequent occurrences of negative total annual returns during the years when the interest payments on the bond were not large enough to offset the bond's price loss for the year. The compound annual return with reinvestment of income for the entire period was 2 percent—less than half that of Treasury bills' compound annual return of 4.1 percent. Current yields obviously were much higher, indicating that the low total return was caused by a protracted capital loss.

Without the reinvestment of income, the investment experience of long-term government bondholders was devastating. The capital appreciation component of long-term government bonds' cumulative return, which had reached its peak of $1.42 at the end of 1945, declined to its 73-year low of $.48 by the end of 1981. This was a principal loss of nearly two thirds *before* one considers the additional damage imposed by inflation. (Refer to the top graph in Figure 2–5.) The interest rate risk that worked for government bondholders prior to 1946 was working against them from 1946 through the end of 1981.

A government bond's yield has three components: an inflation component, a real riskless interest rate, and a premium for bearing interest rate risk. A policy of consistently spending all three components is a prescription for long-term trouble. No period of history more clearly demonstrates the danger of buying "safe" long-term government bonds and spending the interest for living expenses.

As Treasury bill returns were peaking in 1981 at a historical high of 14.7 percent, many investors were swearing that they would never again invest in long-term government bonds. The premium they expected to receive for bearing interest rate risk had not been delivered. The deterioration in bond performance had been so dramatic that by the end of 1981, the post-1925 cumulative performance of Treasury bills actually surpassed that of long-term government bonds. This can be seen in Figure 2–1, where the inflation, Treasury bill, and long-term government bond lines converge.

The final period begins in 1982. Inflation and interest rates both dropped precipitously, producing huge gains in long-term government bond prices. The magnitude of these gains is appreciated if one examines the middle graph in Figure 2–5, which shows the pattern of total annual returns. During the 56-year period leading up to 1982, there were only two years, 1932 and 1976, when the total return on long-term government bonds exceeded 15 percent. Then, in 1982, long-term government bonds had a total return of 40 percent, followed later by total returns in excess of 15 percent in 1984, 1985, 1986, 1989, 1991, 1993, 1995, and 1997!

Given the disinflationary environment, Treasury bill returns were declining as expected but were nevertheless high in real terms by historical standards. A comparison of the performance of long-term government bonds for the first versus the second half of the decade ending with 1986 provides an interesting contrast of the good and bad aspects of interest rate risk, coupled with the impact of inflation. Every long-term bond investor should sign a statement indicating that he or she has seen and understands the information presented in Table 2–2. In a changing interest rate environment, long-term debt obligations are definitely risky.

During the entire 73-year period, long-term government bonds provided a compound annual return of 5.3 percent. This is considerably ahead of Treasury bills and inflation, but it took the experience of several spectacular bond years since 1981 for these relative performance relationships to redevelop. We have seen that during periods of deflation and disinflation, long-term

TABLE 2–2

Comparative Bond Performance

	(A)	(B)	(C) = (A) − (B)
Five-Year Period	Long-Term Govt. Bond Compound Return	Compound Rate of Inflation	Inflation-Adjusted Compound Return of Long-Term Govt. Bonds
1977 through 1981	−1.0%	10.1%	−11.1%
1982 through 1986	21.6	3.3	18.3

government bonds provide excellent returns. During periods of moderate inflation, returns are good provided that the inflation is anticipated. During periods of high inflation, however, long-term government bonds, as well as other long-term debt obligations, do poorly.

INTERMEDIATE-TERM GOVERNMENT BONDS

The return indices, total annual returns, and yields for intermediate-term government bonds are shown in Figure 2–6. The data used for constructing this exhibit describe the performance of a noncallable bond, with the shortest maturity of not less than five years. These bonds have less interest-rate-risk sensitivity than do long-term government bonds because of their shorter maturities. The expectation, therefore, is that intermediate-term bonds should produce total returns lower than those of long-term government bonds but higher than those of Treasury bills. Surprisingly, Figure 2–6 shows that $1 invested in intermediate-term government bonds, with full reinvestment of income, grew to be worth $43.93 by the end of 1998. This represents a compound annual return of 5.3 percent, which is equivalent to the compound annual return produced by long-term government bonds.

Comparing the portion of the total return attributed to the income reinvested, we find, as expected, that long-term government bonds' income return was higher than that produced by intermediate-term government bonds. Long-term government bonds, however, had a slight cumulative capital loss over the 73-year period, whereas intermediate-term government bonds appreciated at an average compound rate of .4 percent annually.[3] As a result of these offsetting factors, the compound annual total returns of long-term government bonds and intermediate-term government bonds are nearly identical.

Although the upside on intermediate-term government bonds is less spectacular than that on long-term government bonds, the downside is also correspondingly less. For example, over the 73-year period 1926 through 1998, intermediate-term government

---

3. Some possible explanations for this are discussed in the Appendix to this chapter.

FIGURE 2-6

Intermediate-Term Government Bonds: Return Indices, Returns, and Yields

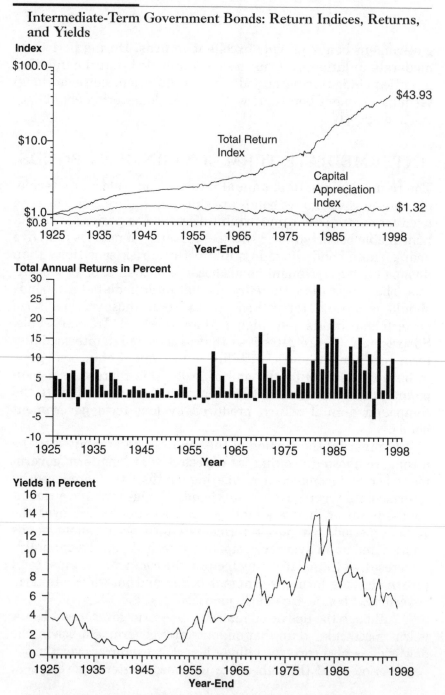

Index

Total Return Index

Capital Appreciation Index

$43.93

$1.32

Year-End

Total Annual Returns in Percent

Year

Yields in Percent

Year-End

Source: *Stocks, Bonds, Bills and Inflation ® 1999 Yearbook,* © 1999 Ibbotson Associates, Inc. Based on copyrighted works by Ibbotson and Sinquefield. All rights reserved. Used with permission.

bonds had negative total returns in only 7 years, compared to 20 years of negative total returns for long-term government bonds. Due to six interest rate hikes imposed by the Federal Reserve, 1994 was one of those loss years for both long-term and intermediate-term government bonds. Figure 2–7 graphically depicts the dramatic upward shift in the yield curve during 1994. The magnitude of these interest rate increases triggered a total return of −5.14 percent for intermediate-term government bonds—the largest annual loss for the entire 73-year period. For long-term government bonds, the 1994 loss of −7.77 percent was the second largest loss on record.

LONG-TERM CORPORATE BONDS

As with long-term government bonds, long-term corporate bonds have long maturities. They are therefore subject to interest rate risk, and investors deserve a corresponding horizon premium for bearing it. Unlike long-term government bonds, however, long-term corporate bonds have credit risk. Investors lack complete certainty that all payments of interest and principal will be made as promised. If held to maturity, a government bond will provide an investor with an expected return equal to the bond's yield to maturity. But because corporate bonds have a possibility of default, the expected return will be less than the yield to maturity. To compensate investors for bearing this credit risk, the return on corporate bonds, after adjustment for any defaults, should be in excess of that available from long-term government bonds. We will call this compensation the *default premium* and define it as the difference between the return on government bonds and the return on corporate bonds with similar maturity after any necessary adjustment for losses due to defaults.

Figure 2–8 shows the pattern of total annual returns, as well as the return index, for long-term corporate bonds. The bonds used in compiling this data series are Aaa- and Aa-rated bonds with maturities of approximately 20 years. As with government bonds, total returns are equal to capital appreciation plus reinvested income. Based on the 73 years of data compiled by Ibbotson Associates, the default premium historically has

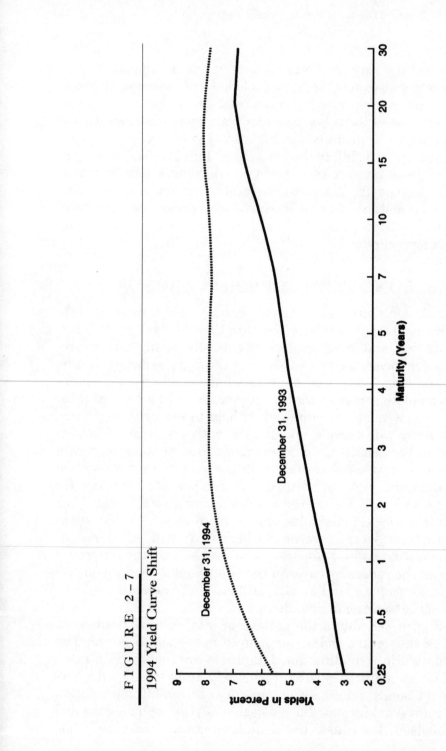

FIGURE 2-7

1994 Yield Curve Shift

December 31, 1994

December 31, 1993

Yields in Percent

Maturity (Years)

FIGURE 2-8

Long-Term Corporate Bonds: Return Index and Returns

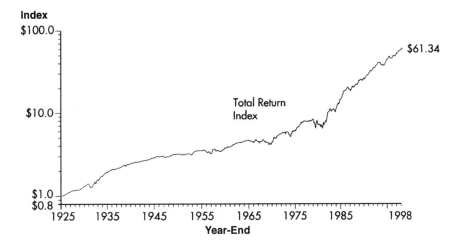

Index

Total Return Index

$61.34

Year-End

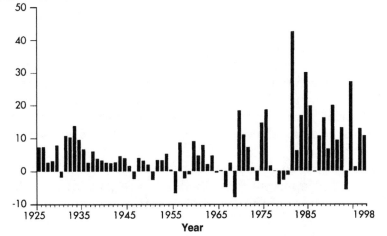

Total Annual Returns in Percent

Year

been .5 percent compounded annually. This is approximated by subtracting long-term government bonds' compound annual return of 5.3 percent from the 5.8 percent compound annual return produced by long-term corporate bonds.[4] This higher return with corporate bonds produced a 1998 ending value of $61.34 for an initial investment of $1 with reinvestment of income.

Corporate bonds vary widely in terms of their creditworthiness, with lower-quality bonds having higher expected returns than high-quality bonds. Returns on low-quality bonds are more volatile because of the greater sensitivity of these bonds to movements in stock prices. Historically, medium- to lower-grade bonds have provided investors with higher net returns over time after adjustments for all capital losses.

LARGE COMPANY STOCKS

Common stock represents ownership interest in a corporation. Investors who buy a share of common stock buy a piece of the company. Unlike fixed-income securities, common stocks have neither fixed maturity dates nor fixed schedules of promised payments. Out of its revenues, a corporation must first pay its expenses, including what it owes to bondholders and other creditors. Obviously, a corporation's creditors have greater certainty regarding their payment than do its shareholders. Common stocks are therefore more risky than are fixed-income securities. Because the bondholders and other creditors of a corporation have a prior claim to the corporation's revenues and assets, common stock shareholders are said to have a *residual ownership interest*.

The return to a shareholder is in the form of dividends and/or capital appreciation. Dividends are paid in accordance with the decisions of the board of directors, which is elected by

---

4. It is more proper to calculate the default premium as the geometric difference in returns calculated as follows:

$$\frac{(1 + \text{Long-Term Corporate Bond Compound Annual Return})}{(1 + \text{Long-Term Government Bond Compound Annual Return})} - 1 = \frac{1.058}{1.053} - 1 = .47\%$$

For conceptual simplicity, throughout the book we will instead approximate this and other premia by subtracting one series' compound return from that of another.

the shareholders. The portion of earnings not paid out in dividends is available for reinvestment by the corporation and provides one source of financing for the future growth of the enterprise. Like any business owner, common stock shareholders share in both the upside potential and the downside risk of the corporation. For assuming greater risk, common stock shareholders expect greater rewards over time. Stock market prices in general reflect investors' assessment of the state of the economy. The better the economic outlook for business, the higher the level of stock prices.

The large company stock performance numbers used for Figures 2–1 and 2–9 are based on the Standard & Poor's 500 Stock Composite Index (S&P 500). The S&P 500 includes 500 of the largest U.S. stocks, as measured in terms of the total market value of shares outstanding. One dollar invested in large company stocks, with reinvestment of income, grew rapidly from the end of 1925 until it reached a value of $2.20 by the end of 1928. The stock market crash and Great Depression followed, taking stock prices down for the next four years. By the end of 1932, the total return index reached its 73-year low of $.79. By comparison, government and corporate bonds were performing quite well. By the end of 1944, large company stocks had made up their lost ground with the total return index reaching $2.91, thereby surpassing the $2.82 total return index for the best-performing interest-generating alternative—long-term corporate bonds. From that point forward through the end of 1998, the total return index for large company stocks would maintain its cumulative performance advantage over corporate bonds, government bonds, and Treasury bills. Although there would be common stock bear markets, most notably in 1973–1974, which would at times narrow the lead, the long-term secular trend was one of an increasing performance advantage for common stocks.

Several years of this period are particularly noteworthy. The bull market, which began in the middle of 1982, produced an advance of more than 260 percent before peaking five years later. Although this was not the largest bull market advance on record, it was one of the most rapid prolonged gains. Measured from the trough to the peak, the total return on large company

FIGURE 2-9

Large Company Stocks: Return Indices, Returns, and Dividend Yields

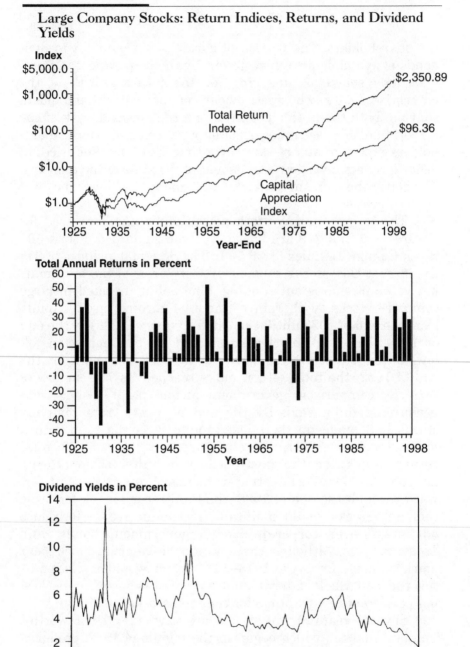

44

stocks was nearly 30 percent compounded annually. This historical first was followed by another. On October 19, 1987, the stock market crashed, with prices falling more than 20 percent—the largest single-day decline on record. Although this was a dramatic loss, stock prices quickly recovered in the next bull market, which began on December 4, 1987. For a prolonged period following 1987, large company stock investors were rewarded with extremely generous returns.

At the end of 1998, the large company stock total return index had a value of $2350.89, produced by a 73-year compound annual total return of 11.2 percent. This performance completely dominates the compound annual returns over the same period of 5.8 percent, 5.3 percent, 5.3 percent, and 3.8 percent for long-term corporate bonds, long-term government bonds, intermediate-term government bonds, and U.S. Treasury bills, respectively.

The "miracle of compound interest" is quite apparent when one realizes that large company stocks had a compound return of only 7.4 percent in excess of Treasury bills yet produced over 157 times the accumulated wealth during the 73-year period. The dramatic, superior long-term performance of large company stocks is matched by a correspondingly higher volatility in annual returns. This is evident in a visual comparison of the total return indices for large company stocks versus long-term government bonds and Treasury bills in Figure 2–1. The center graph in Figure 2–9 also highlights this volatility by showing the year-by-year pattern of total annual returns.

When we examined the historical performance of corporate bonds, government bonds, and Treasury bills, we saw that these investment alternatives could outpace inflation only by reinvesting their income returns. This was not true, however, with large company stocks. Figure 2–9 shows that the capital appreciation return index had a 1998 ending value of $96.36, which is over 10 times the $9.14 CPI value. Thus, even if the dividend yield had been spent for living expenses, large company stocks' capital appreciation on average would have stayed ahead of inflation. In this sense, it is reasonable to consider large company stocks to be a long-term "inflation indexed investment." This is not surprising, given the long-term real growth of the economy.

Assume, for example, that during the next two decades we have annual inflation of 3.5 percent, which will double the price of goods and services within the economy. If we assume that the corporations that produce these goods and services maintain the same level of production over the next two decades and have the same profit margins and price-earnings ratios for their common stocks then as now, corporate earnings and share prices will likewise double, even if all earnings are paid out as dividends.

As with bonds, anticipated inflation is priced into the expected return of common stocks. But with common stocks our performance expectations are different. We expect a broadly diversified common stock portfolio to maintain its purchasing power (i.e., keep up with inflation) while simultaneously generating a stream of dividends, which may start out at a modest level but can likewise grow to maintain its purchasing power on average over time. By contrast, bonds promise only the return of principal in nominal terms, with a fixed-income return that is initially higher than the average dividend yield available from common stocks but which is fixed as to its upper limit. In essence, with bonds' other promises, you also have the assurance that your principal will lose to inflation.

Historically, common stocks do much better in a low-inflationary environment where there is relative stability in consumer prices. Performance has been poor during periods of either deflation or high inflation. It is the *unanticipated* inflation that is especially harmful to common stock performance— particularly in the short run. Over longer periods of time, corporations can make adjustments to inflation, but in the short run, these adjustments are more difficult to accomplish. It is logical to project that barring the collapse of the economic system as we know it, common stocks as an investment vehicle will provide a good alternative for the long-term preservation and enhancement of purchasing power.

SMALL COMPANY STOCKS

The long-term superior performance of small company stocks, relative to all other investment alternatives we have discussed thus far, is evident in Figure 2–1. The stocks used to compile this wealth index are those comprising the fifth (smallest) quintile of the New York Stock Exchange, where stocks are ranked by their market capitalization (market price × number of shares outstanding). One dollar invested in small company stocks at the end of 1925 grew to be worth $5116.65, with full reinvestment of income, by the end of 1998. This represents a compound annual return of 12.4 percent, compared with the next best result of 11.2 percent achieved by large company stocks. We will call the 1.2 percent difference between small and large company stock performance the *small stock premium*.

There are several possible explanations for the superior performance of small company stocks. A comparison of the pattern of total annual returns, as shown in the bottom graph of Figure 2–10, reveals more volatility than that demonstrated by large company stock returns. An increased return for small company stocks is consistent with their higher volatility. Also, small company stocks tend to have higher betas, making them more susceptible to overall stock market movements and thereby again justifying higher returns. Finally, one could argue that large capitalization companies may tend to be in more mature businesses, with their periods of rapid growth behind and not ahead of them.

FIGURE 2-10

Small Company Stocks: Return Index and Returns

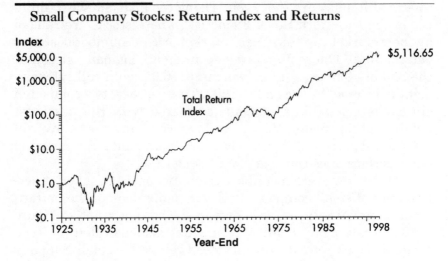

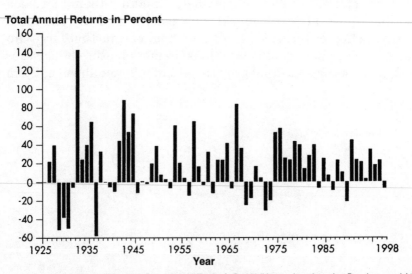

APPENDIX: Bond Duration

Maturity is not the preferred measure of interest-rate-risk sensitivity because it considers only the timing of repayment of principal upon maturity. Maturity accordingly ignores the timing and magnitude of interest payments made in the interim. Because a major portion of the present value of a bond may be attributed to the interest payments, a better measure would take these payments into consideration as well. A bond's *duration* is a measurement that accomplishes this. It is calculated as the weighted average of the lengths of time prior to receipt of interest payments and return of principal, where each payment's weight is determined by dividing its present value by the current market value of the bond. In short, it is the present value weighted average time that the bondholder has money owed to her.

Table 2–3 shows the calculation of duration for a 7 percent coupon bond priced to provide an 8 percent yield to maturity. The duration of 2.81 years is less than the three-year maturity because of the consideration given to the interim interest payments. Had this calculation been performed for a three-year-maturity zero coupon bond, 100 percent of the weighting would have been given to the single-payment return of principal at maturity, and accordingly the duration would have been equal to the maturity of three years.

Because duration is a better indicator of interest-rate-risk sensitivity, a group of bonds with the same duration but varying maturities will respond similarly to a given interest rate move, whereas a different group of bonds with the same maturity but with different durations will have varying price sensitivities. Duration most accurately reflects interest-rate-risk sensitivity for bonds whose prices are close to par. For example, for a bond with a six-year duration, an 8 percent yield, and a market value equal to par, a 50 basis point decrease in the yield to 7.5 percent would cause the price of the bond to increase by approximately six times 50 basis points, or 3 percent, to $10,300.

Earlier in the chapter, we commented that despite the rising interest rate environment, intermediate-term government bonds appreciated at a compound annual rate of .4 percent from

T A B L E   2 – 3

Calculation of Bond Duration

Par Value	$10,000
Coupon Rate	7%
Interest Payments	$700 annually
Years to Maturity	3
Current Market Value of Bond	$9,742
Yield to Maturity	8%

(1)	(2)	(3)	(4)	(5)
Years from Now	Payment	Present Value of Payment at 8%	Present Value of Payment as a Percentage of the Current Market Value of the Bond	Column (1) Times Column (4)
1	$ 700 I	$ 648	.066	.066
2	700 I	600	.062	.124
3	700 I	556	.057	.171
	10,000 P	7,938	.815	2.445
		$9,742	1.000	2.81*

I = interest.
P = principal.
* = duration in years.

1926 through 1998. This may partly result from some unusual characteristics of the bonds selected in building the intermediate-term government bond data series. Another possible explanation involves the positive convexity of most bonds. Positive convexity produces a higher return on average than would be expected, given a bond's yield. This is caused by an inverse relationship between a bond's duration and the direction of interest rate movements. An increase in a bond's yield has the effect of shortening the bond's duration. This occurs because of a corresponding increase in the discount rate used in computing the present value weights for the bond payments. This in turn makes the bond less susceptible to further capital loss. Conversely, a decrease in a bond's yield lengthens duration and thereby makes the bond more susceptible to price change. The changes in duration caused by movements in interest rates are advantageous to the bondholder in both rising and falling interest rate markets. This produces realized returns that are better than would be expected, given the bond's yield.

CHAPTER 3

Comparative Relationships Among Capital Market Investment Alternatives

The best way to suppose what may come is to remember what is passed.

—George Savile, Marquess of Halifax (1633–1695)
Political, Moral and Miscellaneous Reflections, 1750

MODELS FOR THE LONG-TERM COMPOUND RETURNS[1] FROM CAPITAL MARKET INVESTMENT ALTERNATIVES

Treasury bills historically have had a compound annual return of 3.8 percent, which is .7 percent more than the corresponding compound annual inflation rate of 3.1 percent. Some researchers have concluded on this basis that the real (i.e., inflation-adjusted) riskless interest rate is therefore .7 percent. Accepting that assumption, we can use current Treasury bill yields for an approximate indicator of short-term inflation expectations:

Treasury bill yield   =   z%
Minus real riskless interest rate   = $\underline{-.7\%}$
Equals the expected short-term inflation rate = $(z-.7)\%$

---

1. Do not use these models to develop inputs for a computer optimization program. For that purpose, it would be more appropriate to develop models based on historical arithmetic spreads rather than differences in compound returns. For a full discussion of this issue, read Chapter 9, "Portfolio Optimization."

By reorganizing the terms, we can build a simple model of the components of Treasury bill returns:

Expected short-term inflation rate   =   y%

Plus the real riskless rate of interest =   + .7%

Equals the Treasury bill yield   = (y + .7)%

The interest rate risk associated with long-term government bonds deserves compensation in the form of an extra return over what would be available with Treasury bills. The incremental return for bearing interest rate risk is commonly referred to as the *horizon premium*. Historically, long-term government bonds have had a compound annual return of 5.3 percent, compared with the 3.8 percent compound annual return produced by Treasury bills. This indicates an incremental compound annual horizon premium of 1.5 percent.

We know that the pricing mechanism of the marketplace builds into the bond's yield compensation for the risks associated with the *anticipated* inflation rate and level of interest rate volatility. In essence, although investors expect that their bond portfolios will fluctuate in principal value, they do not expect long-term permanent changes in the principal value of their bond portfolios. In modeling future bond returns based on historical data, it is important to examine if there has been any cumulative capital appreciation or loss in the data series. In Table 3–1, the total returns of long-term government bonds are separated into an income component and a capital appreciation component. The capital appreciation component is shown as 0.0 percent. Had this number been anything other than 0.0 percent, the bond portfolio in the data series would have experienced an *unanticipated* cumulative gain or loss in principal value. In this situation, an estimated horizon premium can be inferred from the historical data by adjusting for the bond portfolio's long-term gain or loss in principal value. If there had been cumulative capital appreciation, a downward adjustment would be required to offset the unanticipated capital appreciation. If there had been a cumulative capital loss, an upward adjustment would be needed to offset the impact of the unanticipated capital loss. The formula for the estimated horizon premium is therefore:

TABLE 3-1

Total Returns, Income Returns, and Capital Appreciation of the Basic Asset Classes: Summary Statistics of Annual Returns (1926–1998)

Series	Geometric Mean	Arithmetic Mean	Standard Deviation	Serial Correlation
Large Company Stocks:				
Total returns	11.2%	13.2%	20.3%	0.01
Income	4.5	4.5	1.4	0.84
Capital appreciation	6.5	8.4	19.6	0.01
Small Company Stocks:				
Total returns	12.4	17.4	33.8	0.09
Long-Term Corporate Bonds:				
Total returns	5.8	6.1	8.6	0.10
Long-Term Government Bonds:				
Total returns	5.3	5.7	9.2	−0.01
Income	5.2	5.2	2.9	0.97
Capital appreciation	0.0	0.3	8.0	−0.17
Intermediate-Term Government Bonds:				
Total returns	5.3	5.5	5.7	0.18
Income	4.8	4.8	3.0	0.96
Capital appreciation	0.4	0.5	4.4	−0.19
Treasury Bills:				
Total returns	3.8	3.8	3.2	0.92
Inflation	3.1	3.2	4.5	0.65

Total return is equal to the sum of three component returns; income return, capital appreciation return, and reinvestment return.

Source: *Stocks, Bonds, Bills and Inflation* ® *1999 Yearbook,* © 1999 Ibbotson Associates, Inc. Based on copyrighted works by Ibbotson and Sinquefield. All rights reserved. Used with permission.

Compound annual return from long-term
  government bonds   =   5.3%
Minus compound annual return
  from Treasury bills   = −3.8%
Equals the historical compound annual return
  horizon premium   =   1.5%
Plus (or minus) an adjustment for the compound
  annual loss (or gain) of principal value   =   0.0%
Equals the estimated horizon premium   =   1.5%

On this basis, it is reasonable to project that on average, Treasury bills will provide a compound return of .7 percent in excess of the inflation rate, while long-term government bonds will have a compound return of 1.5 percent in excess of the current Treasury bill yield. We can now specify a model for the estimated compound return on long-term government bonds:

Treasury bill yield   =   x%
Plus the horizon premium   =   +1.5%

Equals the future compound return
  on long-term government bonds   = (x + 1.5)%

If we assume that the default premium will be the same in the future as it has been historically, our model for the estimated compound return on long-term corporate bonds is:

Treasury bill yield   =   x%
Plus the horizon premium   =   +1.5%
Equals the future compound return
  on long-term government bonds   = (x + 1.5)%
Plus the default premium   =   +.5%
Equals the future compound return
  on long-term corporate bonds   = (x + 2.0)%

During the 73-year period we reviewed, large company stocks had a compound annual return of 11.2 percent—7.4 percent more than the compound annual return of 3.8 percent from Treasury bills. The difference between the return from large company stocks and the return from Treasury bills is called the *equity risk premium*. If we assume that the volatility inherent in large company stocks will not be materially different in the future from what it has been in the past, and if we further assume that the market will price large company stocks such that the compensation for bearing that volatility is the same in the future as it has been historically, then 7.4 percent will be a reasonable estimate of the equity risk premium in the future. We can thus build a simple model for the estimated compound return for large company stocks:

Treasury bill yield	=	x%
Plus the equity risk premium	=	+7.4%
Equals the future compound return on large company stocks		= (x + 7.4)%

Finally, with the assumption that the historical small company stock premium is a good estimate of the future small company stock premium, our model for the estimated compound return on small company stocks is:

Treasury bill yield	=	x%
Plus the equity risk premium	=	+7.4%
Equals the future compound return on large company stocks		= (x + 7.4)%
Plus the small company stock premium	=	+1.2%
Equals the future compound return on small company stocks		= (x + 8.6)%

It is important to emphasize that these models are based on long-term, historical relationships among investment alternatives. Accordingly, they represent averages of many distinctly different subperiods during which actual results were very different from what would be predicted by these models. For example, although it is true that on average the yield curve is upward-sloping (as shown in Figure 2–4), there are times when the yield curve is either flat or inverted. During such periods, these models obviously need to be modified.[2]

---

2. There is a tendency over time for inverted or flat yield curves to return to a normal, upward-sloping shape. This occurs through a decline in short-term interest rates, a rise in long-term rates, or a combination of the two.

As another example, Figure 3–1 illustrates how the equity risk premium has varied during the past 73 years. Each point on the graph indicates the difference between the compound annual return for large company stocks and the compound annual return for Treasury bills for the preceding five-year period. The variability is quite apparent and serves as a strong reminder that these models provide only single-point estimates of future security returns. A better description of future performance would incorporate a description of a probabilistic range of outcomes. It is important to share this range of outcomes with clients in order to provide them with a context for evaluating subsequent investment performance.

The relationships described in these models are an important part of the foundation for developing the client's understanding of investment risk and return. They also provide valuable benchmarks that can help clients develop more realistic expectations regarding future investment performance.

SUMMARY COMPARISONS
AND IMPLICATIONS

Clients often misperceive the risks they face in the investment of their money. If these misperceptions go uncorrected, it is very likely that clients will make portfolio decisions that are not in their best interests. This highlights the value of providing to the client a detailed historical review of the capital markets. A client who fully understands inflation, interest rate risk, credit risk, and equity risk is in a much better position to make intelligent investment decisions that are appropriate for his or her financial goals.

Table 3–1 provides an excellent summary of the comparative performance of the major investment alternatives we have reviewed.[3] The column labeled *Geometric Mean* compares the historical compound annual returns for the various investment

---

3. If you are unfamiliar with some of the statistical concepts used in this section, it may be helpful to review the Appendix to this chapter. It provides summary explanations of the terms *geometric mean, arithmetic mean, expected return, standard deviation, probability distribution,* and *serial correlation.*

Equity Risk Premium (1926–1998)

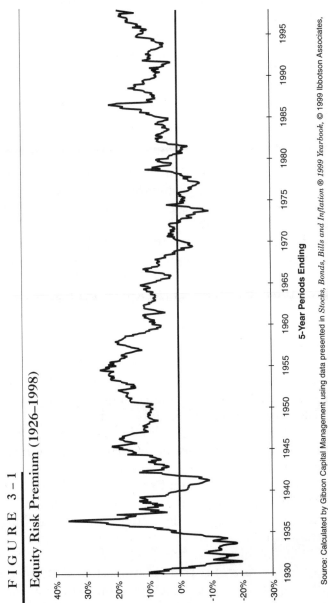

5-Year Periods Ending

alternatives. It is clear that over the long term, equity investments such as common stocks have had better returns than have bonds, which in turn have outperformed Treasury bills. Correspondingly, we can see, by comparing their respective standard deviations, that the higher returns have been obtained at the price of more volatility.

In comparing the returns of these investment alternatives, clients are often surprised by the impact that small, incremental returns have had on wealth accumulation. For example, Treasury bills, with a compound annual return of 3.8 percent, resulted in the growth of a $1 investment to $14.94 by the end of 1998. By contrast, large company stocks had a compound annual return of only 7.4 percent more, yet the initial $1 investment grew to $2350.89 over the same time period. Similarly, small company stocks had an incremental compound annual return of only 1.2 percent in excess of large company stocks, yet this small additional return produced an astounding value of $5116.65 by the end of 1998. These are clear illustrations of the "miracle of compound interest."

Compared to these relatively modest incremental differences in compound annual returns, there are wide differences in the standard deviations of returns among the various investment alternatives. For example, Table 3–1 shows that Treasury bills not only had the lowest historical compound return, they also had the lowest standard deviation. The historical variability of return for Treasury bills should not, however, be interpreted as a short-run measure of uncertainty in return. There are two reasons for this. First, average Treasury bill returns had a multiple-decade upward trend from the late 1930s until peaking in 1981. This upward secular movement in average Treasury bill returns produced higher deviations around the long-term average than would be true around the average for a shorter period of time. In this sense, the long-term standard deviation of Treasury bills overstates their historical short-run volatility. Second, it is possible to completely eliminate the short-run uncertainty in return by purchasing a one-year maturity Treasury bill and thereby lock in the return. For these reasons, it is inappropriate to consider Treasury bills' long-term standard deviation as an indicator of short-run volatility.

Although the wide range of standard deviation numbers shown in Table 3–1 provides a good comparison of relative volatility, a visual comparison is much more striking. Figures 3–2A and 3–2B show the patterns of total annual returns for the various investment alternatives compared directly with each other on a series of graphs with a common vertical scale. This method of presentation gives the client a much better sense of relative volatility.

Table 3–1 breaks down the standard deviation of large company stocks' total returns into income and capital appreciation components. It is very interesting to note that the capital appreciation component has a standard deviation of 19.6 percent compared with 1.4 percent for the income component. Clearly, the variability of return associated with large company stocks is attributable almost entirely to price movements, with the dividend income component being relatively stable.

One possible explanation lies in the manner in which dividend policy is established for most corporations. A corporation's earnings will fluctuate from year to year. Rather than pay a dividend that fluctuates with earnings, however, corporations seek to set dividends at a rate that can be comfortably paid out of earnings through both good and bad years. Corporations do not want to cut a dividend unless cutting is absolutely necessary, and they generally raise dividends only when they are confident that a relatively permanent improvement in earnings justifies a higher payout.[4] This practice leads to a relatively stable and gradually increasing pattern of dividend payouts.

Table 3–1 shows that the capital appreciation component for large company stock returns is 6.5 percent. This is larger than the *total* return of the best-performing interest-generating alternative: long-term corporate bonds. In essence, a common stock investor historically has had long-term capital appreciation sufficient to not only maintain but enhance his or her purchasing power. This leaves the dividend stream available for consumption. Because a common stock portfolio can keep up with inflation *on average over time,* so will its dividend stream. Emphasis is on the phrase *on average over time* because in the short run the much

---

4. For this reason, announcements of dividend changes—good or bad—are said to have *information content* and are of great interest to the investment community.

FIGURE 3-2A

Total Annual Returns in Percent (1926–1998)

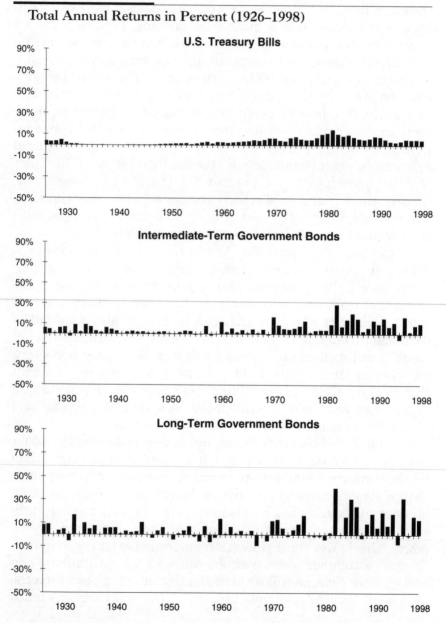

FIGURE 3-2B

Total Annual Returns in Percent (1926–1998)

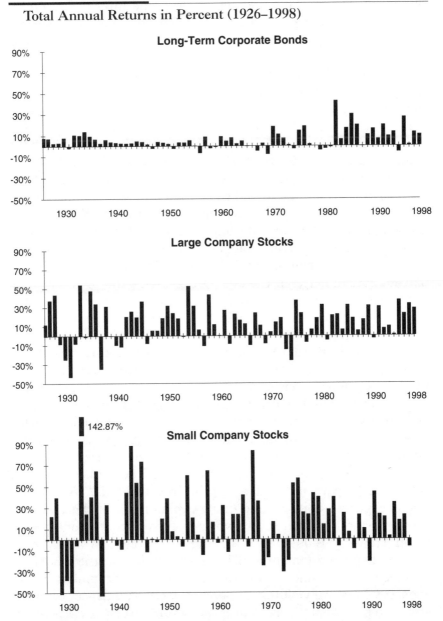

Source: Calculated by Gibson Capital Management using data presented in *Stocks, Bonds, Bills and Inflation*
® *1999 Yearbook*, © 1999 Ibbotson Associates, Inc. Based on copyrighted works by Ibbotson and Sinquefield. All
rights reserved. Used with permission.

higher volatility of common stocks produces great uncertainty in annual returns. Therefore, short-term and intermediate-term results may diverge substantially from the "normal relationships" indicated by examining performance over longer periods of time.

The capacity of a common stock portfolio to produce a relatively stable, growing dividend stream is important for an investor who wants to keep up with inflation. Had the 50-year-old woman previously described in Table 2–1 allocated a portion of her money to common stocks, her portfolio would not have been so susceptible to the devastating impact of inflation.

When reviewing the information in Table 3–1 with clients, it is important to emphasize that the return numbers should be evaluated in terms of their spreads relative to each other. For example, in comparing the 3.8 percent compound annual return of Treasury bills with the 11.2 percent compound annual return of large company stocks, the relationship is best described in terms of the 7.4 percent spread between the two. Occasionally, the relationship is erroneously considered multiplicatively. That is, it is misleading to think of large company stocks' 11.2 percent compound annual return as being 2.9 times that of Treasury bills' 3.8 percent compound annual return. (A review of the security return models we developed for each of the investment alternatives clearly shows the relationships in terms of arithmetic differences or spreads.)

A similar problem arises when looking at the returns outside of their historical context. During the late 1970s and early 1980s, interest rates were at double-digit levels. At that time, clients often asked the question, "Why should I invest in risky common stocks for a compound rate of return of 11.2 percent when I can safely get 12 percent by investing in Treasury bills?" Again, the misconception can be cleared up by explaining that the 11.2 percent return of common stocks was achieved during a time period when Treasury bills were returning 3.8 percent in an average inflationary environment of 3.1 percent. Based on the model we developed for common stock returns, in an environment where Treasury bills are yielding 12 percent, we would expect common stocks to provide an incremental compound return of 7.4 percent, or a total return of approximately 19.4 percent.[5]

---

5. Again, this is under the assumption of a normal yield curve environment.

APPENDIX: Statistical Concepts

Geometric Mean versus Arithmetic Mean

The first column of numbers in Table 3–1 is the *geometric mean,* which is another expression for compound annual return. The *arithmetic mean* shown in the second column refers to the simple average of the returns in the series. An example will illustrate the difference. Assume we invest $100 in a stock, which during the first year increases in value to $125, for a total return of +25 percent. During the second year, the stock has a total return of −20 percent, decreasing in value from $125 back to the original $100. The arithmetic mean of these two annual returns is their sum divided by two:

Year 1 return   = +25%
Year 2 return   = −20%
Sum   = +5%
Arithmetic mean = Sum/2 = 2.5%

The geometric mean (compound annual return), however, is 0 percent; that is, a $100 investment that is worth $100 two years later has a geometric mean return of 0 percent. For any series of numbers, the arithmetic mean will always be greater than or equal to the geometric mean. The difference between the arithmetic and geometric means is larger for a series of highly variable numbers. Only in the situation where the numbers in a series are constant will the arithmetic and geometric means be equal. The disparity between these two measures arises from the fact that it takes a larger percentage of above-average performance to offset a given percentage of below-average performance.

The arithmetic mean is the appropriate measure of typical performance for a single time period. The geometric mean is more appropriate when one is comparing returns over multiple time periods, as it represents the growth rate for an investment that is continually compounded. Often, models that describe the expected returns for various investment alternatives are single-period models, which accordingly incorporate terms using arithmetic means.[6] Because the purpose of this chapter is to develop

---

6. This is the case with input variables for computer optimization models. For a discussion, the reader is referred to Chapter 9, "Portfolio Optimization."

a framework for establishing long-term (i.e., multiple-period) investment policies, the comparison of relative historical performance and models of future investment returns will utilize geometric means (compound annual returns).

Risk Premiums and Inflation-Adjusted Returns

Throughout this book, in order to derive a risk premium or inflation-adjusted return, the geometric return of one investment alternative has been *arithmetically* subtracted from another or from inflation. For example, large company stocks' geometric mean of 11.2 percent was subtracted from Treasury bills' geometric mean of 3.8 percent to derive the equity risk premium of 7.4 percent. Ibbotson Associates, which provided the historical data on Treasury bills, bonds, and stock returns used in this book, prefers to state risk premiums and inflation-adjusted returns as the geometric difference between various return series. For example, the geometric difference between 5 percent and 12 percent is not 7 percent but 6.7 percent, computed as follows:

$$\frac{(1.12)}{(1.05)} - 1 = 6.7\%$$

The models developed in this book are to be used to provide a *conceptual* understanding of investment performance for both advisor and *client*. For this reason, in developing models the arithmetic difference rather than the geometric difference has been used in order to be consistent with the way a client typically thinks. (Most people think of the difference between 5 percent and 12 percent as being 7 percent, not 6.7 percent.) This simpler approach does not impair the conceptual value of the model and avoids the problem of getting sidetracked in explanations of geometric versus arithmetic differences.

Expected Return and Standard Deviation

The *expected return* of an investment is calculated as the weighted average of its possible returns, where the weights are the corresponding probability for each return. Thus, both the value of each outcome and its probability of occurrence are incorporated into this single statistic.

For example, Figure 3–3 describes an investment in common stock XYZ, which, depending on three alternative economic scenarios, will have a return of either −5 percent, 10 percent, or 25 percent. We can express the probability of each economic scenario in decimal form. For example, scenario A has a 25 percent likelihood of occurrence and is therefore assigned a probability of .25. Table 3–2 shows the mathematics for calculating the 10.75 percent expected return from an investment in common stock XYZ.

FIGURE 3 – 3

Probability of Various Returns from an Investment in Common Stock XYZ

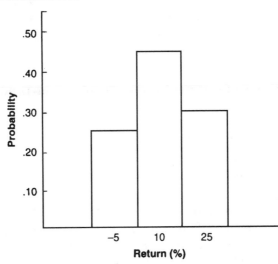

TABLE 3 – 2

Calculating the Expected Return for Common Stock XYZ

(1) Economic Scenario	*(2)* Probability of Occurrence	*(3)* Return	*(4) = (2) × (3)* Calculation of Expected Return
A	.25	−5%	−1.25%
B	.45	10	4.50
C	.30	25	7.50
	1.00		10.75%=Expected Return

TABLE 3-3

Calculating the Standard Deviation of Returns for
Common Stock XYZ

(1) Economic Scenario	(2) Probability of Occurrence	(3) Return	$(4)=(3)-10\ 75\%$ Deviation	$(5)=(4)^2$ Deviation Squared	$(6)=(2)\times(5)$ Probability Times Deviation Squared
A	.25	−5%	−15.75%	248.06	62.02
B	.45	10	−.75	.56	.25
C	.30	25	14.25	203.06	60.92
				Variance =	123.19
			Standard deviation = Square root of variance =		11.10

Alternative investments vary in terms of their expected returns, but an investment's expected return is only one aspect of future performance. It is equally important to simultaneously consider the volatility of an investment. The more widely an investment's return may vary from its expected return, the more volatile it is. The *standard deviation* is a commonly used measure of this volatility. To calculate the standard deviation, deviations are derived by subtracting the expected return from each possible return. These deviations are then squared and multiplied by their corresponding probabilities before being added together. The resulting sum is the *variance* (or probability weighted average squared deviation). The square root of the variance is the standard deviation. In our example, the standard deviation of return is 11.1 and is calculated as shown in Table 3–3.

Probability Distribution

In the real world, the possible returns from an investment cannot usually be divided into three discrete possibilities, as in the previous example. Rather, the range of possible returns forms a continuous curve, or *probability distribution,* similar to that shown in Figure 3–4. Because the distribution of returns is continuous, probabilities are described for various ranges of outcomes. For example, the probability that the return from common stock ABC will fall between 5 and 10 percent can be determined by calculating what portion of the total area under the curve lies between 5 and 10 percent on the horizontal axis. If, for example, the blackened area represents 9 percent of the area underneath the curve, then there is a 9 percent likelihood (or .09 probability) that the return from common stock ABC will fall between 5 and 10 percent.

The probability distribution shown in Figure 3–4 is the familiar bell-shaped curve, or *normal distribution*. A normal distribution has attractive statistical properties. For example, it can be completely specified by using only two numbers: the mean and the standard deviation. That is, given only these two numbers, anyone would draw the same bell-shaped curve. The curve is symmetrically centered on its mean, with 68 percent

FIGURE 3–4

Probability of Various Returns from an Investment in Common Stock ABC

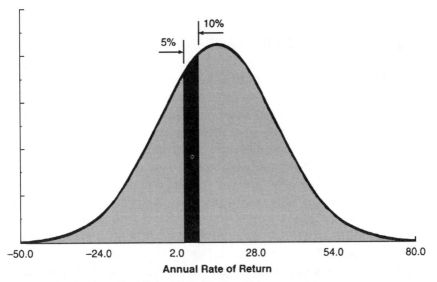

Annual Rate of Return

Source: Figure produced using Vestek Systems, Inc. software.

(approximately two-thirds) of the area underneath the curve lying within one standard deviation of the mean and 95 percent lying within two standard deviations.

In the example of common stock ABC in Figure 3–4, the mean is the expected return of 15 percent and the standard deviation of 20 percent is the measure of volatility, which describes the dispersion of possible returns around the expected return. Given the properties of a normal distribution, we know that the chances are roughly 2 out of 3 (i.e., a probability of .68) that the realized return will be between −5 percent and +35 percent (i.e., 15 percent ± 20 percent), and the chances are roughly 95 out of 100 that the realized return will be between −25 percent and +55 percent (i.e., 15 percent ± 40 percent).

Often, an assumption is made that certain components of security returns are normally distributed when they are actually better described by a lognormal distribution, which has a longer "right tail." This is the case because security returns often do not have an upside limit but nevertheless have a downside limit of −100 percent. For simplicity, we will assume normal rather than lognormal distributions where appropriate.

Serial Correlation

The last column in Table 3–1 specifies *serial correlations*. This statistic describes the extent to which the return in one period is helpful in predicting the return in the following period. A series of returns with a serial correlation near 1.0, for example, would be highly predictable from one period to the next and indicative of a trend. If the serial correlation is near −1.0, the series is highly cyclical. If the serial correlation is near 0, the series has no predictable pattern and is described as a *random walk*. The high values assigned for the income returns produced by stocks and bonds indicate that each follows a trend from year to year. The patterns of total returns from stocks and long-term bonds, however, more closely resemble random walks, as evidenced by their correspondingly low serial correlations. This is caused by the variability of the principal value that is characteristic of stocks and long-term bonds.

Although not shown in this exhibit, the serial correlation for the small stock premium is .39, which suggests that it tends to follow a trend. A review of the historical comparative performance of large company stocks versus small company stocks confirms that there are often prolonged periods of time when one of these investment alternatives outperforms the other.

CHAPTER 4

Market Timing

The evidence on investment managers' success with market timing is impressive — and overwhelmingly negative.

> —*Charles D. Ellis (1937–   )*
> Investment Policy, 1985

He that cannot abide a bad market, deserves not a good one.

> —*John Ray (1627–1705)*
> English Proverbs, 1678

Put all your eggs in one basket and—WATCH THAT BASKET.

> —*Mark Twain (1835–1910)*
> Pudd'nhead Wilson, 1894

The nightingale which cannot bear the thorn
It is best that it should never speak of the rose.

> —*Anwar-i-Suhaili*
> The Lights of Canopus

Common stocks have volatile returns. One consequence of that volatility is that investors have historically suffered negative annual returns approximately 27 percent of the time. Obviously, if there were a way to avoid the stock market's bad years, wealth would accumulate much more rapidly. Assume, for example, that it is December 31, 1925, and we are consulting a market timer who has made forecasts of 1926 security returns for Treasury bills, long-term corporate bonds, large company stocks, and small company stocks. He correctly predicts that of these four investment alternatives, large company stocks will produce the best total return for 1926. We invest $1, which by the end of 1926 grows to be worth $1.12. Impressed with our market timer's predictive abilities, we again meet with him on December 31, 1926, for his advice as to where to position our money for the following year. Year after year our market timer, with perfect predictive accuracy, advises us concerning which investment alternative is appropriate for our market-timed portfolio.

Through this compounding of our wealth, our initial $1 investment would have grown to be worth over $20 million by the end of 1998. This is quite a result compared with the best-performing investment alternative, small company stocks, with its ending value of $5117 and with the more modest ending value of approximately $15 for Treasury bills! To contextualize this phenomenal result, consider the outcome had $1 million been initially invested at the end of 1925. By the end of 1998, the portfolio would have been worth over $20 trillion—substantially more than the $13 trillion market value of all shares outstanding of all publicly traded common stocks in the United States. In essence, our 1925 millionaire would now own all of corporate America and approximately half of all non-U.S. companies from around the world!

Clearly, such market timing ability does not exist. Why, then, the persistent interest in market timing? People want to believe it is possible. Its appeal is truly seductive. When clients look at the long-term historical performance of common stocks, the hope of market timing is reinforced by what appears to be predictive trends: sustained periods of either above-average or below-average returns.[1] The resolution of this seeming contradiction lies in the recognition that a random series of numbers does not always look random! A simple experiment will verify this. Take a coin, flip it 100 times, and record the pattern of heads and tails produced. As you reach the end of the experiment, quite likely you will notice occasional runs of heads or runs of tails. Your knowledge of the nature of the coin flipping process prevents you, however, from inappropriately presuming the existence of predictive trends for either heads or tails. Each flip is independent of the preceding one.

When we examine the pattern of returns for common stocks, we see the same phenomenon. The run of heads in our

---

1. Despite appearances to the contrary, common stock returns do not follow a trend. This is indicated in Table 3–1, which shows that the serial correlation for large company stock returns is .01.

coin flipping experiment can represent a prolonged period of above-average stock returns. The run of tails corresponds to a period of below-average stock returns. With a prolonged bear market, such as occurred in 1973–74, we tend to berate ourselves after the fact by concluding that we should have known that the bear market would have continued once prices started falling. It is easy for investors to fall into this self-punishing attitude because they are continuously bombarded by discouraging commentaries in the financial press and on the evening news concerning the magnitude of the stock market decline.

On the other hand, common stock prices bottomed out during the summer of 1982, prior to one of the biggest bull markets in history. With the benefit of retrospect, people tend to conclude that everyone should have known that stocks were cheap during the summer of 1982 and poised for a big rise. The fact is that investors, in the aggregate, did not know stocks were a great bargain; otherwise, their prior buying activity would have prevented the stocks from becoming such bargains in the first place! As was the case with our coin flipping experiment, the timing and duration of these bull and bear markets are not predictable in advance.

An efficient market incorporates into current security prices relevant known information as well as consensus expectations regarding the unknown. Thus, when it comes to predicting short-term stock market movements, it is not of any value to know whether we are at war or at peace, have a Republican or a Democrat in the White House, or have been in an economic expansion or a contraction. What, then, moves the market? It is moved by information relevant to the pricing of investments that was not previously known. In essence, it is the surprises that no one sees coming that trigger price movements to establish new equilibriums in the markets. These surprises themselves are random events. Occasionally there are more good surprises than bad, and we have a bull market. Other times the reverse is true, and we have a bear market. There will always be bulls and bears, but the evidence indicates that there is no consistent way to predict the turning points.

Before engaging in a review of the research studies on market timing, it is helpful to review some statistics on stock market cycles, as summarized in a research paper by Trinity Investment Management Corporation. The data cover the nine peak-to-peak cycles since World War II. The first cycle began May 29, 1946, and the last cycle ended August 25, 1987.[2] Trinity observed:

1. There are about 1.7 times as many up months as down months: 309 versus 187.
2. The average bull market is up 104.8 percent versus the average bear market's drop of −28 percent.
3. Bull markets last nearly three times as long as bear markets: 41 months for the up legs versus 14 for the down legs.
4. Even within the bear markets, on average, about 3 to 4 months out of 10 are up months.

Trinity makes the further observation that during bull markets, on average, only 8 months (out of the 41-month average bull market duration) accounted for more than 60 percent of the total return achieved.

Clearly, the average advance in a bull market is more than sufficient to regain the ground lost during a typical bear market. The fact that in bear markets 3 to 4 months out of 10 are up months reinforces the notion that it is often difficult to know that a bear market is occurring until one is looking back after the fact. According to a research study by William F. Sharpe,

> a manager who attempts to time the market must be right roughly three times out of four, merely to match the overall performance of those competitors who don't. If he is right less often his relative performance will be inferior. There are two reasons for this. First, such a manager will often have his funds in cash equivalents in good market years, sacrificing the higher returns stocks provide in such years. Second, he will incur transaction costs in making switches, many of which will prove to be unprofitable.

2. Some analysts argue that a bear market occurred from July 16, 1990, to October 11, 1990, during which the S&P 500 suffered a price decline of −19.9 percent. A bear market is defined as a price-only decline of at least 20 percent over a six-month horizon. Having met neither the loss criterion nor the duration criterion, this decline is classified as a correction in the bull market that began on December 4, 1987. As of the end of 1998, this bull market was still intact and had become the longest bull market of the twentieth century.

Regarding the potential gains from market timing, Sharpe concluded:

> Barring truly devastating market declines similar to those of The Depression, it seems likely that gains of little more than four per cent per year from timing should be expected from a manager whose forecasts are truly prophetic.[3]

A study by Robert H. Jeffrey concluded:

> No one can predict the market's ups and downs over a long period, and the risks of trying outweigh the rewards.

He goes on to comment:

> The rationale for being a full-time equity investor is not that there are more positive real return periods than negative ones in most time frames, but rather that most of the "positive action" is compressed into just a few periods, which (perversely but understandably) tend to follow particularly adverse times for stocks.[4]

With reference to Ibbotson Associates' examination of security returns from 1926 through 1998, suppose that a common stock investor had missed the seven best years for common stocks, during which time she alternatively had invested in Treasury bills. Because this investor was on the sidelines in cash equivalents during this critical 10 percent of the time period, $1 initially invested in stocks at the end of 1925 would have declined from what would have been $2351 with continuous investment in large company stocks to only $202 as a consequence of having missed these seven superlative years.

The superior returns available from common stocks do not accrue in a uniform manner. Rather, they can be traced to a few periods of sudden bursts of strength. It is interesting to observe that these positive surges often occur when pessimism is running high. This is consistent with expectations, because a market bottom is reached when pessimism reaches its maximum. It is at that point that the potential sellers have sold, leaving the market with nowhere to go but up. Again, though, it is important

---

3. William F. Sharpe, "Likely Gains from Market Timing," *Financial Analysts Journal,* March–April 1975, pp. 60–69.

4. Robert H. Jeffrey, "The Folly of Stock Market Timing," *Harvard Business Review,* July–August 1984, pp. 102–110.

to stress that these market turning points can be recognized only in retrospect.

For example, at the end of 1990, both investors and money managers were pessimistic. Common stocks had just posted a negative return of -3.71 percent—the first loss in nearly a decade. To make matters worse, recession was upon us and we were on the brink of the Persian Gulf War. Many of my clients, including money management firms for which I have consulted, argued that it had to be a good time to be out of the stock market, with money parked safely in Treasury bills. I urged them to remain invested— not because I believed the market was poised for an advance but rather because it is impossible to know when the particularly rewarding periods of equity investing will occur. As it turned out, 1991 was such a year, posting an advance of 30.55 percent,[5] and a good portion of that return occurred quickly after the beginning of the Persian Gulf War. Investors who, out of fear and pessimism, tried to protect themselves by selling stocks and parking the proceeds in cash missed a wonderful market advance.

Consider a market timer who has a 50/50 forecasting ability—that is, he is wrong in his predictions as often as he is right. Depending on which years he is wrong, his investment experience will vary widely. If he is lucky, he will be in the wrong place at the wrong time when the spread in returns between Treasury bills and the S&P 500 is narrow, thereby not suffering significantly from the error. If, however, his mistakes more often than not occur during time periods when the spread is quite large, the results can be disastrous. Based on the capital market experience from 1926 through 1982, Jeffrey concluded that

> if the theoreticians are correct about the inefficiency of market timing (that is, it will generally be accurate only 50 percent of the time), the probable outcome is a best-case real dollar return only about two times greater than what would come from continuous investment in the S&P, while the worst case produces about one hundred times less!
>
> The point of these...statistics is simply to emphasize that a market-timing strategist has tremendous natural odds to over-

---

5. Annual returns in excess of 30 percent have occurred only seven times in the past four decades.

come, and that these odds increase geometrically with the length of the time frame and with the frequency of the timing interval. There is probably no situation where caveat emptor is more apropos for the portfolio owner than in interviewing prospective timing managers.[6]

Much of the problem with market timing concerns the fact that a disproportionate percentage of the total gain from a bull market tends to occur very rapidly at the beginning of a market recovery. If a market timer is on the sidelines in cash during this critical time, she is apt to miss too much of the action.

In another study, Jess S. Chua and Richard S. Woodward approached the subject from another angle in attempting to ascertain whether it is the inability to avoid bear markets or the tendency to miss the early part of a market recovery that accounts for the poor results achieved from market timing. They concluded:

> Overall, the results show that it is more important to correctly forecast bull markets than bear markets. If the investor has only a 50 percent chance of correctly forecasting bull markets, then he should not practice market timing at all. His average return will be less than that of a buy-and-hold strategy even if he can forecast bear markets perfectly.

These researchers concluded that for market timing to pay:

> Investors require the forecast accuracies of at least:
> 80 percent bull and 50 percent bear;
> 70 percent bull and 80 percent bear; or
> 60 percent bull and 90 percent bear....[7]

This is particularly interesting because professional market timers most often stress capital preservation and the ability to avoid bear markets as the major benefit to be derived from their services.

---

6. Jeffrey, "The Folly of Stock Market Timing," pp. 107–108.

7. Jess H. Chua and Richard S. Woodward, *Gains from Stock Market Timing*, Monograph 1986–2 of *Monograph Series in Finance and Economics,* ed. by Anthony Saunders (New York: Salomon Brothers Center for the Study of Financial Institutions at the Graduate School of Business Administration of New York University), pp. 12–13.

In his wonderful book *Investment Policy,* Charles D. Ellis referred to an unpublished study of 100 large pension funds, stating that

> their experience with market timing found that while all the funds had engaged in at least some market timing, not one of the funds had improved its rate of return as a result of its efforts at timing. In fact, 89 of the 100 lost as a result of "timing"—and their losses averaged a daunting 4.5 percent over the five-year period.[8]

Although long-term gains from market timing are highly unlikely, there will always be investors who have positive results from timing activities—particularly in the short run. This is the case because over any given time period there will be a wide dispersion of investor experiences, with some investors doing very well and some doing very poorly. Statistically, this is what we expect. The danger is the leap of logic which presumes that the good market timing result is caused by superior predictive ability. In the aggregate, market timing does not work, and most investors' experiences have been and will be negative. Those market timers who have most recently made the right moves, however, are written up in financial publications and interviewed on television. This fuels the hopes of those who wish there were a way to get the advantage of a bull market while avoiding the pain of a bear market. Meanwhile, unsuccessful market timing firms fade away as clients reallocate what is left of their portfolios to the newly identified market timing guru.

Many investors prefer to live with false hope rather than critically examine whether market timing is possible at all. As Aristotle observed: "A plausible impossibility is always preferable to an unconvincing possibility." To face the question of whether market timing is possible forces an investor to acknowledge that he may have to either periodically face the pain of a bear market or, alternatively, forgo investing in common stocks altogether and thereby sacrifice the possibility of real capital growth. There is a pervasive human tendency to reinterpret one's experience to fit preconceptions. This is often the case with

---

8. Charles D. Ellis, *Investment Policy* (Burr Ridge, IL: Irwin Professional Publishing, 1985), p. 13.

market timing, where hope springs eternal that somewhere, someone will somehow be able to consistently catch the bull while safely avoiding the bear.

The alternative to market timing is to simply buy and hold common stocks. As William Sharpe points out:

> A manager who keeps assets in stocks at all times is like an optimistic market timer. His actions are consistent with a policy of predicting a good year every year. While such a manager may know that such predictions will be wrong roughly one year out of three, such an attitude is nonetheless likely to lead to results superior to those achieved by most market timers.[9]

This chapter opens with a quote from Charles D. Ellis, and I'll close the discussion with another of his observations:

> In investment management, the real opportunity to achieve superior results is not in scrambling to outperform the market, but in establishing *and adhering to* appropriate investment policies over the long term—policies that position the portfolio to benefit from riding with the main long-term forces in the market.[10]

---

9. Sharpe, "Likely Gains from Stock Market Timing," p. 67.

10. Ellis, *Investment Policy,* pp. 22–23.

CHAPTER 5

Time Horizon

He who wishes to be rich in a day will be hanged in a year.

—Leonardo da Vinci (1452–1519)
Notebooks, c. 1500

Money is of a prolific generating nature. Money can beget money, and its offspring can beget more.

—Benjamin Franklin (1706–1790)
Letters: To My Friend, A. B., 1748

Time is Archimedes' lever in investing.

—Charles D. Ellis (1937–)
Investment Policy, 1985

If you were charged with the task of dividing all the investment alternatives we have reviewed thus far into two groups on the basis of their investment characteristics, how would you do it? One way would be to rank them on the basis of their historical returns and look for a natural dividing line. With reference to the information in Table 3–1, we see that the biggest gap in historical returns exists between long-term corporate bonds and large company stocks. Using this as our dividing line, we would find that one group of investments would consist of Treasury bills, intermediate-term government bonds, long-term government bonds, and long-term corporate bonds—all of the interest-generating alternatives. The second group would consist of large company stocks and small company stocks—the equity alternatives with high historical returns.

If we instead approached the task by ranking the investment alternatives on the basis of volatility as measured by their historical standard deviations, we would draw the natural dividing line in exactly the same place: between interest-generating

investments and equity investments. Let us now contrast
the investment characteristics of these two broad groupings.

An interest-generating investment is a loan that provides a
return in the form of interest payments, with the promise that
the principal will be returned at a stated maturity date. The
primary advantage of this kind of investment is that the cash
flows (interest payments and principal return) are specified in
advance. The major disadvantage is that these investments
tend to be very susceptible to inflation. Historically, interest-
generating alternatives have not been capable of producing an
income stream while maintaining purchasing power.

By comparison, large company stocks and small company
stocks are equity ownership interests in businesses. An equity
investment provides return in the form of dividends and/or capital appreciation. It does not have a stated maturity, and there
is no promise that the principal will be returned some day. But
it also has no upper limit on its return possibilities. The primary
advantage of an equity investment is the prospect for real (i.e.,
inflation-adjusted), long-term capital growth. The major disadvantage of an equity investment is the high short-run volatility
of principal value.

In essence, these two broad categories, interest-generating
investments and equity investments, represent the two alternative ways of putting money to work. It is the traditional distinction of being either a "loaner or an owner." A low return is the
price paid by the "loaner" who wants the advantage of a more
predictable outcome. Short-run volatility of principal is the price
paid by the "owner" who wants the long-term capital growth possible with equities. This is simply an acknowledgment of the
volatility/return relationship among investment alternatives.
We previously discussed a wide variety of risks. In my judgment,
however, the two most important money management risks are:

1. Inflation—which is most damaging to interest-generating investments.
2. Volatility—which is most pronounced with equity
   investments.

To focus our discussion, let us use Treasury bills as a proxy
for interest-generating investments and large company stocks
as a proxy for equity investments. In summary:

	Treasury Bills	**Large Company Stocks**
Advantage	Stability of principal value	Long-term real capital growth
Disadvantage	Susceptibility to inflation	Volatile returns

Given the higher returns produced by equity investments, one could conclude that investors have greater fear of stock market volatility than they have of inflation. This is evidenced by the lower returns they willingly accept with Treasury bills in order to have stable principal values. Many investors are over-concerned with the volatility of common stock returns and underconcerned regarding the damaging effects of inflation. There are several reasons for this. First, inflation is insidious, taking its toll little by little over the long term.

Second, investors who are not aware of the impact of inflation over time tend to view their investment results in nominal terms and generally prefer interest-generating alternatives. For example, during 1979 and 1980, when inflation reached a peak of 12 to 13 percent, Treasury bill returns were at a historical high of 10 to 11 percent. Treasury bill investors tended to look at the accumulation of interest, ignoring the fact that these high nominal returns were insufficient to compensate for the impact of inflation. Many investors still look at 1979 and 1980 as "the good old days" of high money market returns and deplore the lower, single-digit returns that became available as interest rates fell through the 1980s. Yet these investors were actually much better off in the lower interest rate environment. Returns were much higher in *real* terms then than they were during 1979 and 1980. It would be interesting to see how perceptions would change if Treasury bill investors had their returns routinely reported to them in inflation-adjusted terms.

Third, common stock volatility by comparison can do much more damage in the short run. On October 19, 1987, for example, we saw common stocks drop more than 20 percent *in one day,* compared with the highest recent *annual* inflation rate of 13 percent in 1979. Unfortunately, many investors focus too narrowly on the short term and incorrectly conclude that common stock losses are permanent. Some investors who suffered through the 1973–74 bear market for common stocks sold their equities near the bottom and therefore missed participating in

one of the best bull markets in this century. In their discour-
agement they said to themselves, "Common stocks?—never
again!" In the short run, the possible negative consequences of
stock market volatility will be much greater than the damage
likely from inflation.

Is the fear of common stock volatility warranted? In some
circumstances it is, and in other situations, perhaps not. As we
look into the future, there are two things we can count on. First,
short-run common stock returns will remain unpredictable and
volatile. Second, people will prefer predictability over uncertainty. For example, consider a choice between the following
investment alternatives. Investment A has an expected return
of 7 percent, with a standard deviation of 2 percent. Investment
B has an expected return of 7 percent, with a standard deviation
of 4 percent. Both investments offer the same expected return,
but investment B has twice as much volatility as investment A.
Rational investors are volatility-averse. Given these alternatives, such investors will choose investment A. There is no
incentive for bearing the higher volatility of investment B.

Economists refer to the "declining marginal utility of wealth"
as underlying the explanation for this volatility aversion. That is,
each additional dollar that is acquired always increases one's
well-being, but it does so at a declining rate. An extra $100 means
more to you if your net worth is $1000 than it does if you are a
millionaire. In an investment context, this means that the additional dollar you make with a good outcome is not as valuable as
the dollar that is lost with a bad outcome. In the real world,
investors would sell investment B to buy investment A. By their
doing so, the price of A would rise and the price of B would fall. In
equilibrium, investment B would have a higher expected return
to compensate for its greater volatility.

The same is true in our comparison of Treasury bills and
common stocks. The buying and selling activities of investors in
the marketplace cause common stocks to be priced to provide
higher expected returns than Treasury bills, as compensation
for bearing the volatility of equities.

In the last chapter we presented evidence that indicated
that market timing does not work. Consider what would happen, however, if there were an easy way to time the stock market. Investors would buy stocks in advance of a market rise and

sell them in advance of a foreseen decline. This buying and selling activity, however, would change the pattern of future stock
price behavior by smoothing out the market's ups and downs.
There is only one problem: When common stock volatility disappears, so does the reward for bearing it! I therefore *prefer* a
world where common stocks retain their short-run, unpredictable volatility. It is part of the foundation on which their
long-term higher returns are built. Implicit in the market
timer's worldview is the notion that money is made in common
stocks *despite* the volatility. In contrast, the worldview presented here rests on the notion that money is made in common
stocks *because* of the volatility.

Now, the question becomes, "Under what conditions is the
volatility worth bearing?" If we allocate the 7.4 percent equity
risk premium across each of the 365 days in the year, we find
that the daily performance advantage of common stocks relative
to Treasury bills practically disappears. On any given day, the
chances are basically 50/50 that common stocks will outperform
Treasury bills. Given the ever present volatility of common
stocks, there is no incentive to assume equity risk on the basis
of a one-day time horizon. The same is true for one-month and
one-year investments in common stocks. The standard deviation
of large company stocks has historically been 20.3 percent (refer
to Table 3–1). This is much larger than the equity risk premium
we expect to receive on average from holding common stocks. In
the short run, although we expect to have higher returns on
common stocks, the high volatility will swamp recognition of the
equity risk premium. This is particularly troublesome for unsophisticated investors who often confuse this volatility for evidence of an irrational marketplace.

Time is one of the most important dimensions of the money
management process. It is also often the least understood by
investors. In assessing investment alternatives, time horizon
determines appropriateness. If it is known that an investor will
need $20,000 next month to buy a car, a money market fund is a
reasonable investment in the interim. A pension plan with
known future nominal obligations (i.e., there's no provision for
inflation-adjusted benefits) may decide to match the duration of
those obligations with similar duration bonds or follow an immunization strategy.

Most longer-term investment situations, however, do not involve objectives with specific future nominal needs. There is simply too much uncertainty in the direction and magnitude of inflation. More often, the goal is therefore the preservation and/or accumulation of wealth in real terms. This requires the utilization of equity investments. Whereas in the short run we concluded that the volatility of equities is too great relative to the expected reward, this changes as the time horizon lengthens. For example, based on Ibbotson Associates' capital market data, from 1926 through 1998 large company stocks outperformed Treasury bills in 47 of the 73 years, or 64 percent of the time. If we compare the performance over longer holding periods of 5 years, 10 years, and 20 years, however, we find that large company stocks increasingly dominate Treasury bills 81 percent, 84 percent, and finally 100 percent of the time, respectively.

Assume for a moment that we have a stable inflation and interest rate environment. As the time horizon lengthens, the expected return from common stocks will not change, but the variability of holding period compound returns will decline dramatically. The longer the holding period is, the more opportunity there is for good years to offset bad years, with the result that the range of compound returns converges toward the middle.

In Table 5–1, for example, comparisons are made among compound returns for large company stocks, long-term corporate bonds, long-term government bonds, Treasury bills, and inflation for 1-, 5-, 10-, and 20-year holding periods. In examining the information for one-year holding periods, we see that in 43 of the 73 years (59 percent of the time) large company stocks outperformed the other three investment alternatives. But the returns ranged from −43.3 percent to 54.0 percent. Hence, although we expect large company stocks to outperform the other three investment alternatives in any given year, the penalty for underperformance can be quite high. The ranges of returns for other investment alternatives are narrower, as expected given their lower standard deviations.

As we stretch the time horizon to 10 years, large company stocks now dominate the other investment alternatives in 50 out of 64 periods, or 78 percent of the time. Not only has our confidence in being right with large company stocks increased, the penalty for a bad outcome is considerably less. The worst

10-year large company stock experience produced a compound average return of −.9 percent. On that basis, a $10,000 investment would have declined to $9136 with full reinvestment of income. In 98 percent of the 10-year holding periods, the outcome was better than that!

Finally, we see that with 20-year holding periods, large company stocks outperformed the other three investment alternatives in 51 out of 54 periods, or 94 percent of the time. Although this is nearly 100 percent of the time, it is important to recognize that there have been three 20-year periods when long-term corporate bonds provided returns superior to those of large company stocks. These were the 20-year periods beginning 1928, 1929, and 1930. The extreme market conditions accompanying the Great Depression were the cause of this unusual result. Although this is not shown in Table 5–1, if we stretched the holding periods to 25 years, we would find that large company stocks dominated the other three investment alternatives 100 percent of the time.

The volatility of common stocks is undoubtedly an enemy in the short run, but it is the basis for their higher expected returns. Time transforms this short-run enemy into a friend for the long-term investor.

In Table 5–1 we noted that an investor's performance results will vary depending on the calendar year with which her holding period begins. Few clients, however, establish an investment position exactly at the beginning of a calendar year. The utilization of annual return data understates the range of returns for various holding periods. By changing the beginning point for various holding periods to a monthly rather than a calendar-year basis, Figure 5–1 provides a more comprehensive comparison of the range of returns for Treasury bills versus large company stocks. The graph utilizes data from 1926 through 1998 and compares the range of returns for holding periods of 12 months (1 year) to 240 months (20 years). Observe the potentially high penalty for being in large company stocks for holding periods as short as 12 months to 60 months.

As the holding period lengthens, however, the range of compound annual returns converges dramatically. Note that *all* 240-month holding periods had positive compound annual returns. It is also quite interesting to observe that the median return for

T A B L E   5 – 1

Comparison of Investment Results for Various Holding Periods (1926–1998)

	Large Company Stocks	Long-Term Corporate Bonds	Long-Term Government Bonds	Treasury Bills	Inflation
73 One-Year Holding Periods					
Highest annual percent return	54.0	42.6	40.4	14.7	18.2
Lowest annual percent return	−43.3	−8.1	−9.2	−0.0	−10.3
Number of periods with negative returns	20	16	20	1	10
Number of periods with best of four returns	43	11	7	12	N/A
Percentage of periods with best of four returns	59	15	10	16	N/A
69 Five-Year Holding Periods					
Highest compound annual percent return	24.1*	22.5	21.6	11.1	10.1
Lowest compound annual percent return	−12.5	−2.2	−2.1	0.1	−5.4
Number of periods with negative compound returns	7	3	6	0	7
Number of periods with best of four returns	52	10	3	4	N/A
Percentage of periods with best of four returns	75	15	4	6	N/A

64 Ten-Year Holding Periods

Highest compound annual percent return	20.1*	16.3	15.6	9.2	8.7
Lowest compound annual percent return	−0.9	1.0	−0.1	0.1	−2.6
Number of periods with negative compound returns	2	0	1	0	6
Number of periods with best of four returns	50	8	0	6	N/A
Percentage of periods with best of four returns	78	13	0	9	N/A

54 Twenty-Year Holding Periods

Highest compound annual percent return	17.7*	10.9*	11.1*	7.7	6.4
Lowest compound annual percent return	3.1	1.3	.7	.4	.1
Number of periods with negative compound returns	0	0	0	0	0
Number of periods with best of four returns	51	3	0	0	N/A
Percentage of periods with best of four returns	94	6	0	0	N/A

*The most recent holding period produced the highest compound return since 1926.

Source: Calculated by Gibson Capital Management using data presented in *Stocks, Bonds, Bills and Inflation* ® *1999 Yearbook*, © 1999 Ibbotson Associates, Inc. Based on copyrighted works by Ibbotson and Sinquefield. All rights reserved. Used with permission.

FIGURE 5–1

Large Company Stocks versus Treasury Bills: Range of Compound Annual Returns for Various Holding Periods (1926–1998)

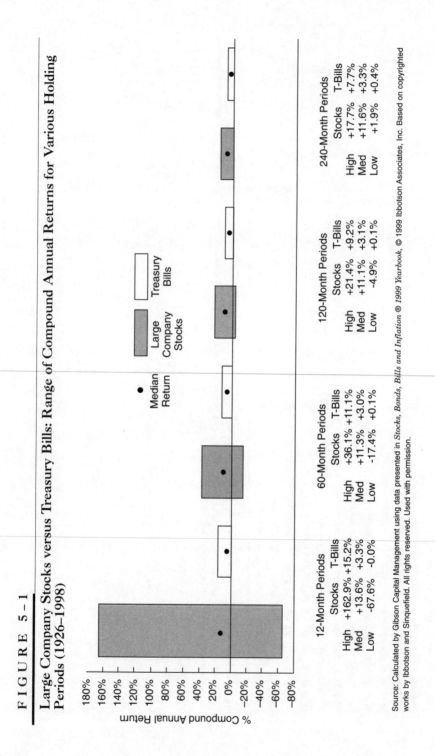

12-Month Periods

	Stocks	T-Bills
High	+162.9%	+15.2%
Med	+13.6%	+3.3%
Low	-67.6%	-0.0%

60-Month Periods

	Stocks	T-Bills
High	+36.1%	+11.1%
Med	+11.3%	+3.0%
Low	-17.4%	+0.1%

120-Month Periods

	Stocks	T-Bills
High	+21.4%	+9.2%
Med	+11.1%	+3.1%
Low	-4.9%	+0.1%

240-Month Periods

	Stocks	T-Bills
High	+17.7%	+7.7%
Med	+11.6%	+3.3%
Low	+1.9%	+0.4%

Source: Calculated by Gibson Capital Management using data presented in *Stocks, Bonds, Bills and Inflation* ® *1999 Yearbook*, © 1999 Ibbotson Associates, Inc. Based on copyrighted works by Ibbotson and Sinquefield. All rights reserved. Used with permission.

large company stocks was approximately the same across the 12-, 60-, 120-, and 240-month holding periods. The median return for Treasury bills was, of course, much lower than that for large company stocks but was similarly relatively constant.

Figures 5–2A and 5–2B communicate the same message in a different form. Here, we can directly compare relative returns in a contemporaneous way for various holding periods. Again, we see that if stock market volatility is the disease, time is the cure.

The "miracle of compound interest" is also at work in the pattern of the increasing dominance of large company stocks over time. What seems like a modest 7.4 percent equity risk premium produces huge differences in wealth accumulation over long time periods. During the period 1926 through 1998, the 7.4 percent incremental return with large company stocks produced more than 157 times the wealth accumulation from Treasury bills. Assume Treasury bills now yield 5 percent, with the corresponding estimated compound return for large company stocks at 12 percent. In Table 5–2, we see that in only 11 years the cumulative wealth from an investment in large company stocks would double that of a corresponding investment in Treasury bills. By 17 years, large company stocks would be worth three times the value of an investment in Treasury bills.

In summary, volatility swamps the expected payoff from common stocks in the short run, making them a risk not worth taking. But in the long run, common stocks emerge as the winner because of the convergence of average returns around common stocks' higher expected return, coupled with the miracle of compounding interest.

Time horizon is the key variable in determining the appropriate balance of interest-generating versus equity investments in a portfolio. This is summarized in the following comparison:

	Interest-Generating Investments	Equity Investments
Advantage	Less volatility	Long-term real capital growth
Disadvantage	Inflation susceptibility	High volatility
Appropriate for	Short time horizons	Long time horizons

FIGURE 5-2A

Large Company Stocks versus Treasury Bills: Compound Annual Returns for Various Holding Periods (1926–1998)

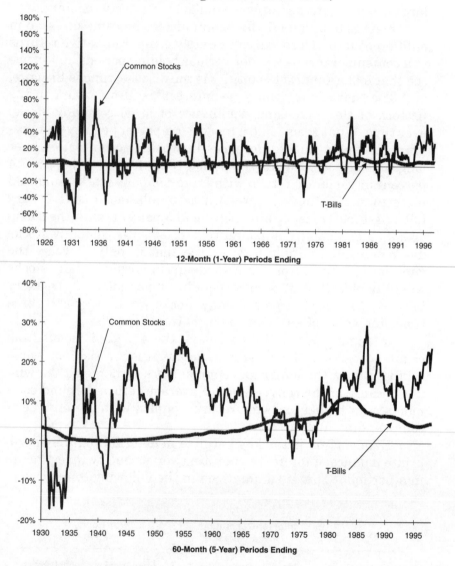

FIGURE 5-2B

Large Company Stocks versus Treasury Bills: Compound Annual Returns for Various Holding Periods (1926–1998)

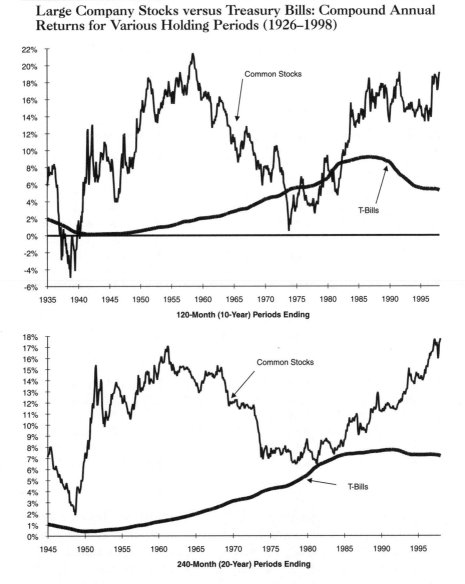

Source: Calculated by Gibson Capital Management using data presented in *Stocks, Bonds, Bills and Inflation* ® *1999 Yearbook*, © 1999 Ibbotson Associates, Inc. Based on copyrighted works by Ibbotson and Sinquefield. All rights reserved. Used with permission.

T A B L E 5 – 2

Growth of $1 at Interest

Years	4%	5%	6%	7%	8%	9%	10%	11%	12%	13%
1	1.04	1.05	1.06	1.07	1.08	1.09	1.10	1.11	1.12	1.13
2	1.08	1.10	1.12	1.14	1.17	1.19	1.21	1.23	1.25	1.28
3	1.12	1.16	1.19	1.23	1.26	1.30	1.33	1.37	1.40	1.44
4	1.17	1.22	1.26	1.31	1.36	1.41	1.46	1.52	1.57	1.63
5	1.22	1.28	1.34	1.40	1.47	1.54	1.61	1.69	1.76	1.84
6	1.27	1.34	1.42	1.50	1.59	1.68	1.77	1.87	1.97	2.08
7	1.32	1.41	1.50	1.61	1.71	1.83	1.95	2.08	2.21	2.35
8	1.37	1.48	1.59	1.72	1.85	1.99	2.14	2.30	2.48	2.66
9	1.42	1.55	1.69	1.84	2.00	2.17	2.36	2.56	2.77	3.00
10	1.48	1.63	1.79	1.97	2.16	2.37	2.59	2.84	3.11	3.39
11	1.54	1.71	1.90	2.10	2.33	2.58	2.85	3.15	3.48	3.84
12	1.60	1.80	2.01	2.25	2.52	2.81	3.14	3.50	3.90	4.33
13	1.67	1.89	2.13	2.41	2.72	3.07	3.45	3.88	4.36	4.90
14	1.73	1.98	2.26	2.58	2.94	3.34	3.80	4.31	4.89	5.53
15	1.80	2.08	2.40	2.76	3.17	3.64	4.18	4.78	5.47	6.25
16	1.87	2.18	2.54	2.95	3.43	3.97	4.59	5.31	6.13	7.07
17	1.95	2.29	2.69	3.16	3.70	4.33	5.05	5.90	6.87	7.99
18	2.03	2.41	2.85	3.38	4.00	4.72	5.56	6.54	7.69	9.02
19	2.11	2.53	3.03	3.62	4.32	5.14	6.12	7.26	8.61	10.20
20	2.19	2.65	3.21	3.87	4.66	5.60	6.73	8.06	9.65	11.52
21	2.28	2.79	3.40	4.14	5.03	6.11	7.40	8.95	10.80	13.02
22	2.37	2.93	3.60	4.43	5.44	6.66	8.14	9.93	12.10	14.71
23	2.46	3.07	3.82	4.74	5.87	7.26	8.95	11.03	13.55	16.63
24	2.56	3.23	4.05	5.07	6.34	7.91	9.85	12.24	15.18	18.79
25	2.67	3.39	4.29	5.43	6.85	8.62	10.83	13.59	17.00	21.23

Investors generally tend to underestimate their relevant time horizons. For example, consider new clients, a husband and a wife, both age 60, who when discussing their time horizon comment: "We both work now but want to retire at age 65. Because we are only five years from retirement, our time horizon is very short. Equities were fine when we were young and building assets for retirement, but now that retirement is approaching, we should be cashing out of stocks to move into certificates of deposit and bonds so that we can use the interest for living expenses during retirement."

This couple has confused their retirement horizon with their investment portfolio time horizon. The latter is *much* longer. If they plan to rely on their portfolio to support them through retirement, their time horizon extends until the death of the survivor of them. For a man and woman of average health, both age 60, the life expectancy of the survivor of them is more than 25 years. As we have seen, over a 25-year time horizon, the danger of inflation is greater than the risk of common stock volatility, and accordingly, equities should be meaningfully represented in their portfolio.

The tendency for investors to underestimate their time horizons leads to portfolios that are inappropriately underweighted in equities and therefore overexposed to inflation. This tendency is reinforced by the client's desire to measure performance over quarterly and annual time periods. Such measurement intervals are much too short to get a realistic assessment of progress toward the achievement of long-term objectives.

A proper understanding of time horizon as it relates to the investment process can dramatically alter a person's volatility tolerance. The next chapter builds a simple model for guiding clients in making the most important decision impacting portfolio performance: the balance between interest-generating and equity investments.

CHAPTER 6

A Model for Determining Broad Portfolio Balance

Everything should be made as simple as possible, but not simpler.

—Albert Einstein (1879–1955)

You pays your money and you takes your choice.

—Punch, 1846

The client/advisor relationship begins with the data-gathering session. The purpose of this process is to get to know the client. Much of the information solicited is factual in nature and can be objectively determined. For personal clients, this information includes the value of assets and liabilities, sources of income and expenditures, tax situation, family composition, employment information, and so on. For institutional clients, such as qualified retirement plans and endowments, this information includes a list of investment positions, anticipated contributions to and withdrawals from the portfolio, and a description of legal or regulatory constraints.

Another area of data gathering is subjective in nature and requires a more qualitative approach. This is the realm of client psychology, hopes and dreams, opinions and preferences regarding investments, and tolerance for various types of risk. Specifically, let us discuss the challenges involved in assessing the client's:

- Specific goals
- Investment objectives
- Investment knowledge
- Risks
- Volatility tolerance

SPECIFIC GOALS

Examples of goals for an individual money management client include:

- Early retirement
- College education for children
- Buying a vacation home
- Providing for an aging parent with declining health

For institutional money management clients the goal might be to:

- Provide retirement benefits to participants in a qualified plan
- Fund the charitable pursuits of an endowment fund

When these goals are expressed, they often lack specificity. The advisor needs to help the client flesh out the goals in more detail. For example, does early retirement mean age 50, age 55, or age 60? What lifestyle does the client want in retirement, and what level of income will be necessary to sustain it? If the client wants to send three children to college, will they attend high-priced private institutions or less expensive public universities? Will scholarships be likely? Will the children get jobs in order to help pay their own expenses? If the children are young, at what rate will tuition rise in the interim?

Is a vacation home purchase a short-term or a long-term goal? Approximately what price range is the client considering? What would be the expenses associated with a vacation home? Does the client anticipate renting it when it is not in use? What kind of rental income could be obtained?

In the situation of the aging parent, is support currently being provided by the client? What sources of income does the parent currently have, and are there assets that can be sold to provide additional funds if needed? What kind of health insurance coverage does the parent have, and will he or she qualify for some form of government assistance for medical bills or income needs? Similarly, greater specificity can be developed for institutional clients who have quantifiable needs to fund future benefit payments.

INVESTMENT OBJECTIVES

Once the client goals have been specified, the next step is to develop investment objectives that correspond to those goals. Much of this can be described mathematically in a relatively straightforward manner. Subject to reasonable assumptions, for example, we can calculate the annual investment necessary at a specified growth rate to accumulate a predetermined future sum of money.

Very often, however, client goals are more ambitious than can realistically be achieved. We have all known investors who decide to get serious about their retirement goals a few years prior to retirement. They are ready to modify their lifestyles as necessary to free up funds for investment in order to be assured a comfortable retirement. By that point, however, the lifestyle supportable at retirement has been largely determined. If that lifestyle is found to be seriously inadequate, there is probably little that can be done to materially improve it.

Human desires tend to exceed the resources available to fund them. In developing investment objectives, goals must therefore be prioritized and often compromised in the process of determining what is realistically possible in any given situation. Sound investment objectives are built on realistic capital market assumptions and reflect the limitations of the client's available income and resources.

INVESTMENT KNOWLEDGE

The best clients understand the general principles of money management and the characteristics of alternative investments. The long-term success of the investment management process depends to a large extent on the client's understanding of how his or her portfolio is structured and the manner in which it will behave. In the data-gathering process, it is helpful to have clients describe their good and bad experiences with investments. From their comments the breadth and depth of their knowledge can be gleaned. Often, advisors use questionnaires that exhaustively list many different types of investment alternatives. Clients are asked to indicate their familiarity with, preference for, and prior use of each investment alternative. I think it is important to recognize the primary purpose of such questionnaires and to be aware of their limitations.

A client who indicates on a questionnaire familiarity with, preference for, and/or knowledge about common stocks, for example, does not necessarily understand them sufficiently to make informed decisions regarding their use. At best, such questionnaires are a beginning point for an educational process that meaningfully involves the client. A significant danger exists in inappropriately using the responses to such questions as a basis for either inferring volatility tolerance or choosing building blocks for constructing a portfolio. A client who says he has never invested in bonds and prefers not to use them may only be expressing unfamiliarity with them. It would be inappropriate to develop a portfolio excluding bonds solely on the basis of such a response.

By analogy, consider a person who consults a physician because of an ache or pain. The physician will not recommend a course of treatment based on the patient's familiarity with various prescription drugs. Investment preferences are often based on incomplete or erroneous information and should therefore not be used as the basis of a portfolio strategy or assessment of volatility tolerance.

RISKS

In investment management, risk is often equated with the uncertainty (variability or standard deviation) of possible returns around the expected return. Clients, however, do not typically think in terms of expected return and standard deviation. More often, clients think of risk as it is defined in the dictionary: the chance of loss. Many investment counselors agree that it is more accurate to think of investors as typically being "loss-averse" rather than "risk-averse." For example, the variability of returns investors experience from one year to another may not be particularly troublesome so long as there are no *negative* returns. Beneath the psychology of "loss aversion" lurks a conviction among some investors that negative returns represent permanent capital losses.

Another problem with loss-aversion psychology is that clients tend to think in terms of nominal rather than real returns. For example, many investors would feel better about earning 5 percent after taxes in a 12 percent inflationary environment than they would about losing 1 percent after taxes in a 4 percent inflationary environment. The positive nominal gain of 5 percent in this example creates the illusion of getting ahead, although adjusted for the 12 percent inflation, there is a real loss of 7 percent. In actuality they would be better off losing 1 percent in the 4 percent inflationary environment for a smaller real loss of 5 percent.

Many clients are fearful of equity investments. In working with them, the task is not to convert them from "risk avoiders" to "risk takers." As we concluded earlier, it is very rational to be risk-averse. Rather, the task is to sensitize the client to all the risks he or she faces and then to prioritize the relative dangers of those risks *given the context of the situation.* This is why we explored in detail the impact the time horizon has on the investment management process.

It was only in reference to the relevant time horizon that we could determine whether volatility or inflation was the greater risk. For the long-term investor, volatility is not the major risk; inflation is. Because risk is time-horizon dependent, I will use the expression *volatility tolerance* when discussing the investor's ability to live with the ups and downs of investment markets. Although this may seem to be a subtle distinction, it is an important one. Occasionally, traditional investment terminology contributes to investor confusion. Although it is true that people prefer stability over uncertainty and therefore are "volatility-averse," it is not necessarily true that volatility is the major risk confronting the investor. Hence, it is a mistake to interchangeably use the words *risk* and *volatility.* This distinction avoids the labeling of equity-oriented long-term investors as risk takers! In my judgment, the equity-oriented investor with a long time horizon is following the *low-risk strategy* by holding a portfolio that offers protection from the biggest risk she faces—inflation!

Without guidance, most clients do not know how to realistically assess the risks they face. By default, they tend to assume that the familiar and comfortable path is the safe path, whereas anything unfamiliar or uncomfortable must be risky. For example, I have worked with a number of real estate professionals who consider themselves very risk-averse and fearful of common stocks. Yet they are heavily invested in real estate (another equity) using high financial leverage. When the risk of such highly leveraged equity investing is pointed out to them, the response is often: "There's no risk there. I *understand* real estate and am *comfortable* with it!"

VOLATILITY TOLERANCE

Investment advisors use a variety of methods to assess a client's ability to tolerate volatility. Given the problems we have discussed regarding using the terms *risk* and *volatility* interchangeably, it is obviously not advisable to simply ask clients to describe themselves as being either risk avoiders or risk takers. Given that choice, rational investors should answer that they are risk avoiders. The real issue is the amount of volatility that the client can tolerate. Some investment advisors look for volatility tolerance cues based on the client's business and personal lifestyles. For example, a person who likes the security of working for one employer for a lifetime and prefers recreational horseshoes may be more volatility-averse than a person who changes jobs relatively frequently in advancing his career and likes to parachute on the weekend.

The problems with these approaches are that they are highly subjective and are difficult to translate into a measurement of volatility tolerance. An examination of the client's current investment portfolio provides some clues, but again, the danger is that this may be more indicative of client familiarity and comfort with various investments than it is a measure of volatility tolerance.

Whatever approach is used to assess volatility tolerance, it is important to remember that it is not a fixed, inherited characteristic like blue eyes that stay blue for the rest of one's life. Accordingly, it is dangerous to develop an investment strategy on the basis of an initial assessment of volatility tolerance, regardless of how accurate the reading may be. To do so inappropriately presumes that clients already know what is in their best interest. If clients' risk perceptions are inaccurate, they cannot make wise decisions. The investment advisor's task is to provide a frame of reference that enables clients to correctly perceive risks within the context of their situations. Surprisingly, a client's volatility tolerance can change within a rather broad range, based on an improved understanding of the investment management process. The informed modification of volatility tolerance is one of the investment advisor's major responsibilities to his or her clients and represents a great opportunity to add value. The modification of volatility tolerance often takes the form of helping clients become more comfortable with equity investments for long time horizons. In other situations, however, clients may gain increased awareness that the incremental return expected from common stocks is not sufficient to compensate for the volatility of returns if the investment time horizon is short. For these clients, volatility tolerance is appropriately lowered with a corresponding reduction in equity investments as their perceptions become more realistic.

Figure 6–1 is an effective visual aid for contrasting the return/volatility characteristics of Treasury bills versus large company stocks. Treasury bills' stable pattern of positive, annual total returns looks like the skyline of a large city. Superimposed on this is the wildly fluctuating pattern of annual total returns for large company stocks. A solid horizontal line is drawn across the graph corresponding to the 13.2 percent arithmetic mean. It is interesting to note that over the entire 73-year period, 1981 was the only year when Treasury bills had a return in excess of large company stocks' arithmetic mean return of 13.2 percent. That does not, however, justify common stock investing for short time horizons. Over one third of the time, large company stocks' annual returns lagged those of Treasury bills, often by a significant margin.

It is easy to identify on Figure 6–1 the particularly bad years for large company stocks. It is also fairly easy to spot the bad 2- and 3-year periods. It is more difficult to identify bad 5- and 10-year periods, since good years invariably became averaged in with the bad years. The passage of time therefore mitigated the risk posed by volatility while providing an opportunity for the equity risk premium to compound its advantage.

The high level of large company stocks' volatility is quantified in Table 3–1 by the standard deviation statistic of 20.3 percent. With the simplifying assumption that large company

FIGURE 6-1

Treasury Bills versus Large Company Stocks (1926–1998)

Annual Total Returns

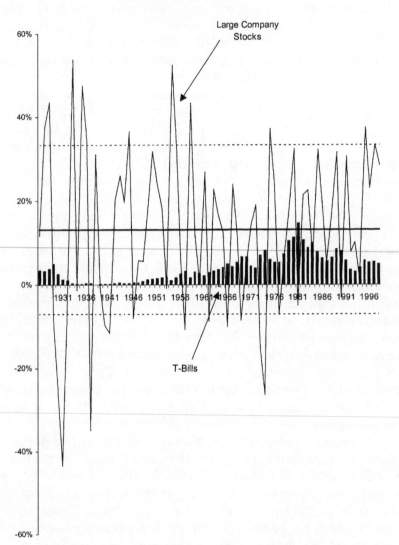

stock returns are normally distributed, roughly two thirds of the yearly return observations should fall within plus or minus 20.3 percent of the arithmetic mean of 13.2 percent. In Figure 6–1, dashed horizontal lines are drawn one standard deviation above and below large company stocks' arithmetic mean of 13.2 percent at 33.5 percent and −7.1 percent, respectively. These upper and lower dashed horizontal lines form an envelope that contains approximately two thirds of the annual return observations. The other one third of the annual return observations falls outside the envelope.[1] The relative range defined by one standard deviation is 40.6 percentage points wide. Historically, the reward for bearing this volatility has been an incremental compound return of 7.4 percent above that available from stable principal value, Treasury bills. Now, which number is bigger: the 40.6 percentage points of relative volatility or the 7.4 percentage points of reward?

The relationship between these two numbers has great significance in properly managing client expectations. The expected reward for bearing volatility risk is small relative to the level of volatility. Therefore, it will always be impossible for the client to have any short-run recognition of the higher average return she expects to receive from making equity investments. The high volatility of common stock returns will simply swamp the short-term expected reward. A corollary of this observation is that short-term common stock performance is meaningless for a truly long-term investor. A quarterly or annual "performance report" does not measure return as much as it measures volatility around a long-term growth path completely obscured by the volatility. This growth path will become clear only in retrospect toward the end of the client's investment time horizon.

THE PORTFOLIO BALANCE MODEL

Admittedly, there is a gap between the money manager's world of "expected returns and standard deviations" and the client's world of "wanting to make lots of money without taking risks."

---

1. With a normal distribution, approximately two thirds of the observations fall within one standard deviation of the arithmetic mean and approximately 95 percent of the observations fall within two standard deviations of the arithmetic mean.

The first part of this book is devoted to a discussion of the long-term historical performance of various investment alternatives. On the basis of this information, we developed simple models to estimate the long-term compound annual returns and risks associated with these investment alternatives. As clients are guided through this capital market review, their perceptions and expectations become more realistic and their capacity for making improved investment decisions develops. Without this process, few clients are equipped to make the right decisions for themselves.

The most important decision that the client makes deals with the allocation of portfolio assets between interest-generating investments and equity investments. This decision determines the basic volatility/return characteristics of the portfolio and quantifies both the likelihood of realizing financial goals and the range of possible outcomes. A methodology is needed that forces the client to deal realistically with the trade-off between volatility and return. The model we will develop uses simplistic assumptions. Although some rigor may be lost in this simplicity, the effectiveness of the model should ultimately be judged by the criterion of whether it effectively helps the client understand the volatility/return trade-off. If the client makes better decisions and more confidently adheres to an appropriate long-term strategy, the model accomplishes its purpose.

In Chapter 5, we divided the investment world into two categories: interest-generating investments and equity investments. We concluded that each category has a primary advantage and disadvantage. Interest-generating investments provide promises regarding the payment of interest and principal but are susceptible to purchasing-power erosion as a consequence of inflation. By contrast, equity investments have historically been able to build purchasing power through capital growth but have the disadvantage of high volatility.

To highlight these differences, we chose Treasury bills as a proxy for interest-generating investments in general and large company stocks as a proxy for the wide variety of equity investments. We concluded that the appropriateness of Treasury bills versus large company stocks was primarily determined by the investment time horizon. For long time horizons, inflation poses a larger risk than does stock market volatility, and accordingly, a portfolio should be oriented more heavily toward common stocks and other forms of equity investments. For short time horizons, stock market volatility is more dangerous than inflation, so portfolios should be more heavily positioned in Treasury bills and other interest-generating investments that have more predictable returns.

By adding the historical equity risk premium of 7.4 percent to the Treasury bill yield, we derived an estimate of the future compound annual return for large company stocks. Given the high volatility of common stocks, we also know that the realized equity risk premium will vary widely. (Refer to Figure 3–1, which shows the historical volatility of the equity risk premium on a rolling five-year basis.) Unfortunately, the actual equity risk premium is not subject to direct measurement.

Some forecasters use macroeconomic models to try to predict the equity risk premium with greater accuracy. This, of course, presumes that the careful analysis and manipulation of macroeconomic data can provide a unique insight missed by the capital market participants as a whole—a very difficult achievement in highly efficient markets. Other forecasters evaluate the current economic environment and attempt to find similar conditions at other times in history to develop a better prediction of how the capital markets may behave. For example, if there is a concern regarding the prospects of accelerating inflation, historical returns are examined from other periods of history when accelerating inflation was experienced. This selective use of history presumes that we can correctly determine in retrospect what caused the markets to behave as they did and that current market behavior will be determined by the same causal relationships. Again, this is quite difficult to do successfully.

The easy way out may also be the best way out. This is to simply assume that the historical equity risk premium of 7.4 percent is a reasonable estimate of what the equity risk premium should be. This has been the historical reward received for bearing equity risk, based on a long time horizon encompassing periods of both war and peace, economic expansions and contractions, high and low inflation, Republican and Democratic administrations, and so on. There will always be unusual events, and arguably an estimate built on the basis of long-term experience may be the safest approach. The precision of this estimate of the equity risk premium is not particularly important for two reasons. First, in the short run, the high standard deviation of common stock returns will always swamp recognition of the equity risk premium. Therefore, whether the actual equity risk premium is 7 percent or 8 percent makes little difference. Second, the purpose of the methodology is not to derive accurate estimates of future returns but rather to develop a systematic way of making broad portfolio balance decisions that acknowledge the volatility/return trade-off.

Let us discuss the steps involved in our methodology for guiding clients in making this most important investment policy decision impacting portfolio performance.

Step 1: *Verify that the client fully understands the volatility / return characteristics of Treasury bills and large company stocks.* (Refer to Figure 6–1 and Table 6–1.)

Step 2: *Review with the client the importance of time horizon in assessing risks and evaluating the appropriateness of interest-generating investments versus equity investments.*

Step 3: *Determine the current value of the client's total investment portfolio.* This includes:

   A. All liquid and nonliquid investments (e.g., investment real estate) even though the latter cannot be easily converted to cash.

   B. The value of employer-sponsored retirement plans, even though the client may not have investment discretion of the funds.

   C. The present value of annuitized streams of income. Although these are not normally thought of as investment assets and are seldom reflected on the balance sheet, they are nevertheless important economic assets that should be considered in structuring portfolios.

   This third step helps the client think of his or her portfolio in the broadest terms and focuses the client's attention on the "big picture."

TABLE 6-1

Volatility/Return Characteristics of Treasury Bills versus Large Company Stocks

Modeled Return	Volatility*	Comments
Treasury Bills		
5%	±0%	The modeled return of 5% is the yield on a one-year bill as shown in *The Wall Street Journal.* The volatility is shown as ±0% because the return can be locked in with no uncertainty.
Large Company Stocks		
12%	±20%	The modeled return of 12% is derived by adding the historical equity risk premium of 7% (rounded to the nearest percentage) to the current Treasury bill yield of 5%. The volatility of ±20% is the historical standard deviation of returns for large company stocks from 1926 through 1998.

*The odds are approximately two out of three that the actual return will fall within a range defined by the modeled return plus or minus the volatility.

Step 4: *Instruct the client to hypothetically convert his or her entire investment portfolio to cash.* This conversion overcomes inertia by freeing the client from the ghosts of past investment decisions.

Step 5: *Describe a hypothetical investment world where there are only two investment alternatives: Treasury bills and large company stocks. Ask the client to allocate the cash from his or her liquidated investment portfolio between these two alternatives.* In doing so, the client should keep in mind the volatility/return characteristics of each alternative and his or her relevant investment time horizon.

In reviewing the range of choices available to the client, consider a portfolio composed entirely of Treasury bills. Of all possible alternatives, this portfolio has the lowest modeled return. This is the price paid for the elimination of short-run volatility. As we begin to allocate money to large company stocks, the volatility of the resulting portfolio increases in direct proportion to the percentage invested in stocks. Table 6–2 shows the volatility/return characteristics of five portfolios ranging from 100 percent Treasury bills through 50 percent Treasury bills/50 percent large company stocks to 100 percent invested in large company stocks.

Investment decisions are made under terms of uncertainty. For this reason, it is better to forecast portfolio results in terms of typical ranges around modeled returns. For example, rather than simply saying that portfolio 2 has a modeled return of 7.1 percent, it is much more meaningful to indicate that the odds are approximately two out of three that the actual return will be within plus or minus 6 percent of the modeled return of 7.1 percent. This implies a typical range of results from 1.1 percent to 13.1 percent.

TABLE 6–2

Example Portfolio Choices

	Portfolio Balance		Modeled Portfolio Performance		
	Treasury Bills	Large Company Stocks	Modeled Return*	Volatility*	Typical Range of Results**
1	100%	0%	5.0%	±0.0%	5.0%
2	70	30	7.1	±6.0	1.1% to 13.1%
3	50	50	8.5	±10.0	−1.5% to 18.5%
4	30	70	9.9	±14.0	−4.1% to 23.9%
5	0	100	12.0	±20.0	−8.0% to 32.0%

*Calculated as the weighted average of the modeled returns and volatilities of Treasury bills and large company stocks. For example, for portfolio 2 above, which is made up of 70 percent Treasury bills and 30 percent large company stocks:

$$\text{Portfolio modeled return} = .70(5\%) + .30(12\%) = 7.1\%$$
$$\text{Portfolio volatility} = .70(0\%) + .30(20\%) = 6.0\%$$

**The odds are approximately two out of three that the actual return will be in a range defined by modeled return plus or minus the volatility.

Note: As the percentage allocated to large company stocks increases, the portfolio volatility increases much more rapidly than does the incremental increase in modeled return. The longer the time horizon, the more worthwhile it is to bear higher levels of short-run volatility. In deciding how they would divide their investment funds between Treasury bills and large company stocks, clients are forced to acknowledge and deal with the volatility/return trade-off issue.

Clients bring to the client/advisor relationship their own expectations regarding the returns and volatility levels associated with various investment alternatives. Often, clients believe that returns are more easily achieved with less volatility than is indicated here. Such clients struggle with the portfolio choices presented in Table 6–2. If so, that is good. If there is going to be a struggle over the nature of the volatility/return trade-off, it is best to deal with it at this point in the investment decision-making process. Generally, clients will accept the framework because the alternative requires the rejection of over seven decades of historical relationships in favor of a different investment worldview.[2]

By dividing the 20 percent standard deviation of large company stocks by the 7 percent presumed equity risk premium, we see that for every 1 percent increase in the portfolio's modeled return, portfolio volatility will increase by approximately plus or minus 2.9 percent. For example, portfolio 1 has 100 percent of its assets in Treasury bills and has a modeled return of 5 percent. In order to increase the modeled return by only 2.1 percent more, we need to shift 30 percent of the portfolio out of Treasury bills and into large company stocks. Doing so, however, increases portfolio volatility by an additional plus or minus 6 percent!

Awareness of this trade-off forces the client to focus more attention on his or her ability to tolerate short-run portfolio volatility. This process is healthy because in determining overall portfolio balance it is more important to concentrate on volatility tolerance than on return requirement. Most clients require unusually high rates of return to achieve all of their goals. These high rates of return often are not realistically possible given reasonable capital market expectations. Even if they are possible, they should not be pursued unless the client has both the objective and subjective capacity to tolerate the associated volatility.

Having reviewed the historical performance of the capital markets, a client should have developed an awareness that the higher returns from equity investments are the compensation

---

2. We will see later that on a portfolio basis using multiple asset categories, incremental returns are possible with less volatility than this simple "two-investment alternative world" implies. In working with clients, however, it is better to avoid holding out such hope at this point in the decision-making process.

one expects to receive in exchange for the volatility assumed. A client's volatility tolerance, in this framework, is simply the added volatility he is willing to accept in exchange for an extra unit of modeled return. If the return associated with a client's maximum volatility tolerance is insufficient to realize the client's goals, he should either modify his goals or acknowledge that they will most likely not be realized. If the return associated with the upper limit of the client's volatility tolerance is more than is needed to accomplish his goals, it is easy to move down to a more stable portfolio if that is the client's preference.

Psychologically, it is easier to tolerate volatility if the final outcome occurs in the distant future. A proper understanding of time horizon, therefore, increases volatility tolerance for the long-time-horizon investor. Unfortunately, however, the liquidity of the capital markets provides constant revision of security prices and a heightened awareness of short-run performance. The trick is to avoid attaching too much significance to short-run performance numbers if the relevant outcome is truly associated with a long-term time horizon.

Table 6–2 by itself may be sufficient for use by those clients who have a good, intuitive grasp of the impact that the passage of time has on narrowing the range of portfolio compound returns. Other clients may need to have the range of returns over time for each portfolio specified in more detail. For them, Figures 6–2 through 6–6 can be used in conjunction with Table 6–2 to communicate the impact time has on the choice of portfolio balance. For those who like graphs, the distribution of returns for a one-year time horizon is shown in Figures 6–3A through 6–6A for portfolios 2 through 5. No such distribution is shown for portfolio 1 because it has a fixed annual return of 5 percent. Figures 6–3B through 6–6B show in tabular form the "distributions of portfolio annualized returns," which describe the likelihood of achieving various returns over 1-, 3-, 5-, 10-, 15-, and 25-year time horizons. Finally, Figures 6–2 and 6–3C through 6–6C show the path of wealth accumulation over time for each of the five portfolios for the 10th, 50th, and 90th percentile compound return probabilities.

As we review the distribution of portfolio annualized returns for portfolio 3 in Figure 6–4B, we see that −3.97 percent

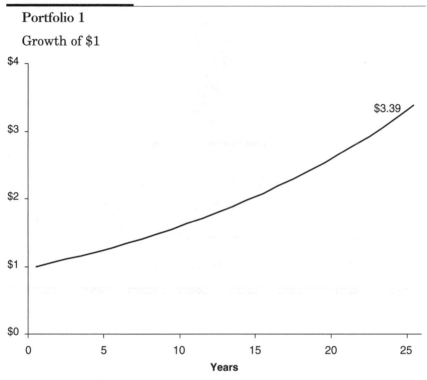

FIGURE 6-2

Portfolio 1

Growth of $1

Source: Illustrations produced using Vestek Systems, Inc., software.

is shown at the 10th percentile for a one-year time horizon. This means that there is a 90 percent likelihood that the actual return will be higher than −3.97 percent and a 10 percent likelihood that it will be lower. Under the 10th percentile column for a five-year time horizon, however, we see a value of 2.49 percent. That is, there is a 90 percent likelihood that for a five-year holding period, this portfolio will have a compound annual return in excess of 2.49 percent. For a 25-year horizon, there is a 90 percent likelihood that the compound annual return will be greater than 5.52 percent—an interesting outcome when one considers that the return available from Treasury bills is 5 percent. In other words, with a 25-year investment horizon, the chances are 9 out 10 that a 50/50 mix of Treasury bills and large company

FIGURE 6-3

Portfolio 2
A. Distribution of Returns: One-Year Time Horizon

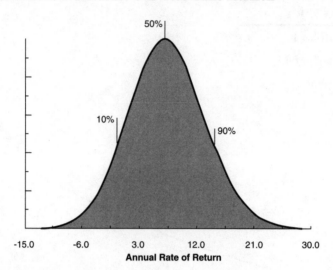

B. Distribution of Portfolio Annualized Returns

Year	1st%	10th%	25th%	50th%	75th%	90th%	99th%
1	-6.12	-0.47	2.97	6.93	11.04	14.89	21.80
3	-0.81	2.59	4.63	6.93	9.29	11.46	15.28
5	0.88	3.55	5.14	6.93	8.75	10.42	13.34
10	2.62	4.53	5.66	6.93	8.22	9.39	11.43
15	3.40	4.97	5.90	6.93	7.98	8.93	10.59
25	4.18	5.41	6.13	6.93	7.74	8.48	9.75

C. Growth of $1

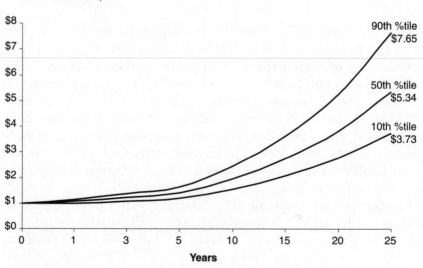

Source: Illustrations produced using Vestek Systems, Inc. software.

Portfolio 3
A. Distribution of Returns: One-Year Time Horizon

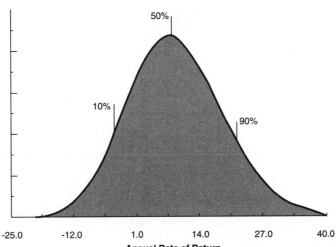

Annual Rate of Return

B. Distribution of Portfolio Annualized Returns

Year	1st%	10th%	25th%	50th%	75th%	90th%	99th%
1	-12.77	-3.97	1.55	8.04	14.95	21.56	33.81
3	-4.51	0.93	4.24	8.04	11.98	15.65	22.25
5	-1.82	2.49	5.09	8.04	11.08	13.89	18.89
10	0.97	4.09	5.94	8.04	10.18	12.15	15.60
15	2.24	4.80	6.33	8.04	9.79	11.38	14.18
25	3.52	5.52	6.71	8.04	9.39	10.62	12.76

C. Growth of $1

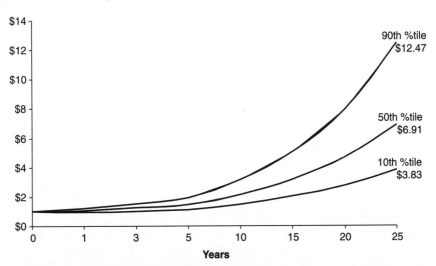

Years

Source: Illustrations produced using Vestek Systems, Inc. software.

FIGURE 6-5

Portfolio 4
A. Distribution of Returns: One-Year Time Horizon

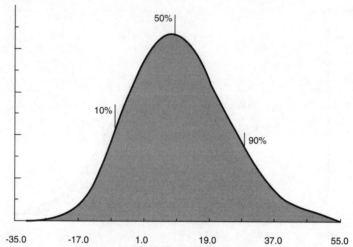

B. Distribution of Portfolio Annualized Returns

Year	1st%	10th%	25th%	50th%	75th%	90th%	99th%
1	-18.84	-7.35	0.08	9.02	18.75	28.28	46.44
3	-8.06	-0.75	3.77	9.02	14.54	19.75	29.27
5	-4.46	1.37	4.93	9.02	13.27	17.24	24.40
10	-0.69	3.55	6.11	9.02	12.01	14.77	19.68
15	1.02	4.54	6.64	9.02	11.45	13.70	17.65
25	2.77	5.53	7.17	9.02	10.90	12.62	15.65

C. Growth of $1

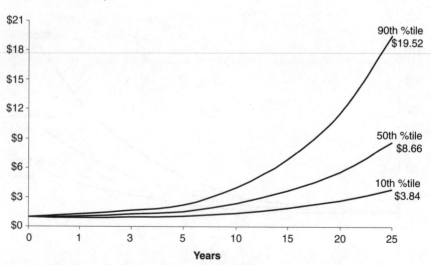

Source: Illustrations produced using Vestek Systems, Inc. software.

FIGURE 6-6

Portfolio 5
A. Distribution of Returns: One-Year Time Horizon

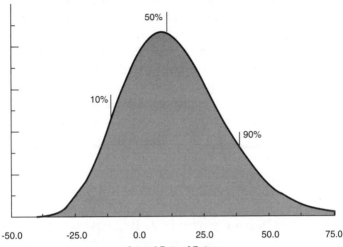

B. Distribution of Portfolio Annualized Returns

Year	1st%	10th%	25th%	50th%	75th%	90th%	99th%
1	-26.98	-12.15	-2.15	10.26	24.24	38.37	66.49
3	-13.09	-3.29	2.91	10.26	18.13	25.71	39.87
5	-8.30	-0.39	4.52	10.26	16.30	22.04	32.57
10	-3.22	2.61	6.17	10.26	14.50	18.47	25.60
15	-0.87	3.98	6.91	10.26	13.71	16.92	22.63
25	1.53	5.36	7.65	10.26	12.92	15.38	19.73

C. Growth of $1

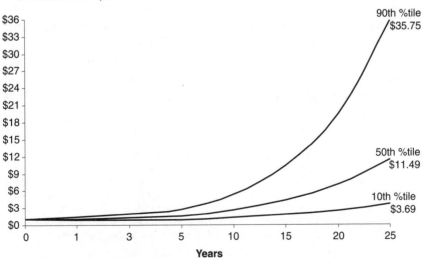

Source: Illustrations produced using Vestek Systems, Inc. software.

stocks will outperform an all-Treasury bill portfolio. As expected, with longer time horizons, there are more opportunities for good and bad years to offset each other, thereby narrowing the range of outcomes and mitigating the downside risk posed by volatility.

The 25th percentile column provides a less severe and more likely picture of the downside risk of the portfolio. For example, under the 25th percentile column we find a value of 1.55 percent for a one-year time horizon. That indicates that the chances are three out of four that the portfolio return will exceed 1.55 percent over a one-year time horizon, and so forth.

If we compare portfolio 2 with portfolio 3, we will find that the median (50th percentile) return is lower and that the range of possible outcomes for any comparative time period is correspondingly smaller for portfolio 2. By contrast, portfolio 4 will have wider ranges of outcomes with a correspondingly higher median (50th percentile) return.[3]

A comparison of these exhibits shows the variation in short-run volatility based on the percentage of the portfolio allocated to large company stocks. It also clearly demonstrates that the passage of time dramatically narrows the range of compound returns for each portfolio. This is consistent with the conclusions reached in Chapter 5, which dealt with the importance of the time horizon.

Investment objectives are usually solicited from clients during the initial data-gathering session. Occasionally, a client will express an objective of "12 percent compound returns with little or no risk," which qualitatively translated would be "very high returns with stable principal values." This is not one investment objective; it is two competing objectives, and to the extent to which one objective is pursued, the other must be sacrificed. This is simply the volatility/return trade-off implicit among the choices in Table 6–2.

---

3. With a normal distribution, the range of returns is symmetrically distributed around the expected return. In reality, security returns are better described by a lognormal distribution which has a longer right tail. This is the case because it is impossible to lose more than 100 percent of your money, but the upside is open-ended. With a "right-tailed" lognormal distribution, the range is *not* symmetrically distributed around the expected return. The graphs and tables in Figures 6–3 through 6–6 utilize the more realistic lognormal distribution assumption.

We now have an appreciation of the necessity of educating clients and providing them with a context for making good decisions. According to Charles D. Ellis, portfolio-balance decisions are investment policy decisions, which are the nondelegatable responsibility of the *client*. Within the framework developed, the client's choice of a portfolio from Table 6–2 is an indirect measure of the client's *informed* volatility tolerance.

This model is not without its drawbacks. The notion of the standard deviation is not well understood by most clients. For this reason, the model has been designed to be as simple and straightforward as possible. There is also a risk of the choices being too hypothetical and therefore not realistic to clients. This can be overcome by incorporating discussions of historical capital market experiences such as the 1973–74 bear market, when common stocks lost more than 40 percent of their value. Such market declines have occurred in the past and will surely happen again in the future. Clients should be educated to expect that.[4]

This exercise for determining broad portfolio balance should be engaged in periodically with clients. Over time, their experiences with investments will change and their reactions may differ from what was initially expected. For example, some clients who thought they thoroughly understood common stock volatility and could live with it may temper their opinions following a stock market crash like that of October 1987. Various life events can also occur that alter volatility tolerance. Examples are changes in family composition, job or career changes, and health problems.

---

4. Another dilemma with the model is that technically, the standard deviation should be measured around the arithmetic average return rather than the compound return. To use the arithmetic return in the model, however, may mislead the client into thinking that his or her money will compound at that rate. (As we discussed in the Appendix to Chapter 3, the arithmetic return will always be higher than the corresponding compound return for a variable pattern of returns.) Use of the compound return number avoids this problem. In my judgment, the technical inaccuracy serves the more important consideration of the client's conceptual understanding. Within a time horizon context, clients will naturally think of compound returns, yet their experience of volatility will be in the near term. A fuller discussion of these issues appears in Chapter 9, "Portfolio Optimization."

Through these changes, this decision-making model will continue to emphasize the fact that to increase the portfolio's modeled return, one must willingly accept increased volatility. The balance chosen between interest-generating investments, as represented by Treasury bills, and equity investments, as represented by large company stocks, is the most important investment decision the client will make. It simultaneously determines both the general volatility level and the return characteristics of the portfolio. Subject to this broad portfolio balance decision, the advisor can proceed to design a more diversified portfolio, utilizing multiple asset classes. This brings us to the next chapter, which deals with diversification.

CHAPTER 7

Diversification: The Third Dimension

Better a steady dime than a rare dollar.

—*Anonymous*

Diversification in its naive sense means simply avoiding putting all of your eggs in one basket. Certainly there is value in averaging out one's risks in a number of different investments, but diversification is both more powerful and more subtle than this. In this chapter we will explore the concept of diversification and find that our prior two-dimensional world that describes an investment in terms of its volatility and return[1] is inadequate. We also need to describe investments along a third dimension, which we will call the *diversification effect*.

Figure 7–1 shows two investments, A and B, each of which has similar volatility/return characteristics. They also move in lockstep with one another; as investment A moves up, so does investment B. As investment A loses value, so does investment B. A statistician would describe this relationship as one of "perfect positive cross-correlation." If we invest half our money in investment A and half in investment B, we will have a portfolio result that follows the path of the dotted line in Figure 7–1. The return on this portfolio will simply be a weighted average of the returns of the two investments that constitute the portfolio. Similarly, *because they move in lockstep with one*

---

1. Throughout this chapter, the term *return* refers either to a single-period expected return or to the simple average return of a multiple-year time period.

another, the volatility of the portfolio will be a weighted average of the volatilities of the two investments. In this example we have only an averaging of volatilities: Our eggs are in two baskets rather than one. As we will define the term, there is no diversification effect as these assets are combined to form a portfolio.

In Figure 7–2 we again have two investments, C and D. As in Figure 7–1, they have the same return characteristics. They also have the same volatility as measured by their respective standard deviations. However, unlike the situation in Figure 7–1, investments C and D move in opposite cycles. As investment C gains value, investment D loses value and vice versa. This is an example of "perfect negative cross-correlation." With half of our money allocated to investment C and half allocated to investment D, this countercyclical pattern of returns produces a marvelous portfolio result, as indicated by the dotted line in Figure 7-2. The return on the portfolio is again simply a

FIGURE 7–1

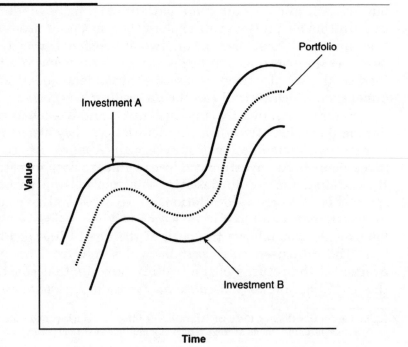

weighted average of the returns of the two investments that compose the portfolio, but rather than simply averaging our volatilities as we did in Figure 7–1, we have completely eliminated the volatility of the portfolio in Figure 7–2. Diversification effect is at a maximum as these assets combine to build a portfolio. Such perfectly negatively correlated investments generally do not exist in the real world. If they did, no one would buy a volatility-free Treasury bill yielding 5 percent when he or she could buy two volatile assets and combine them in such a manner as to produce a stable 8 percent return.

In Figure 7–3, we have two more investments, E and F, with similar volatility and return characteristics. This is the

FIGURE 7-2

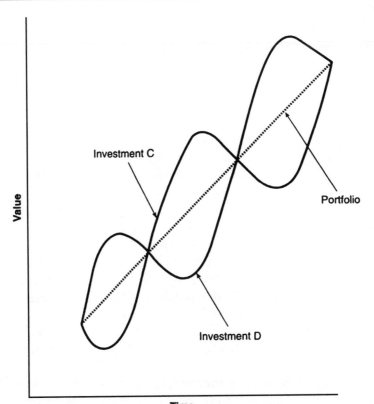

FIGURE 7–3

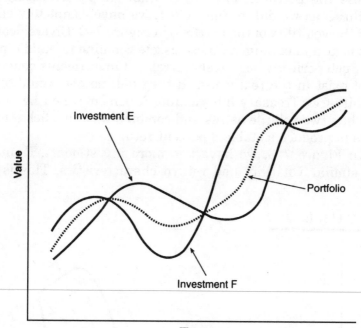

middle-ground situation, where the investments are neither perfectly positively nor perfectly negatively correlated. We can see periods of time when the investments tend to move together and the diversification effect is weak and other times when they move in different directions, with a stronger diversification effect on the portfolio. This is more representative of real-world investment situations. As in the other two examples, the portfolio return is a weighted average of the returns of the investments that compose the portfolio, but the diversification effect associated with the dissimilar patterns of return has resulted in a level of portfolio volatility below the weighted average of the volatilities of investments E and F. Visually, this diversification effect can be seen as a somewhat smoothed pattern of returns for the portfolio.

Statisticians use the measurement called *cross-correlation* (or simply correlation) *of returns* between two investments to indicate the extent to which knowledge of one return provides information regarding the behavior of the other. For example, the perfect positive correlation, such as the one found between investments A and B in Figure 7–1, is described by a correlation of +1.0. The perfect negative correlation between investments C and D in Figure 7–2 is described by a correlation of −1.0. All correlation measures are bound by these two extremes. Patterns of return that are unrelated to one another (i.e., neither positive nor negative correlation) have correlations near 0.[2]

In each of the examples above, the portfolio return is simply a weighted average of the returns of the investments that compose the portfolio. This will always be the case, regardless of the pattern of returns among the investments. The portfolio volatility, however, will be *less* than the weighted average of the volatility levels of the assets in the portfolio in all cases except the rare situation of perfect positive correlation among investments. This is due to the diversification effect of investments whose patterns of returns partially offset one another, thereby somewhat smoothing portfolio volatility.

Diversification is much more than simply not putting all of your eggs in one basket. We can also see clearly why measures of the volatility and return characteristics of individual investments are inadequate in describing what happens when investments are combined in forming portfolios. The diversification effect, as measured by the correlation of returns among investment alternatives, provides the third measurement dimension needed.

How do these concepts apply in the real world? Consider the portfolio possibilities created by various combinations of large company stocks and long-term corporate bonds. To map out the volatility and return characteristics of different stock/bond portfolio allocations, we need estimates of the expected return and the standard deviation for both large company stocks and long-term corporate bonds as well as the correlation statistic that

2. The *covariance* of two investments' returns is a weighted average of the products of the deviations of the returns around their expected returns, where the probabilities of the deviations are used as weights. The *cross-correlation* of two investments' returns is equal to their covariance divided by the product of their standard deviations.

measures the degree of dissimilarity in the patterns of returns between the two. In Chapter 3 we learned that from 1926 through 1998, large company stocks had an arithmetic (simple average) annual return of 13.2 percent with a standard deviation of 20.3 percent, whereas long-term corporate bonds had a simple average annual return of 6.1 percent with a standard deviation of 8.6 percent. The correlation between bond and stock returns over this same period was +.26. If we assume that the future will be like the past (a big assumption, as we will see), the range of portfolio possibilities using large company stocks and long-term corporate bonds is described by the curved solid line in Figure 7–4. Point B represents an all-bond portfolio, and point S represents an all-stock portfolio. The straight dashed line connecting B and S shows the performance of the portfolio possibilities if stocks and bonds are perfectly positively correlated. In this situation, there is no "diversification effect" as we have defined it. The portfolio's volatility is equal to the weighted average of the volatility levels of its components.

Because stocks and bonds are *not* perfectly positively correlated, however, each stock/bond portfolio allocation has

FIGURE 7 – 4

Corporate Bond/Common Stock Portfolio Possibilities

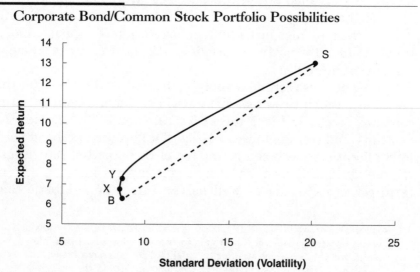

Source: Illustration produced using Vestek Systems, Inc., software.

less volatility than the weighted-average volatility of its components. As a result, the set of portfolio possibilities is described by the solid line that bows out from the straight dotted line. The horizontal distance between the dotted and solid lines measures the beneficial diversification effect for any portfolio. This diversification effect is driven by the relatively low stock/bond correlation of +.26.

Somewhat surprisingly, the minimum volatility portfolio is not composed entirely of long-term corporate bonds! Point X on the graph corresponds to the minimum volatility portfolio. Its allocation is 93 percent to bonds and 7 percent to stocks. It has a standard deviation of 8.5 percent, which is lower than the 8.6 percent standard deviation of long-term corporate bonds, and its expected return of 6.6 percent is one half percentage point higher! Ultraconservative investors, lacking an understanding of the power of diversification, often hold portfolios allocated entirely to bonds. This illustration indicates that such investors have an opportunity to simultaneously improve expected returns and lower their volatility risk by means of modest diversification into equity investments. If they are already comfortable with the volatility level of an all-bond portfolio, they can choose portfolio Y, allocated 85 percent to bonds and 15 percent to stocks. Its standard deviation of 8.6 percent is equivalent to that of an all-bond portfolio, but its expected return is 7.1 percent, a full percentage point higher than bonds. This is an example of the power of diversification.

The volatility/return characteristics of and correlation between stocks and bonds as described in the preceding paragraph are based on the entire 73-year period 1926 through 1998. It is important to keep in mind, however, that there has been and will continue to be considerable variability in these relative performance numbers. For example, Figure 7–5 compares the 60-month (5-year) compound annual returns of large company stocks and long-term corporate bonds on a rolling monthly basis. The dominance of common stock returns over corporate bonds is very apparent, but we can also see that over periods as short as five years, the higher volatility associated with common stocks will result in many instances when their returns will lag those available from bonds.

FIGURE 7 – 5

Common Stocks versus Corporate Bonds: Compound Annual Returns (1926–1998)

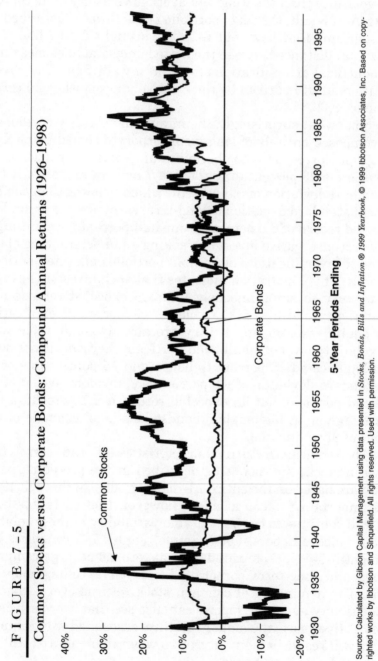

5-Year Periods Ending

Source: Calculated by Gibson Capital Management using data presented in *Stocks, Bonds, Bills and Inflation* ® *1999 Yearbook*, © 1999 Ibbotson Associates, Inc. Based on copyrighted works by Ibbotson and Sinquefield. All rights reserved. Used with permission.

   This highlights the danger of putting too much attention on the long-term relationships among expected returns for various investment alternatives without simultaneously considering the uncertainty in those relationships. This is true particularly in the short run, when high standard deviations can produce short-term and intermediate-term experiences that differ considerably from the long-term experience. It is therefore important for advisors to guide their clients through the exercise of developing models of long-term relationships among investment alternatives while simultaneously emphasizing that short-term experiences will vary widely.

   Figure 7–6 graphs on a rolling monthly basis the 60-month (5-year) standard deviations of returns for large company stocks and long-term corporate bonds. Table 3–1 previously indicated that based on the entire period 1926 through 1998, the standard deviation of returns was 20.3 percent for large company stocks and 8.6 percent for long-term corporate bonds. We can see, however, from Figure 7–6 that the volatility of both stocks and bonds has varied widely over time. Common stocks had their highest volatility during the period preceding World War II. Bonds, on the other hand, had low volatility until the mid-1960s, when their volatility began to increase dramatically through the 1980s as a result of a rapidly changing interest rate environment.

   The 60-month (5-year) correlation between large company stocks' and long-term corporate bonds' returns is graphed on a rolling monthly basis in Figure 7–7. For this entire 73-year period, the correlation was +.26, but we can see that it actually varied widely from a high of +.62 to a low of −.28. It is during the periods of negative correlation that the strongest diversification effect will be produced, offering investors great advantages in volatility reduction from having both represented in a portfolio.

   In the next chapter we will discuss the mathematics of portfolio optimization, which identifies "ideal asset mixes" *based on the inputs* to a computer program. The output from such programs is highly sensitive to the inputs. One purpose in reviewing Figures 7–5 through 7–7 is to increase one's awareness of the uncertainty inherent in the inputs on which these computer programs rely. At best, historical data are *helpful* in understanding investment

FIGURE 7-6

Common Stocks versus Corporate Bonds: Standard Deviations of Returns (1926–1998)

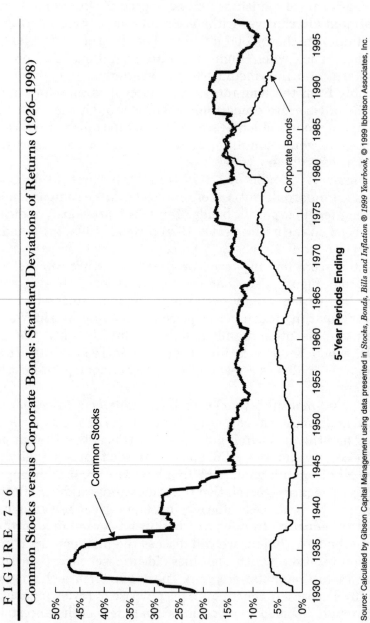

5-Year Periods Ending

FIGURE 7-7

Common Stocks versus Corporate Bonds: Cross-Correlation of Returns (1926–1998)

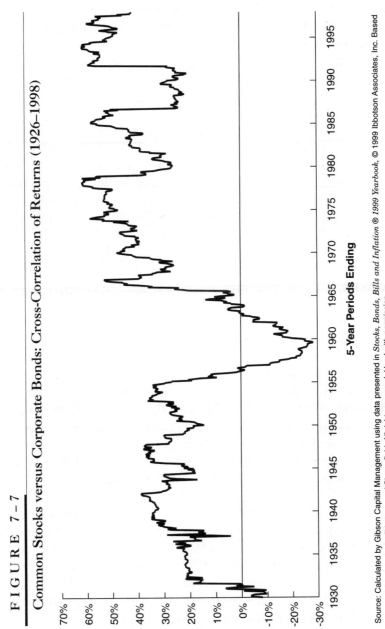

5-Year Periods Ending

Source: Calculated by Gibson Capital Management using data presented in *Stocks, Bonds, Bills and Inflation* ® *1999 Yearbook*, © 1999 Ibbotson Associates, Inc. Based on copyrighted works by Ibbotson and Sinquefield. All rights reserved. Used with permission.

asset volatility/return characteristics and relationships. It cannot, however, be massaged in such a way as to extract "the truth" from what is basically an uncertain process. Precise answers are simply not possible.

When we examine the range of portfolio possibilities utilizing only two investment alternatives, each level of portfolio expected return has a unique asset allocation associated with it. This is not true when we consider the range of portfolio possibilities utilizing three or more investment alternatives. A wide range of asset allocations may be identified, all of which produce the same portfolio expected return but with different levels of volatility. Obviously, the optimal asset allocation for a particular portfolio expected return is that unique allocation which minimizes portfolio volatility. Other asset allocations are undesirable because of their unnecessarily high levels of volatility. By definition, a portfolio that minimizes portfolio volatility for a given expected return (or equivalently maximizes portfolio expected return for a given level of volatility) is said to be *efficient*. If we join together all the efficient portfolios for a given set of investment alternatives, we form what is called the *efficient frontier*.

We intuitively understand the wisdom of not putting all of our eggs in one basket, and we know that it is important to understand the volatility/return characteristics of each basket we use. Earlier in this chapter we gained an appreciation of the importance of also considering how the various baskets behave relative to one another in reducing volatility on a portfolio basis through the diversification effect. Now we have gone an additional step by emphasizing that it is also important to determine the *right amount* to place in each of the baskets in order to have an efficient portfolio.

The implications of this last realization are important. There are good and bad allocations of assets within any portfolio, and the objective is to allocate assets in such a way as to own a portfolio that lies on the efficient frontier. These portfolios have less volatility than any other portfolio with equivalent expected return or, alternatively, have more expected return than any other portfolio with equivalent volatility.

Inefficient portfolios should be avoided because they have levels of volatility that could be reduced with proper reallocation. Sometimes, the idea of an inefficient portfolio sounds like evidence against the notion of the volatility/return trade-off we worked so hard to establish and describe in Chapter 6. Before, we concluded that the only way to increase expected return is to assume a higher level of volatility. Now, we are told that we can improve the expected return on an inefficient portfolio without increasing volatility. Isn't this a contradiction? No. The volatility/return trade-off is alive and well, living on the efficient frontier! That is, assuming that you now have an efficient portfolio, the only way to increase the expected return (if constrained to a given set of investment alternatives) is to increase portfolio volatility.

Another possible reaction to the notion of inefficient portfolios is the apparent existence of an economic free lunch. Here is a situation where it is possible to pick up incremental return for free. Yet in an efficient market there are no free lunches. Rather than this situation being thought of as a free lunch, an inefficient portfolio can be more appropriately considered as a situation where volatility is needlessly incurred without compensation or, alternatively, incremental returns are unnecessarily sacrificed.

If we extend our diversification example by adding a fourth investment alternative with volatility/return characteristics different from those of the other three, we now have even more options to consider in building our portfolios. The new investment alternative provides the *possibility* of further portfolio volatility reduction at various levels of expected return. (I emphasize *possibility* because the addition of a new investment alternative does not guarantee the advisability of its utilization.) If the volatility/return characteristics of this fourth investment alternative provide less volatile ways of building portfolios for various levels of expected return, a new efficient frontier will be formed above the old one, as shown in Figure 7–8.

Expanding the menu of investment alternatives to be used as possible building blocks for the portfolio adds more opportunities to earn increasingly higher returns at whatever level of volatility one can tolerate. Alternatively, we can view the increasing number of alternatives as providing more opportunities to reduce volatility at whatever level of expected return one seeks. The message is clear: Although it is not always advisable

FIGURE 7-8

Three versus Four Investment Alternative Efficient Frontiers

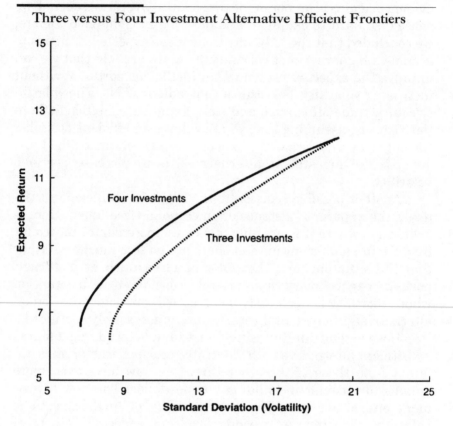

to utilize all the investment alternatives provided in a given situation, it is always preferable to have more, rather than fewer, investment alternatives from which to choose. Any time investment alternatives are artificially restricted, the risk is incurred that the investor will be confined to a choice along a lower efficient frontier than would otherwise be possible.

Although the diversification effect is usually thought of in terms of volatility reduction, it equivalently can be viewed in terms of return enhancement. This is important because aggressive investors are often not interested in discussing diversification strategies because they believe that diversification will impair returns. This is not necessarily so! In essence, the diversification effect enables the more aggressive investor to improve returns through the commitment of an even greater percentage of his or her portfolio to equity investments than would otherwise be possible without the smoothing effect of partially offsetting patterns of returns.

If we wanted to eliminate as much volatility as possible from our portfolio, we might consider taking diversification to its logical conclusion by representing all major investment alternatives in our portfolio. This would provide the greatest opportunity for dissimilar patterns of returns among investments to partially offset one another. Would this, however, eliminate all portfolio volatility? No. The remaining volatility exists despite diversification; we will call it *nondiversifiable volatility*. When we think about bearing unavoidable volatility, we expect to be commensurably rewarded. For example, in Chapter 6 we devised a hypothetical world composed of only two investment alternatives: Treasury bills and large company stocks. In this world, the only route to an improved expected return was through the assumption of the volatility of common stocks. Therefore, we expect to be rewarded for bearing unavoidable volatility.

But what about the kind of volatility that can be easily eliminated through diversification? We will call this *diversifiable volatility*. Should we be rewarded for bearing it? By analogy, consider a firefighter who deserves to be well compensated because of the risks inherent in that occupation. One day he heroically enters a burning building to successfully save a child from the flames. For this and other similar acts of courage and skill he receives a promotion with a pay raise. During a subsequent fire he hears the screams of another young child, but before entering the burning building, he takes off his asbestos suit and, wearing only his underwear, rescues the child. The next day he approaches the fire chief and asks for a raise because of the increased risks he took in rescuing the child. What will be the fire chief's response?

One big lesson of modern portfolio theory is that in an efficient market, there is no compensation for bearing volatility that can be easily avoided. Diversifiable volatility therefore deserves and receives no compensation. For example, Figure

7–9 describes the volatility characteristics of two stocks, A and B. Initially, one might naively conclude that stock A, with its greater total volatility, will be priced to provide for a greater expected return than that of stock B. But we can see that in this example stock B has more nondiversifiable volatility than stock A and, accordingly, will be priced by the marketplace to produce a higher expected return than stock A!

One very practical implication of what we have discussed is the volatility unnecessarily assumed by anyone who commits a disproportionately large share of his or her portfolio to one investment position. Consider a client who has 90 percent of her investment portfolio allocated to the stock of one large publicly traded corporation. She obviously has retained much diversifiable volatility *which is not priced by the marketplace to reward her or anyone else.* This is like the firefighter who takes off his asbestos suit to run into a burning building to save a child from

FIGURE 7–9

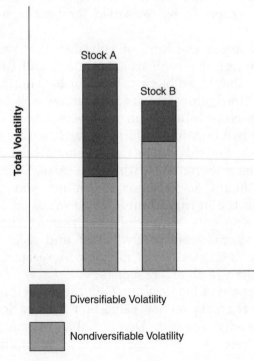

the flames. The pricing mechanism of an efficient market, in effect, assumes that investors are smart enough to eliminate diversifiable volatility through broad diversification. Those who do not diversify pay the price of assuming an unnecessarily high level of volatility. The argument for diversifying a client's portfolio away from overconcentration in one stock obviously goes beyond the notion of simply not putting all of your eggs in one basket.

The Appendix that follows is written for readers who are interested in a more detailed discussion of the concepts developed in this chapter. Those who are not interested in further elaboration can proceed safely to the next chapter.

APPENDIX: A More Detailed Discussion of Diversification Concepts

Consider two investments, X and Y, with expected returns and volatilities as measured by their standard deviations of:

Investment	Expected Return	Standard Deviation
X	10%	18%
Y	8%	10%

Figure 7–10 shows both investments plotted in volatility/return space. Initially, one might presume that investment portfolios built using those two investments would plot along the straight line connecting points X and Y. This would be true, however, only if the correlation of returns between X and Y were perfectly positive, as it was for the two investments in Figure 7–1. To get an expected return of 9 percent, for example, one would have to be willing to accept a volatility level of 14 percent. (This can be seen by noting the distance on the horizontal axis corresponding to the point where a horizontal line drawn from an expected return of 9 percent intercepts the straight line connecting points X and Y.)

The opposite extreme is where X and Y are perfectly negatively correlated in a fashion similar to the two investments in Figure 7–2. Let us start at point Y with 100 percent of the portfolio committed to investment Y. As we begin to reallocate some money to investment X, we begin moving the portfolio along the line connecting point Y to point W. At point W, we have approximately 64 percent of our money in investment Y, with the remainder in investment X. With this asset allocation, the perfect countercyclical pattern of returns has completely eliminated volatility on a portfolio level: portfolio W has an expected return of 8.7 percent with no volatility! As we further increase the percentage of the portfolio allocated to investment X, the portfolio moves along the line connecting point W to point X, until the point is reached where 100 percent of the portfolio is committed to investment X.

FIGURE 7-10

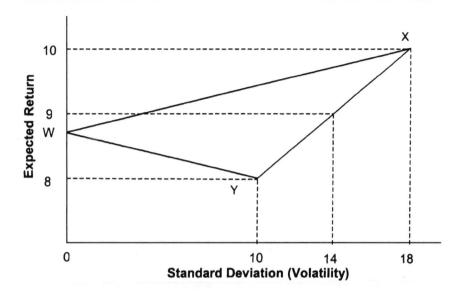

The curved line in Figure 7–11 connecting points Y and X describes the more typical situation of neither perfectly positive nor perfectly negative correlation. Assume, for example, that we want to achieve a 9 percent expected return from a portfolio composed of investments X and Y. A horizontal line drawn from the 9 percent point on the vertical axis intercepts the curved line at a point corresponding to a volatility level of 11 percent. Note that this horizontal line would intercept a straight line connecting points Y and X at a volatility level of 14 percent. In essence, the difference between this 14 percent volatility level (which assumes perfect positive correlation and, hence, no diversification effect) and the 11 percent volatility level implied by the curved line represents the reduction in portfolio volatility associated with the diversification effect.

Although the diversification effect is usually thought of in terms of volatility reduction, it can equivalently be viewed in terms of return enhancement. Returning to Figure 7–11, for example, if we were willing to live with a volatility level of 14 percent, we would have to accept an expected return of 9 percent

FIGURE 7-11

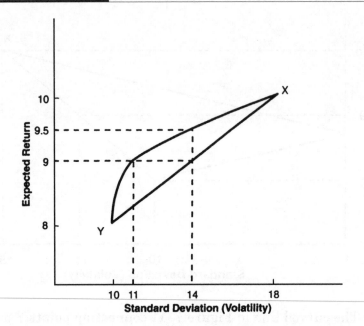

if X and Y were perfectly positively correlated. Because they are not, we can obtain an expected return of 9.5 percent. This is the vertical height corresponding to a point where a vertical line drawn from a volatility level of 14 percent intercepts the curved line. This extra .5 percent in expected return is equivalently attributable to the diversification effect.

Thus far, we have discussed diversification in the context of two investment alternatives. In this situation, each unique combination of the two investments is associated with a particular expected return. For example, in Figure 7-11, an expected return of 9 percent is associated with only one specific combination of investments X and Y. Lowering the percentage allocated to X produces a lower expected return for the portfolio, while increasing the percentage allocated to X increases the expected return.

Let us now consider diversification in a situation involving multiple investment alternatives, X, Y, and Z, with the following volatility/return characteristics:

Investment	Expected Return	Standard Deviation
X	10%	18%
Y	8%	10%
Z	6%	2%

With three investment alternatives, we need to specify three correlations. This is usually done in the form of a correlation matrix:

	X	Y	Z
X	1.00		
Y	.50	1.00	
Z	.10	.30	1.00

With three or more investment alternatives, we no longer have unique solutions associated with various expected returns. For example, we can build any number of different investment portfolios to obtain an expected return of 8 percent. Some examples are:

Portfolio	Percentage Allocation to Investment			Portfolio Expected Return	Portfolio Standard Deviation
	X	Y	Z		
1	0	100	0	8	10.0
2	50	0	50	8	9.2
3	30	40	30	8	8.3
4	25	50	25	8	8.4

Of the four choices listed, portfolio 3 is the best because it produces the expected return of 8 percent with the least volatility, as measured by the portfolio standard deviation. Can this portfolio be improved? Is there some other asset allocation that can produce the same expected return of 8 percent with even less portfolio volatility? Although there are an infinite number of different portfolio allocations that can produce the desired expected return of 8 percent, there is only one specific allocation that will push portfolio volatility to its minimum possible value.

The same is true for any specific expected return between the maximum return of 10 percent associated with investment X and the expected return associated with the lowest-volatility portfolio that can be constructed using investments X, Y, and Z as possible building blocks. Due to the diversification effect, it is possible that this lowest-volatility portfolio may have a higher expected return *with less volatility* than investment Z! With respect to *any* specific expected return within that range, there are an infinite number of portfolio allocations that can produce a specified expected return, but there is only one unique allocation that optimally produces the specific expected return with a minimum of portfolio volatility.

The specific allocation that minimizes portfolio volatility for a given expected return is considered *optimal*. By definition, these optimal portfolios are said to be *efficient*. Other portfolios that produce the same expected return, but with greater volatility, are said to be *inefficient*. If we connected each of the optimal portfolios associated with each possible level of expected return, we would form what is called the *efficient frontier.*

Let us now approach the subject of diversification from yet another direction. Assume we have a large collection of volatile assets. Figure 7–12 shows each asset plotted in terms of its volatility/return characteristics. As we consider the nature of the volatility/return trade-off, we would perhaps expect to see these assets form a pattern that slopes upward to the right. Yet we see no such pattern. The reason for this will become clear later.

Now consider the portfolio possibilities based on various combinations and weightings of these volatile assets. Figure 7–13 shows this set of possible portfolios as the shaded area bound on the upper left by the efficient frontier connecting points A and B. Obviously, we again see that for any given expected return, there are good (efficient) and bad (inefficient) ways to combine assets to build portfolios. If we are limited to choosing from only these volatile assets in building our portfolios, we should choose a portfolio lying somewhere along the curved efficient frontier connecting point A with point B.

What would happen if we changed the example by permitting investors to either borrow money or invest it at some volatility-free rate of interest, R_f? Figure 7–14 shows a line

FIGURE 7-12

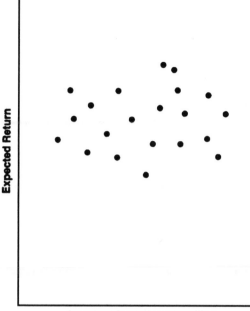

Standard Deviation (Volatility)

drawn from point C corresponding to R_f on the vertical axis to the point of tangency M on the efficient frontier. In this situation, it is advantageous for *all* investors to hold the same optimal volatile portfolio M, in combination with either borrowing or investing at the volatility-free rate of interest in accordance with their volatility tolerance.

Investors who are more volatility-averse would invest part of their money at the volatility-free rate of interest and hold the balance in the volatile portfolio M. Depending on the percentage invested at the volatility-free rate of interest, their portfolio would lie somewhere on the straight line connecting point C, corresponding to the volatility-free rate of interest, and point M, the optimal volatile portfolio. Investors with greater volatility tolerance could hold investment portfolios lying along line MX by borrowing money at the volatility-free rate of interest in order to provide additional funds for making larger investments

FIGURE 7-13

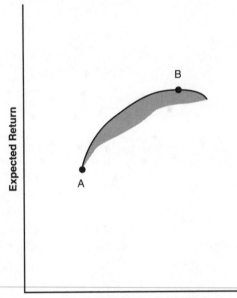

Standard Deviation (Volatility)

in the optimal volatile portfolio M. Note that with the added possibility of borrowing or lending, the portfolio possibilities on line CMX lie above, and are therefore superior to, those lying on the prior efficient frontier connecting points A and B, where borrowing or lending is not possible.

This leads to a discussion of the Capital Asset Pricing Model (CAPM), which was developed in the mid-1960s by William F. Sharpe in conjunction with other researchers.[3] It provides a powerful description of the relationship between volatility and expected return in an efficient capital market. As is the case with most models, simplifying assumptions are made to abstract the essence of the relationship being modeled. With the CAPM, several such assumptions are made:

---

3. I have modified the language normally used in discussing the CAPM by often substituting the word *volatility* for *risk*. This is consistent with my decision to carefully choose the contexts within which those words are used throughout the book.

FIGURE 7–14

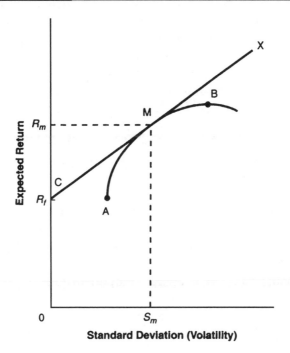

Standard Deviation (Volatility)

1. All investors are assumed to have the same investment
   information and to hold identical expectations regarding the future.
2. The market is perfectly competitive.
3. There are no transaction costs for buying and selling
   securities.
4. Investors live in a tax-free world.
5. Investors can either invest or borrow at the same
   volatility-free rate of interest.
6. Investors are volatility-averse.

In such a world, all investors would create and hold the
same efficient portfolio of volatile assets. This is called the *market portfolio* and is composed of all volatile investment assets,
each weighted in terms of its outstanding market value. In order
to accommodate individual differences in volatility tolerance,

investors can either borrow or invest at the volatility-free rate of interest in combination with holding the market portfolio. Let us now define point M in Figure 7–14 to be the market portfolio. The volatility associated with the market portfolio is the nondiversifiable volatility inherent in the market as a whole. This volatility is quantified by the distance OS_m on the horizontal axis. The expected return on the market is labeled on the vertical axis at R_m. Line CMX is known as the *Capital Market Line*. It reflects the upward-sloping relationship between volatility and expected return among the efficient investment strategies that lie on this line. The slope of the capital market line can be thought of as the reward one expects to receive per unit of volatility borne.

Each volatile asset in the market portfolio can have its total volatility (standard deviation) broken down into diversifiable and nondiversifiable components. One conclusion of the CAPM is that only the latter, nondiversifiable component of total volatility justifies extra compensation. Beta, β, is the measure of an asset's nondiversifiable volatility relative to the market portfolio. It is computed by a statistical comparison of the asset's pattern of returns relative to the return of the market portfolio.

We can now explain why the volatile assets in Figure 7–12 do not form a pattern that slopes upward to the right. If diversifiable volatility is not rewarded by the marketplace, we should plot expected return against nondiversifiable volatility (i.e., β) rather than against total volatility, as we did in Figure 7–12. A plot of this new relationship forms what is called the *Security Market Line* (SML), shown in Figure 7–15. The SML begins at R_f and passes through point M, which corresponds to the market portfolio. In equilibrium, the buying and selling activities of investors in an efficient capital market will price securities such that they fall on the SML. In other words, according to the CAPM, a security's expected return is a function of the volatility-free rate of interest, the expected return on the market, and its nondiversifiable volatility as measured by β. This is mathematically expressed by:

$$R_i = R_f + (R_m - R_f)\,\beta_i$$

FIGURE 7-15

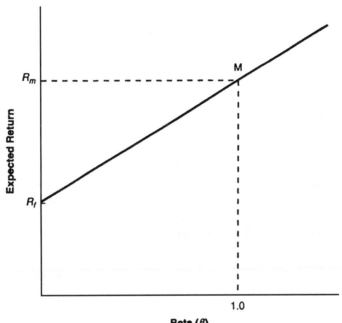

where

R_i = Expected return on security I
R_f = Volatility-free rate of interest
R_m = Expected return on the market portfolio
β_i = Beta value for security I

Most often, a broad-based stock index such as the S&P 500 is used as a proxy for the market portfolio. In this context, β is a measure of how an individual stock's return covaries with the S&P 500. Arguably, however, the S&P 500 is much too narrow a proxy for the market portfolio. By definition, the market portfolio should contain all volatile investment assets, each weighted in terms of its outstanding market value. Hence, it would be more appropriate to describe the market portfolio in global terms, including both domestic and international stocks and bonds, real estate, and all other major investment asset classes.

Such a market portfolio would look similar to Figure 1–1. In this context, β would be a measurement of each investment's pattern of return relative to this world market portfolio. By implication, all investors should hold the same world market portfolio and adjust for differences in volatility tolerance through either investing or borrowing at the volatility-free rate of interest.

Various extended models of the original CAPM have been developed since the mid-1960s, as well as other models concerning security pricing. For example, Arbitrage Pricing Theory asserts that multiple factors, in addition to market volatility, are involved in security pricing. The CAPM has been criticized on the basis of its unrealistic assumptions and for not providing a completely accurate description of real-world security pricing. It nevertheless remains a powerful model that highlights the importance of diversification and the relationship between non-diversifiable volatility and security expected returns.

CHAPTER 8

The Rewards of Multiple-Asset-Class Investing

My ventures are not in one bottom trusted,
Nor to one place; nor is my whole estate
Upon the fortune of this present year;
Therefore, my merchandise makes me not sad.

—*William Shakespeare (1564–1616)*
Merchant of Venice
Act I, Scene 1

Twenty-five years ago, U.S. stocks and bonds constituted the majority of the world's total equity and debt markets. Our capital markets not only were the largest, they were also the most liquid and efficient. Our economy was broadly diversified, dynamic, and resilient. It is not surprising, therefore, that U.S. investors have traditionally held portfolios composed predominantly of domestic stocks and bonds. Would investors be better off in the long run by following a more broadly diversified investment strategy?

Imagine for a moment that we have two competing investment organizations that are alike in every way except that one firm can invest globally whereas the other is restricted to U.S. stocks and bonds. Each firm is well staffed by highly qualified, talented professionals with ready access to quality research services. Which firm is likely to deliver the better risk-adjusted performance results? All other things being equal, the global firm with its broader set of investment possibilities has a greater chance for superior performance. The worst case for the global money management firm is that it will find no attractive investment opportunities outside of the United States. In this unlikely situation, it still has a 50/50 chance of outperforming the money management firm that is restricted to U.S. stocks and bonds. If, however, it finds attractive investment opportunities not available to the domestic money management firm, the expectation is that its performance will be superior.

Figure 1–1 shows the estimated allocation of the world's total investable capital as of the end of 1998. The non-U.S. capital markets are now as large, and therefore as important, as the U.S. capital markets. Why not take diversification to its logical conclusion and design portfolios that use all of these major world asset classes? This would create more opportunities for the ups and downs of one asset class to partially offset the ups and downs of another. Multiple-asset-class portfolios should give investors a better relationship between the returns they want and the volatility they wish to mitigate.

INTERNATIONAL BONDS

Let's begin with interest-generating investments and examine the impact of international diversification on a domestic bond portfolio. Figure 8–1 graphs the comparative performance over rolling 20-year periods of a 100 percent U.S. long-term corporate bond portfolio and portfolios with 10 percent, 20 percent, and 30 percent international bond allocations. Salomon Brothers, Inc., provided the international bond index performance numbers used in these graphs. These index numbers measure the total return from a broad representation of international bonds from several foreign countries.

There are seven lines on the chart, one for each 20-year rolling period ending 1992 through 1998. In every case except the 20-year period ending with 1998, bond portfolio return increased and volatility decreased as the allocation to international bonds increased from 10 percent to 30 percent. For the most recent period ending 1998, bond portfolio return was slightly impaired as a result of international diversification. Nonetheless, there was an offsetting advantage secured with a sizable reduction in bond portfolio volatility.

FIGURE 8-1

International Diversification of a Bond Portfolio

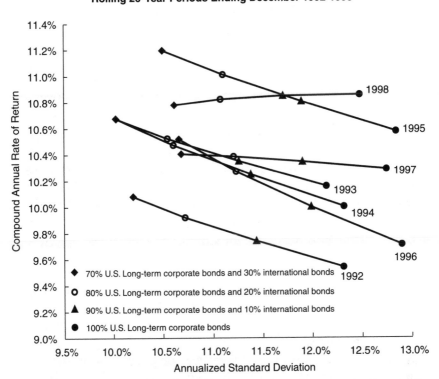

Rolling 20-Year Periods Ending December 1992-1998

Historically, international bonds have provided returns that are competitive with those of U.S. bonds, but it is important to realize that the very high coupon returns from some international bonds are not fully realizable by U.S. investors. The "theory of interest rate parity" provides an explanation for this. It suggests that a higher foreign interest rate is often associated with a higher foreign inflation rate. This triggers depreciation in the foreign currency relative to our dollar, thus impairing the realizable returns. In the end, some international bonds' dollar-adjusted interest rates may not be as advantageous as their high coupons would indicate. The evidence suggests, however, that international diversification of a U.S. bond portfolio probably will improve long-term volatility-adjusted returns.

INTERNATIONAL STOCKS

International stock investing has increased substantially in the wake of wider acceptance over the past couple of decades. This has been triggered by a variety of factors. First, the international markets account for a larger percentage of world Gross National Product and world market capitalization than was the case 20 years ago. Second, many of the world's major corporations are non-U.S. and offer significant opportunities in certain market sectors. For example, Canada, South Africa, and Australia have major natural resource companies and Germany, Japan, and Sweden all have major automobile manufacturing corporations. Many other countries have higher rates of savings, capital formation, and economic growth. The work ethic is also stronger in some countries, particularly in the Pacific Basin. Finally, there are periods when international stock markets outperform the U.S. stock market, and the relatively low cross-correlation of returns between the U.S. and international markets provides for a significant diversification effect in moderating portfolio volatility.

Figure 8–2 examines the impact of international diversification on a domestic common stock portfolio. Morgan Stanley Capital International provided the EAFE international stock index performance statistics used in this graph. The EAFE Index measures the total return of a sample of common stocks of companies representative of the market structure of 20 European and Pacific Basin countries. The data for international common stock returns begin three years earlier than the data for international bonds, and we therefore have 10 rolling 20-year periods to examine.

In all but two 20-year periods, the international diversification steadily improved the portfolio returns as the commitment increased from 0 percent to 30 percent. The notable exceptions were the 20-year periods ending 1997 and 1998. Over these time periods, domestic stock returns were sufficiently

F I G U R E   8 – 2

International Diversification of a Stock Portfolio

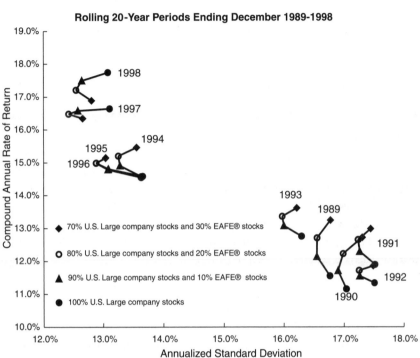

Rolling 20-Year Periods Ending December 1989-1998

Source: Based on data from Morgan Stanley Capital International; Standard & Poor's.

higher than international stock returns so as to slightly impair the portfolio returns as we added international stocks to the domestic stock portfolio.[1] This is not an argument against international diversification. Rather, these exceptions highlight the fact that there will be time periods when domestic stocks generate higher returns than international stocks. But unless you possess the market timing skills to predict which asset class will

---

1. Diversification into an asset class with lower returns does not necessarily result in a lower portfolio return. Depending on the magnitude of the difference in returns and the correlations among the portfolio components, diversification into a lower-returning asset class may actually result in an increase in portfolio return. Later in the chapter, we will see several examples of this in the section titled "Multiple-Asset-Class Investing."

be superior, a diversified approach remains the best strategy. Over every 20-year period, portfolio volatility was lower with a 10 percent or 20 percent international commitment. Also, in almost every period, volatility remained lower with a 30 percent international commitment compared to an all-domestic common stock portfolio.

International investing is not without its special problems, however. Accounting practices in foreign countries differ from our own and often provide less complete disclosure to investors. Many international markets are not as liquid or as well regulated as the U.S. stock market. This often results in high transaction costs and possible delays in the settlement of security transactions. Foreign nations may suffer from political instability, which adds another dimension of risk to the investment management process. Foreign governments can also tax and/or in various ways restrict the flow of investment capital. Finally, the currency risk of a rising dollar can result in a poor dollar-denominated return even when the securities perform well in terms of their native currency. In essence, every international investment is two investments: one in the security itself and the other in the native foreign currency.

The risks cited above are even more pronounced with investments in the capital markets of rapidly developing third world economies. Nevertheless, the long-term rewards from investing in emerging markets can be significant. Many of these countries have economic growth rates twice that of the United States, and modest diversification into these markets should be considered.

Despite the special problems, international common stock investing is likely to become more prevalent in the future due to the increasing interdependence of the world's economies and the benefits to be derived from this important form of diversification.

REAL ESTATE

Real estate is quite different from the other investment alternatives we have discussed. Each real estate property is unique in its geographic location, physical structure, tenant mix, and a variety of other attributes. The purchase and sale of real estate properties are negotiated transactions, which can become very complex.

Because the real estate market is composed of noninterchange-able, unique, nonliquid properties, it is probably less efficient than the stock and bond markets. This inefficiency may give rise to exploitable opportunities for skilled investors to secure superi-or investment results. At the same time, however, the search and transaction costs involved with real estate investments are often high relative to other investment alternatives.

As an equity investment, real estate's capital appreciation has generally served as an effective hedge against inflation over long time horizons. Well-purchased real estate often also pro-duces generous current cash flow. Many investors prefer to leverage their real estate investments with borrowed money. Although this increases the risk of the investment and diverts cash flow for debt service, it also magnifies the potential gains on the upside. In the past, tax benefits further enhanced the attractiveness of real estate investing. Unfortunately for the high-tax-bracket investor, the Tax Reform Act of 1986 largely eliminated real estate's favorable tax treatment. Despite this, real estate remains a major asset class that should be meaning-fully represented in a well-diversified portfolio. Because each real estate investment is unique and nonliquid, it is very impor-tant that real estate investments be adequately diversified. This can be accomplished by having ownership interests in different types of real estate investments, such as office buildings, resi-dential apartment complexes, shopping centers, and/or raw land, in a variety of geographic locations.

Equity Real Estate Investment Trusts (REITs) provide an alternative method of real estate diversification. Equity REITs are similar to closed-end funds of real estate properties. Like investment companies, they avoid corporate taxation by serving as a conduit for earnings on investments. The stocks of many equity REITs are traded on securities exchanges. The liquidity and the trading activity provide constant market consensus pricing of these investments. Some argue that because REITs provide an indirect form of ownership, they are therefore not pure real estate investments. Indeed, equity REITs are some-thing of a "no-man's-land" in the investment world. Real estate professionals claim ignorance about them because they trade like common stocks, while stock portfolio managers often ignore them because they consider equity REITs to be real estate investments rather than common stocks! This thinking is beginning to change, however, as a result of the increasing securitization of real estate and wider acceptance of REITs as a viable form of real estate ownership.

The diversification achievable with REITs is of particular value to investors. Unlike the case with direct real estate ownership, a REIT investor can easily diversify a relatively small sum of money both geographically and across different types of real estate investments, such as shopping centers, office buildings, and residential apartment complexes.

By stock market standards, equity REITs tend to generate above-average yields and to have smaller capitalizations. For these reasons, the performance of equity REITs not only will be determined by the real estate market in general but also will be impacted by changes in interest rates and by the relative performance of small company stocks.

MULTIPLE-ASSET-CLASS INVESTING

Let's now examine multiple-asset-class investing in a broader equity context. The equity side of the portfolio is usually responsible for great portfolio returns when they occur. The equity side of the portfolio is also most often responsible for significant losses. Figure 8–3 shows the performance of 15 different equity portfolios over the period 1972 through 1997. The portfolios are intentionally unlabeled to allow us to conduct a "blindfolded" exercise. Of these 15 portfolios, 4 are identified by squares, 6 by triangles, 4 by diamonds, and 1 by a circle. As you move to the right along the chart, portfolio volatility increases. Likewise, returns increase as you move from bottom to top. Assume that you have a reliable crystal ball and know with certainty that each one of these portfolios will have the same performance over the next 26 years that it had over the period 1972 through 1997. Now answer these questions:

- If you had to choose between owning a randomly chosen portfolio identified by a square and owning one identified by a triangle, which would you choose: square or triangle?

FIGURE 8-3

Fifteen Equity Portfolios (1972–1997)

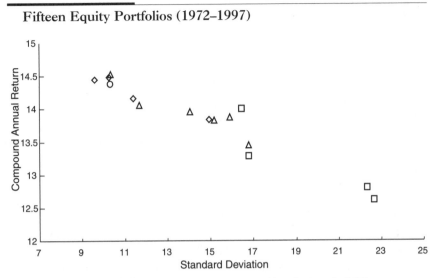

Source: © Roger C. Gibson, "Asset Allocation and the Rewards of Multiple-Asset-Class Investing," 1998.

- If you had to choose between owning a randomly chosen portfolio identified by a triangle and owning one identified by a diamond, which would you choose?
- If you had to choose between owning a randomly chosen portfolio identified by a diamond and simply owning the circle, which would you choose: diamond or circle?

I have posed this series of questions to my clients and to audiences at speaking engagements. The answers are consistent. When given the choice, people prefer the triangles to the squares, the diamonds to the triangles, and the circle to the diamonds.

Now let's take off the blindfold and look at Figure 8–4. Each square is a single-asset-class portfolio.

- A is the Standard & Poor's 500 Composite Index (S&P 500). The S&P 500 currently includes 500 large U. S. stocks, as measured in terms of the total market value of shares outstanding. The index measures the total return of a capitalization-weighted basket of these stocks and, for our purposes, represents the domestic common stock asset class.

FIGURE 8-4

The Rewards of Multiple-Asset-Class Investing (1972–1997)

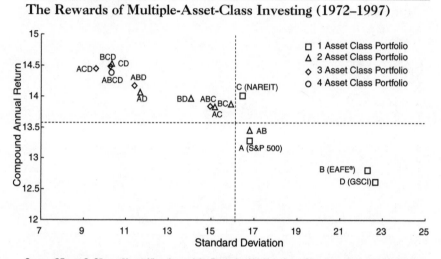

Source: ©Roger C. Gibson, "Asset Allocation and the Rewards of Multiple-Asset-Class Investing," 1998; Standard & Poor's; Morgan Stanley Capital International; Copyright © 1998 by National Association of Real Estate Investment Trusts®. NAREIT® data is reprinted with permission. Statements, calculations, or charts made by the author which use NAREIT® data have not been approved, verified, or endorsed by NAREIT®; *GSCI® performance data used with permission of Goldman, Sachs & Co.*

- B is the EAFE Index (Europe, Australia, and Far East), which measures the total return of a sample of common stocks of companies representative of the market structures of 20 European and Pacific Basin countries. It represents the international common stock asset class.

- C is the National Association of Real Estate Investment Trusts (NAREIT) Equity Index, which measures the total return of equity real estate investment trusts. Equity REITs are similar to closed-end funds of real estate properties. The NAREIT Equity Index is a proxy for the real estate asset class.

- D is the Goldman Sachs Commodity Index (GSCI). This index measures the total return of a collateralized position in the Goldman Sachs Commodity Index futures contract. The GSCI represents a diversified cross section of the major raw and semifinished goods used by producers and consumers. The major components of the index are energy, agricultural products, livestock, industrial metals, and precious metals.

The triangles represent every possible two-asset-class portfolio that investors can construct using the four single-asset classes (A, B, C, and D) as building blocks. Each portfolio is rebalanced annually to maintain an equally weighted allocation among the asset classes. For example, the triangle AB represents the performance of a portfolio weighted equally between the S&P 500 (domestic stocks) and EAFE (international stocks).

The diamonds represent every possible three-asset-class portfolio that investors can construct with the four single-asset classes. The circle is an equally balanced portfolio using all four asset classes.

An investor who chooses a triangle portfolio over a square is indicating a preference for a two-asset-class portfolio over a single-asset-class portfolio. This decision is a rational one, since two-asset-class portfolios, in general, have less volatility and more return than do single-asset-class portfolios. Likewise, the three-asset-class portfolios (diamonds) have better volatility/return characteristics than do the two-asset-class portfolios (triangles). The four-asset-class portfolio (circle) is a better choice than a random placement in one of the three-asset-class portfolios (diamonds). The order of preference moves to the left, in the direction of less volatility, and upward, toward higher returns.

The reduction in volatility observed as we progress from one- to four-asset-class portfolios is not unanticipated. It is to be expected due to the dissimilarity in returns among the portfolio components. The generally rising pattern of returns, however, is surprising. The GSCI, for example, had lower returns with considerably more volatility than did the S&P 500, yet a portfolio allocated equally between the two had a higher return with much less volatility than did either of its components. Indeed, all six of the two-asset-class portfolios had higher returns with less volatility than three out of four of the single-asset classes used to build them.

When comparing the returns of these 15 equity portfolios, single-asset-class portfolios generated the three lowest returns, whereas the highest-returning portfolios were all multiple-asset-class structures. When we compare the volatility levels of these portfolios, we find that four out of the five most volatile portfolios were single-asset-class structures. The low-volatility alternatives are all multiple-asset-class portfolios.

Return for a moment to the four single-asset classes. If we offer investors the opportunity to choose how they would invest their money, given complete certainty that each asset class would perform as indicated on the graph, they probably would pick portfolio C, equity REITs. The choice seems obvious. Equity REITs had both a higher return and less volatility than any of the other asset classes. Yet a portfolio allocated equally among the other three asset classes generated a higher return than did REITs, with approximately 30 percent less volatility. Compare the position of C versus ABD in Figure 8–4. This amazing result occurred despite the fact that each of the other three asset classes had lower returns with more volatility than did REITs!

If we asked an investor to eliminate one of the four asset classes as a building block for the multiple-asset-class portfolios, he would probably choose D, the Goldman Sachs Commodity Index. Of all 15 portfolios on the graph, GSCI has the lowest return with the most volatility, yet the 5 highest-returning portfolios have D as an equal component and the 7 least volatile portfolios have D as an equal component. Obviously, there is more going on here than is captured by the return and volatility statistics in Figure 8–4. We are missing the crucial information about how each asset class's pattern of returns correlates with the others. The GSCI, for example, has a pattern of returns that is the most dissimilar to the other asset classes. Accordingly, it produces the strongest diversification effect when combined with other asset classes.

Table 8–1 shows the performance statistics for the 15 equity portfolios. The data in this exhibit make a very strong case for multiple-asset-class investing. For investors concerned primarily with maximizing portfolio returns, you can see that multiple-asset-class strategies have dominated single-asset-class strategies. For investors who are more concerned about volatility, again multiple-asset-class strategies are dominant. The Sharpe ratios displayed provide a volatility-adjusted performance measurement for each portfolio.[2] Again, we find multiple-asset-class strategies delivering much higher rates of volatility-adjusted returns than do single-asset-class strategies.

At the bottom of Table 8–1 there are summary comparisons for four-, three-, two-, and one-asset-class approaches. This summary provides perhaps the most compelling argument for multiple-asset-class investing. As we move toward broader diversification, rates of return increase, volatility levels decrease, and Sharpe ratios improve. The four-asset-class portfolio has a compound rate of return 1.2 percentage points higher than the average compound returns of its components. That is, a $1 investment in a continuously rebalanced portfolio of all four components has a future value of $32.89 compared with an average future value of $25.18 for the four components standing alone. The four-asset-class portfolio has 47 percent less volatility than the average volatility levels of its components. Also, the Sharpe ratio of the four-asset-class portfolio shows that it has generated nearly twice as much volatility-adjusted return as the average of its components.

It is often difficult to see the beneficial impact on return created by broader diversification because diversification examples mix fixed-income investments with equity investments. In this situation, the large difference between the returns of fixed-income and those of equity investments obscures the increase in portfolio return attributable to the diversification effect. Although one would expect that asset classes with similar volatility levels would have similar long-term growth paths, we are pedagogically fortunate to have the four equity asset class returns in our analysis be as close as they are. As a result, you can see the positive impact diversification has on both dampening volatility and increasing return.

---

2. The Sharpe ratio is a measure of reward relative to volatility. A portfolio's Sharpe ratio can be calculated easily using a simple spreadsheet program. The portfolio's returns are listed in one column, and those for Treasury bills are listed in the next column. The differences between the portfolio returns and Treasury bill returns are computed in the third column. The Sharpe ratio is equal to the average of the differences in column 3 divided by the standard deviation of those differences. The Sharpe ratio affirms the notion that a portfolio should generate some incremental reward for the assumption of volatility; otherwise, it would be better to simply own Treasury bills.

T A B L E 8 – 1

The Rewards of Multiple-Asset-Class Investing (1972–1997)

Performance Statistics for the 15 Equity Portfolios

Compound Annual Returns and Future Values of $1 Ranked High to Low			Standard Deviations (Volatility) Ranked Low to High		Sharpe Ratios Ranked High to Low	
	%	$		%		
CD	14.53	34.00	ACD	9.59	ACD	0.77
BCD	14.48	33.67	BCD	10.26	CD	0.74
ACD	14.44	33.36	ABCD	10.30	BCD	0.72
ABCD	14.38	32.89	CD	10.32	ABCD	0.71
ABD	14.16	31.31	ABD	11.40	ABD	0.64
AD	14.06	30.59	AD	11.68	AD	0.63
C	14.01	30.21	BD	14.05	BD	0.53
BD	13.96	29.88	ABC	14.95	ABC	0.51
BC	13.87	29.31	AC	15.18	AC	0.51
ABC	13.84	29.07	BC	15.92	C	0.49
AC	13.83	29.00	C	16.44	BC	0.49
AB	13.45	26.62	AB	16.79	AB	0.44
A	13.28	25.61	A	16.79	A	0.44
B	12.81	22.94	B	22.30	B	0.34
D	12.61	21.95	D	22.66	D	0.34

Average Performance Statistics: Four-, Three-, Two-, and One-Asset-Class Portfolios

Compound Annual Returns and Future Values of $1 Ranked High to Low			Standard Deviations (Volatility) Ranked Low to High		Sharpe Ratios Ranked High to Low	
	%	$		%		
Four	14.38	32.89	Four	10.30	Four	0.71
Three	14.23	31.85	Three	11.55	Three	0.66
Two	13.95	29.90	Two	13.99	Two	0.56
One	13.18	25.18	One	19.55	One	0.40

Source: ©Roger C. Gibson, "Asset Allocation and the Rewards of Multiple-Asset-Class Investing," 1998; Standard & Poor's; Morgan Stanley Capital International; Copyright © 1998 by National Association of Real Estate Investment Trusts®. NAREIT® data is reprinted with permission. Statements, calculations, or charts made by the author which use NAREIT® data have not been approved, verified, or endorsed by NAREIT®; *GSCI® performance data used with permission of Goldman, Sachs & Co.*

I originally did this research toward the end of 1998. As a result, 1997 was the last calendar of data included in the analysis. The year 1972 was chosen as the beginning point because it was the earliest year for which data were available for all four equity asset classes. As fate would have it, 1998 was a year when there were strikingly different returns across the four asset classes, as shown in Table 8–2. The returns ranged from a stellar 28.58 percent for the S&P 500 to −35.75 percent for the GSCI—the biggest drop in commodity prices in over a century.

As expected, the marked disparity in 1998 returns trigger some significant repositioning of the 15 equity portfolios in volatility/return space, as shown in Figure 8–5. This is a wonderful illustration of "end point sensitivity." As a result of one additional year of data, REITs fell from first place to third in return among the four asset classes while the S&P 500 moved into first place. Among the 15 equity portfolios, the S&P 500 moved from thirteenth place in compound annual return to second! This underscores the danger of naively extrapolating an asset class's relative performance into the future. The performance of the GSCI was so bad that the vertical axis on Figure 8–5 had to be rescaled; otherwise, it would have fallen off the graph. The inclusion of 1998's returns flattened somewhat the pattern of portfolios in volatility/return space. Despite this repositioning,

TABLE 8-2

What a Difference a Year Makes!

	1998 Total Return
S&P 500	28.58
EAFE	20.33
NAREIT	−17.50
GSCI	−35.75

Source: © Center for Fiduciary Studies, 1999; Standard & Poor's; Morgan Stanley Capital International; Copyright © 1998 by National Association of Real Estate Investment Trusts®. NAREIT® is reprinted with permission. Statements, calculations, or charts made by the author which use NAREIT® data have not been approved, verified, or endorsed by NAREIT®; *GSCI® performance data used with permission of Goldman, Sachs & Co.*

however, *the basic conclusion of the analysis remains the same.* Table 8–3 provides the updated performance statistics for all 15 equity portfolios. Even though both REITs and the GSCI had very rough years, the multiple-asset-class strategies delivered superior volatility-adjusted returns relative to less well-diversified strategies and portfolio ABCD was the best, as evidenced by its Sharpe ratio.

Table 8–4 gives another picture of the risk reduction achieved by the breadth of diversification. Here we list the five worst years, from 1972 through 1998, generated by each of the single-asset classes compared with the four-asset-class portfolio. Each of the single-asset-class portfolios had one or more years when the loss was worse than −20 percent. By comparison, the worst year for portfolio ABCD was a modest loss of −7.63 percent. Portfolio ABCD also experienced fewer years of negative returns than did any of the single-asset-class portfolios.

Most of the improvement in downside risk is due to the tendency of the Goldman Sachs Commodity Index to perform

FIGURE 8–5

The Rewards of Multiple-Asset-Class Investing (1972–1998)

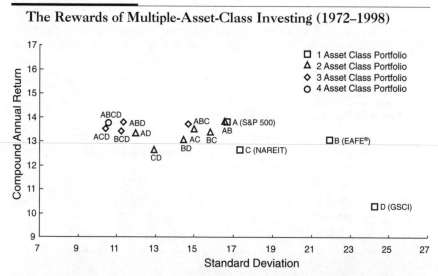

Source: ©Roger C. Gibson, "Asset Allocation and the Rewards of Multiple-Asset-Class Investing," 1998. Updated by author, Roger C. Gibson; Standard & Poor's; Morgan Stanley Capital International; Copyright © 1998 by National Association of Real Estate Investment Trusts®. NAREIT® data is reprinted with permission. Statements, calculations, or charts made by the author which use NAREIT® data have not been approved, verified, or endorsed by NAREIT®; *GSCI® performance data used with permission of Goldman, Sachs & Co.*

T A B L E 8 – 3

The Rewards of Multiple-Asset-Class Investing (1972–1998)

Performance Statistics for the 15 Equity Portfolios

Compound Annual Returns and Future Values of $1 Ranked High to Low			Standard Deviations (Volatility) Ranked Low to High		Sharpe Ratios Ranked High to Low	
	%	$		%		
AB	13.84	33.13	ACD	10.40	ABCD	0.66
A	13.82	32.92	ABCD	10.55	ACD	0.66
ABD	13.79	32.68	BCD	11.23	ABD	0.62
ABCD	13.77	32.53	ABD	11.36	BCD	0.60
ABC	13.71	32.12	AD	11.98	AD	0.57
ACD	13.51	30.62	CD	12.91	ABC	0.51
AC	13.51	30.60	BD	14.45	CD	0.50
BCD	13.42	29.98	ABC	14.69	AC	0.50
BC	13.39	29.73	AC	14.99	A	0.48
AD	13.35	29.50	BC	15.83	AB	0.47
B	13.08	27.61	AB	16.57	BD	0.47
BD	13.07	27.58	A	16.69	BC	0.47
CD	12.65	24.94	C	17.31	C	0.41
C	12.65	24.92	B	21.90	B	0.36
D	10.30	14.10	D	24.25	D	0.25

Average Performance Statistics: Four-, Three-, Two-, and One-Asset-Class Portfolios

Compound Annual Returns and Future Values of $1 Ranked High to Low			Standard Deviations (Volatility) Ranked Low to High		Sharpe Ratios Ranked High to Low	
	%	$		%		
Four	13.77	32.53	Four	10.55	Four	0.66
Three	13.61	31.35	Three	11.92	Three	0.60
Two	13.30	29.25	Two	14.45	Two	0.50
One	12.46	24.89	One	20.04	One	0.37

Source: ©Roger C. Gibson, "Asset Allocation and the Rewards of Multiple-Asset-Class Investing," 1998. Updated by author, Roger C. Gibson; Standard & Poor's; Morgan Stanley Capital International; Copyright © 1998 by National Association of Real Estate Investment Trusts®. NAREIT® data is reprinted with permission. Statements, calculations, or charts made by the author which use NAREIT® data have not been approved, verified, or endorsed by NAREIT®; GSCI® performance data used with permission of Goldman, Sachs & Co.

TABLE 8-4

The Five Worst Years (1972–1998)

A S&P 500		B EAFE®		C NAREIT		D GSCI		ABCD Equal Allocation	
Year	Return	Year	Return	Year	Return	Year	Return	Year	Return
1974	−26.47	1990	−23.19	1974	−21.40	1998	−35.75	1974	−7.63
1973	−14.66	1974	−22.15	1998	−17.50	1981	−23.01	1981	−5.74
1977	−7.18	1973	−14.17	1973	−15.52	1975	−17.22	1990	−3.16
1981	−4.91	1992	−11.85	1990	−15.35	1997	−14.07	1998	−1.08
1990	−3.17	1981	−1.03	1987	−3.64	1993	−12.33	1992	3.71

Source: ©Roger C. Gibson, "Asset Allocation and the Rewards of Multiple-Asset-Class Investing," 1998. Updated by author, Roger C. Gibson; Standard & Poor's; Morgan Stanley Capital International; Copyright © 1998 by National Association of Real Estate Investment Trusts®. NAREIT® data is reprinted with permission. Statements, calculations, or charts made by the author which use NAREIT® data have not been approved, verified, or endorsed by NAREIT®; GSCI® performance data used with permission of Goldman, Sachs & Co.

countercyclically to the other asset classes, an attribute that was of great value during the worldwide bear market for common stocks during 1973 and 1974. Figure 8–6 gives a visual picture of the countercyclicality of the GSCI versus the S&P 500. Even with the elimination of the GSCI as a building block, however, the analysis supports a multiple-asset-class approach with the remaining three asset classes.

WHY ISN'T EVERYONE DOING MULTIPLE-ASSET-CLASS INVESTING?

If multiple-asset-class investing is so wonderful, why isn't everyone doing it? There are three primary reasons. First, investors lack an awareness of the power of diversification. The typical investor understands that diversification may reduce volatility but suspects that it simultaneously impairs returns. As we have demonstrated, diversification tends to improve returns, not diminish them. Investors need to be educated about this dual benefit.

Second, the question of market timing arises. Investors naturally want to believe that there must be some way to predict which asset class will come in first place, and some money managers suggest that they in fact can make such market timing predictions accurately. Let's assume that we have a market timer with whom we consult annually for his prediction of the following year's best-performing asset class among the S&P 500, EAFE, NAREIT, and GSCI. Had he successfully predicted the winning asset class over the 15-year period from 1984 through 1998, an investor following his recommendations would have earned a compound rate of return of 32.19 percent. If such market timing skill exists, there should be evidence of money managers earning these rates of return. A check of Morningstar's database reveals that there is a universe of nearly 600 mutual funds with at least 15 years of performance history. Included is the full variety of professionally managed domestic and international funds, equity and fixed-income funds, and various specialty funds. How many of these funds had compound rates of return in excess of 32.19 percent? None! Not one got remotely close.

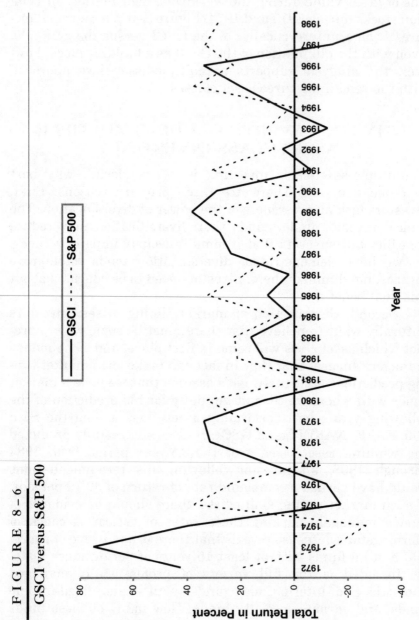

FIGURE 8-6

GSCI versus S&P 500

GSCI —— **S&P 500** - - - - -

Total Return in Percent

Year

Source: GSCI® performance data used with permission of Goldman, Sachs & Co.; Standard & Poor's.

Maybe we are asking for too much proficiency from our market timer. Let's assume that his prediction for the winning asset class each year never finished first but instead came in second among the four asset classes. This does not seem like a particularly impressive achievement, yet it would have generated a 15-year compound annual return of 19.32 percent. Out of nearly 600 funds, only 5 had a better investment performance. This is less than 1 percent of all professionally managed mutual funds, and none of the 5 funds relied on market timing to deliver its impressive returns.

Perhaps this is still asking too much of the market timer. What if we ask him simply to recognize the long periods of dominance of one asset class over another? For example, our market timer might instruct us to invest our funds in EAFE during the portion of the 15-year period that fell in the 1980s and then switch to the S&P 500 for the 1990s. This strategy would have generated a compound return of 23.06 percent. Again, not one mutual fund manager among nearly 600 funds achieved that rate of return. Apparently, successfully predicting the relative performance of asset classes is difficult to do!

The third reason everyone is not doing multiple-asset-class investing involves investor psychology. Investors use their domestic market as a frame of reference for evaluating their investment results. For example, a U.S.-based investor will compare her equity returns to a market index such as the S&P 500. This frame of reference is not a problem in years when the domestic market underperforms other asset classes, since diversification into better-performing markets rewards a multiple-asset-class investor. When the domestic market comes out on top, however, the investor perceives that diversification has impaired her returns. This sense of winning or losing arises primarily from the investor's immediate frame of reference. For example, the four-asset-class portfolio we have been discussing had a 10.4 percent return in 1997. Given either an EAFE or GSCI frame of reference, investors perceive this as a "winning" return, since these asset classes had returns in 1997 of 2.05 percent and −14.07 percent, respectively. This return is lousy from either an S&P 500 or a NAREIT perspective, since these asset classes had returns of 33.36 percent and 20.26 percent, respectively.

Each year, the multiple-asset-class strategy loses relative to some of its component asset classes and wins relative to others. That is the nature of diversification. As of the date of this writing, the S&P 500 is everyone's favorite asset class due to its remarkable performance from 1995 through 1998. Over the 27-year period of our analysis, the GSCI had 5 first-place finishes and EAFE and NAREIT had 7 and 10 first-place finishes, respectively. The S&P 500, by comparison, came in first place only five times. The frame-of-reference problem is particularly acute, however, because three of the S&P 500's first-place finishes happened during the last four years of the analysis. This period of S&P 500 dominance seems like an eternity to investors and fuels dissatisfaction with the lower returns generated over the same time period by a multiple-asset-class strategy. As a friend in the business observed, the problem with diversification is that it works whether or not you want it to!

We should not underestimate this frame-of-reference problem. Investors compare their investment results with their friends' results while playing golf or at cocktail parties. The true multiple-asset-class investor is still in the minority. During periods when the U.S. market prevails, this person will feel particularly vulnerable talking with friends who own a more traditional domestic stock and bond portfolio. Recently, a client told me that he would rather follow an inferior strategy that wins when his friends are winning and loses when his friends are losing than follow a superior long-term strategy that at times results in his losing when his friends are winning. There is pain in being different.

Equity investing is a long-term endeavor, and investors should devise and implement strategies with the long term in mind. Investors naturally attach more significance to recent investment experience than to longer-term performance, but they should resist the temptation to abandon more diversified strategies in favor of chasing yesterday's winner.

The multiple-asset-class investing analysis presented here is a pedagogical illustration that, for simplicity, utilizes equally weighted strategies of various combinations of the S&P 500, EAFE, NAREIT, and GSCI. As a teaching example, my goal is to demonstrate the power of diversification. Although I am a strong proponent of multiple-asset-class investing, I do not recommend an equally weighted equity strategy for my clients. My reasoning is partially rooted in the psychological concerns of this frame-of-reference issue. More suitable equity structures would be allocated most heavily to the domestic common stock asset class, with decreasing commitments to international stocks, real estate securities, and commodities. Although such portfolio allocations may not generate long-term, volatility-adjusted returns as desirable as that of the equally weighted strategy, the portfolio's pattern of returns probably will be easier for clients to live with and much of the advantage of broad diversification will still be retained.

I want to reiterate that this teaching example focuses solely on the equity side of an investor's portfolio in order to illustrate the power of diversification in both improving returns and mitigating volatility. Had interest-generating investments been included in the analysis, the diversification benefits would have been obscured by the significant differences in growth paths among the asset classes. The choice to exclude interest-generating investments from the analysis does not imply that I am an advocate of portfolios that are allocated 100 percent to equity investments. In the majority of client situations, diversification into interest-generating investments is advisable.

Occasionally, a client follows this analysis and questions its merit because it relies on historical data that may be irrelevant when looking into the future. Her or his argument rests on the notion that the world is very different today from what it was during the time period covered by my multiple-asset-class investing analysis; risks and opportunities exist now that have no historical precedent. Although that may be true, investor behavior is much the same as it has always been. Investors prefer predictability to uncertainty, and they face a menu of investment alternatives differentiated according to their levels of volatility. The buying and selling activity of investors establishes security prices that bring supply and demand into equilibrium. For this to occur, more volatile asset classes must have higher expected returns than less volatile asset classes. This leads to competitive, volatility-adjusted returns across investment alternatives.

The diversification benefits of a multiple-asset-class approach rest on dissimilarity in patterns of returns across investment alternatives in the short run and competitive asset class pricing in the long run. These conditions should hold in the future, even in the face of risks and opportunities that are unique to our times. But for the sake of argument, let's assume with the critics that the future is simply unknowable. If there is no basis on which to make predictions about the future, the wisest investment strategy is to broadly diversify portfolios in order to mitigate the risks of unknowable markets. This criticism, in fact, supports the argument in favor of multiple-asset-class investing.

SUMMARY

Asset allocation is vitally important. The benefits of diversification are powerful and robust not just in terms of volatility reduction but also for return enhancement. To evaluate the desirability of an asset class as a portfolio building block, it is not enough to know only its return and volatility characteristics. One must also know how its pattern of returns correlates to the patterns of returns of the other portfolio components. All other things being equal, the more dissimilarity there is among the asset classes within a portfolio, the stronger the diversification effect, providing investors with not only less volatility but also greater returns in the long run.

The beauty of diversification lies in the fact that its benefits are not dependent on the exercise of superior skill. They arise from the policy decision to follow a multiple-asset-class investment approach. Imagine for a moment that each of the portfolios in Figure 8–5 represented the performance of a different common stock manager actively engaged in trying to outperform his competitors through superior skill in security selection. We would want to know what the managers on the left-hand side of the graph are doing to generate such superior volatility-adjusted returns. Amazingly, these marked performance advantages did not rely on skill but rather on a simple policy decision: diversify!

The multiple-asset-class strategy is a tortoise-and-hare story. Over any 1-year, 3-year, or 10-year period, the race will probably be led by one of the component single-asset classes.

The leader will, of course, attract the attention. The tortoise never runs as fast as many of the hares around it. But it does run faster on average than the majority of its competitors, a fact that becomes lost due to the attention-getting pace of different lead rabbits during various legs of the race. It is noteworthy that the time period for the initial multiple-asset-class analysis presented in this chapter is 26 years. The length of a marathon is 26 miles. Think of this 26-year, multiple-asset-class illustration as a marathon. The GSCI rabbit led the first third of the race during the 1970s. The second third of the race was run in the 1980s, when the EAFE rabbit ran the fastest. During the final third of the race, the 1990s, the S&P 500 rabbit was outpacing all others. There is always a hare running faster than the multiple-asset-class tortoise, and depending on the leg of the race, it is usually a different hare that takes the lead. Yet the tortoise, in the long run, leaves the pack behind. We know the moral of the story: Slow and steady wins the race. In the end, patience and discipline are rewarded. To secure the reward, we need to relinquish our domestic frame of reference and invest as citizens of the world.

CHAPTER 9

Portfolio Optimization

All business proceeds on beliefs, on judgments of probabilities and not on certainties.

—Charles W. Eliot (1834–1926)

This chapter is devoted to a discussion of portfolio optimization. It may be particularly valuable to readers who are interested in, or intend to use, computer programs that are designed to identify optimal asset allocations for various client situations. Those readers who are not interested in this technical aspect of asset allocation may want to proceed to Chapter 10.

In Chapter 7 we learned that there are good and bad ways to allocate assets in constructing investment portfolios. Good asset allocations are said to be *efficient*. With an efficient asset mix, the portfolio's expected return is maximized subject to a specific portfolio volatility level. Bad asset allocations are said to be *inefficient*. With inefficient portfolios, it is possible to increase the portfolio's expected return without increasing portfolio volatility (or, equivalently, to reduce portfolio volatility without sacrificing the portfolio's expected return) by simply reallocating funds among the various investment positions. Each asset in a portfolio contributes to both the portfolio's expected return and its volatility. For a given level of portfolio volatility, an inefficient portfolio has some assets that make higher volatility-adjusted incremental contributions to portfolio expected return than do other assets.

For example, if the international bonds in a portfolio contribute more incremental portfolio expected return per unit of portfolio volatility than do the small company stocks, we can improve the portfolio's expected return without increasing portfolio volatility by simply selling some small company stock holdings to provide additional funds for international bond investments. Because such a swap changes the composition of the portfolio, each asset's volatility-adjusted contribution to portfolio expected return also changes and therefore needs to be recalculated. If we again find differences in the volatility-adjusted incremental contributions to portfolio expected return for the various assets, the portfolio's expected return can be further improved (without increasing portfolio volatility) by swapping some of the asset that now makes the smallest volatility-adjusted contribution to portfolio expected return for some of the asset that makes the largest contribution. If we continue in this manner, we will eventually run out of advantageous swaps. The resulting asset mix maximizes the expected return for that particular level of portfolio volatility. Hence, the portfolio is efficient. As a condition of that efficiency, each asset's volatility-adjusted incremental contribution to the portfolio's expected return is equal. (If this were not true, we could obviously continue to improve the portfolio's expected return without increasing portfolio volatility by engaging in more swaps.) By analogy, you know that you are standing on the top of a mountain (i.e., you have maximized your altitude) when you lose altitude regardless of which direction you walk. Similarly, an efficient portfolio is like being at the top of the mountain in that the pursuit of any alternative asset allocation with equivalent portfolio volatility will result in a loss of portfolio expected return.

For any given set of investment alternatives, there is a unique efficient portfolio that corresponds to a given level of portfolio volatility. The collection of all efficient portfolios across the full range of portfolio volatility possibilities is known as the *efficient frontier*. Although all efficient portfolios on the efficient frontier are good because they maximize expected return for any given level of volatility, from a particular client's point of view they are not equally desirable. The reason for this is that people vary in their volatility tolerance. The optimal portfolio for a client is that unique portfolio on the efficient frontier that maximizes the client's expected return subject to his or her particular level of volatility tolerance.

With the aid of computers utilizing sophisticated quadratic programming techniques, it is possible to mathematically identify the asset allocations that correspond to each portfolio lying on the efficient frontier. These computer optimization programs require as inputs estimates of the expected returns and standard deviations for each asset class as well as estimates of the cross-correlation of returns among all of the asset classes. Hopefully, the discussions we have had thus far have underscored the dangers of blindly using historical data to derive estimates of these variables. The fact that measures of uncertainty are incorporated into the inputs does not eliminate this danger. The difficulties are further compounded by the sensitivity of output to small variations in the input variables. The admonition often given to students in introductory computer programming courses is particularly relevant here: "Garbage in, garbage out!"

As a practical matter, most professionals who are experienced with optimization programs use historical cross-correlations and standard deviations as a departure point for developing estimates of future correlations and standard deviations.[1] Historical returns, however, are of less value in estimating future returns. For example, for the 10 rolling 20-year periods ending with 1979 through 1988, large company stocks usually had compound returns that were less than 2 percentage points greater than those of Treasury bills. Given the much greater volatility of large company stocks, we would certainly expect them to outperform Treasury bills in the future by a spread larger than 2 percentage points. Thus, anyone developing future return estimates based on any of these rolling 20-year periods would probably underestimate the incremental return expected from large company stocks. One way around this problem is to use longer-term historical relationships among asset class returns to develop estimates of future expected returns.

Another approach utilizes the implications of modern portfolio theory to derive estimates of the expected returns for various asset classes. For example, modern portfolio theory suggests that it is optimal for an investor with average volatility tolerance

---

1. In using an optimizer, an asset class's input statistic for standard deviation should generally be larger than its anticipated level of volatility in order to take into consideration the uncertainty in the level of future average returns for the asset class.

to hold an investment portfolio with an asset mix that mirrors the percentage allocation of assets of the world investable capital market. The estimation procedure first uses historical data as a basis for developing estimates of the standard deviations and cross-correlations for the various asset classes. Then the allocation of the world investable capital market is determined. (For example, see Figure 1–1, which shows an estimate of this allocation as of December 31, 1998.) Under an assumption that this asset mix is optimal for an investor with average volatility tolerance, it is possible to work backward to solve for the expected return for each asset class.

Once the inputs for expected return, standard deviation, and cross-correlation have been estimated for the asset classes, it is a straightforward, although sophisticated, mathematical calculation to derive the asset allocations for portfolios on the efficient frontier. It is then necessary to select the specific portfolio along the efficient frontier that is most appropriate for the client in question. One method for doing this is to describe the expected return/volatility characteristics of a representative sample of portfolios from the efficient frontier and then have the client select one. The client's choice will be an indirect indication of his or her volatility tolerance. Because there is no way to directly measure a client's volatility tolerance, this process of choosing an optimal portfolio will always have a subjective dimension.

Many computer optimization programs have a built-in feature that selects the optimal portfolio based on an input variable that attempts to describe a client's volatility tolerance. To do this, the computer identifies the efficient portfolio that optimizes the portfolio's *utility* for the investor. Utility is an expression borrowed from economic theory that, loosely translated, means "psychological satisfaction." In an optimization program, utility is calculated as the portfolio's expected return minus a penalty for volatility. The volatility penalty in turn is a function of two things: the portfolio's volatility, which can be mathematically quantified, and the client's volatility tolerance, which can only be subjectively estimated. To indirectly assess a client's volatility tolerance, some computer optimization programs utilize a decision-making procedure like the one we developed in Chapter 6, which requires the investor to choose a preferred portfolio allocation between Treasury bills and large company stocks. The percentage allocated to large company stocks serves as the input value for the investor's volatility-tolerance variable. For example, a volatility-tolerance input of 80 corresponds to a preferred 80 percent commitment to large company stocks and hence indicates high volatility tolerance, whereas a volatility-tolerance input of 25 corresponds to a large company stock commitment of 25 percent, which indicates low volatility tolerance.

The portfolio optimization program described in the next section uses a different approach. The client is asked to specify how much additional expected return over Treasury bill yields he or she would require to actively choose a 50 percent Treasury bill/50 percent large company stock portfolio balance. An investor with low volatility tolerance, for example, might require large company stocks to have an expected return that is 20 percentage points higher than Treasury bills in order to actively choose a 50/50 portfolio balance. The *volatility-premium* input variable would therefore have a value of 20. An investor with higher volatility tolerance may require large company stocks to have an expected return only 3 percentage points higher than Treasury bills to actively choose a 50/50 portfolio balance. The volatility-premium input variable would in this case be assigned a value of 3.

COMPUTER OPTIMIZATION PROGRAMS

A computer optimization program is a very sharp tool, which can easily cut the hand of an inexperienced user. The purpose of this discussion is to highlight the dangers and limitations of this powerful technology without losing an awareness of the contribution it can make to the portfolio management process.

Let us now observe a computer optimization program in action.[2] Although the reader is advised to exercise judgment in the specification of input values, for pedagogical reasons we will simply use unmodified historical performance statistics for our first optimization illustration. The input values shown in Table 9–1 are based on the 22-year time period from 1973

---

2. All computer optimizations were performed on Vestek Systems, Inc., software.

through 1994. In addition to the seven asset classes listed, there are two specific investment alternatives: a real estate separate account and a precious metals mutual fund. I have included the real estate separate account to provide an example of the dangers of incorporating a nonliquid investment in an optimization. The precious metals mutual fund is included as an example of an investment that historically has been used as a hedge against inflation and/or political instability. After we run the series of optimization illustrations, we will compare the expected return input for each asset class with its subsequent performance over the time period that followed from 1995 through 1998.

The historical simple average return for the 22-year period rather than the compound annual return is used as the input value for the expected return of each asset class. The expected return is an estimate for a single-period return and is best approximated by the simple average return. Another reason for using the simple average return is that the standard deviation statistic is measured relative to the simple average return, not the compound return. In actuality, the compound annual return statistic contains within itself information regarding the volatility of the pattern of returns. Accordingly, the erroneous use of the compound annual return statistic as the input value for the expected return would have the effect of double counting the volatility.

In the Appendix to Chapter 3, we discussed the fact that for a variable pattern of returns, the compound annual return is always less than the simple average return. This occurs because it takes a larger above-average return to offset the impact of any given below-average return. Expressed another way, a given margin of above-average performance is not sufficient to offset an equal margin of below-average performance. An illustration will clarify this. Table 9–2 shows three different investments. Each has a simple average return of 8 percent, a below-average return in year 2, and an above-average return in year 3. Note that although the three investments vary in terms of their volatility, for each one the margin of above-average performance equals the margin of below-average performance. In all three cases, the compound annual return is lower than the corresponding simple average return of 8 percent because the return for

TABLE 9 – 1

Computer Optimization Program Input Values

Expected Return Input Value	Standard Deviation Input Value	Asset Class	Cross-Correlation Matrix Input Values								
			(1)	(2)	(3)	(4)	(5)	(6)	(7)	(8)	(9)
7.34	0.81	(1) U.S. Treasury bills	1.00								
9.57	10.08	(2) Long-term corporate bonds	.05	1.00							
11.29	11.63	(3) International bonds	-.09	.35	1.00						
12.09	15.71	(4) Large company stocks	-.06	.39	.12	1.00					
17.83	21.51	(5) Small company stocks	-.08	.24	.02	.79	1.00				
14.95	17.94	(6) International stocks	-.09	.24	.64	.48	.38	1.00			
14.40	13.95	(7) Equity REITS	-.09	.27	.13	.65	.75	.41	1.00		
8.78	3.48	(8) Real estate separate account	.32	-.08	.00	.03	.03	.08	.04	1.00	
23.03	33.78	(9) Precious metals mutual fund	-.06	-.02	.20	.21	.19	.31	.16	-.02	1.00

the above-average year was not sufficient to offset the return in the below-average year. Also note that investment A, which is the most stable, has the smallest spread between its simple average return of 8 percent and its compound annual return of 7.99 percent, whereas investment C, which is the most volatile, has the largest spread between its simple average return of 8 percent and its compound annual return of 7.39 percent.

We see the same relationship among the compound annual return, simple average return, and standard deviation statistics in Table 3–1. Those asset classes with the highest standard deviations have the biggest spreads between their simple average return and compound annual return statistics. Conversely, those asset classes with the lowest standard deviations have the smallest spreads between their simple average return and compound annual return performance numbers.[3] This discussion regarding the relationship among the compound annual return, simple average return, and standard deviation provides further

TABLE 9-2

Relationships among Simple Average Return, Compound Annual Return, and Volatility

	Investment A	Investment B	Investment C
Year 1 return	8%	8%	8%
Year 2 return	6%	0%	−6%
Year 3 return	10%	16%	22%
Simple average return	8%	8%	8%
Compound annual return	7.99%	7.80%	7.39%
Volatility	Low	Medium	High

---

3. The arithmetic mean is approximately equal to the geometric mean plus one half of the variance. For example, in Table 3–1, we see that large company stocks have an arithmetic mean (simple average) return of 13.2 percent, a geometric mean (compound annual) return of 11.2 percent, and a standard deviation of 20.3 percent. The arithmetic mean of 13.2 percent is approximately equal to the geometric mean of 11.2 percent plus one half of the variance (standard deviation squared):

$$13.2 \text{ percent} = .132 \approx .112 + .5\,(.203)^2 = .133 = 13.3 \text{ percent}$$

clarification of the issues reviewed in footnotes 1 and 6 of Chapter 3 and footnote 4 of Chapter 6.

Assume that we have a client with whom we have thoroughly reviewed the concept of time horizon and that she understands the expected return/volatility characteristics of Treasury bills and large company stocks. We describe to her a portfolio composed of 50 percent Treasury bills and 50 percent large company stocks and ask her this question: "With Treasury bills currently yielding 7.3 percent, how much additional expected return would you require from large company stocks in order for you to actively choose a portfolio allocation of 50 percent Treasury bills/50 percent large company stocks?" The client's response will be an indirect measure of her volatility tolerance and will give us a value for the volatility-premium input variable in the computer optimization program. For our example optimizations, we will assume that the client has responded that she requires common stocks to have an expected return of 17.3 percent—10 percentage points more than Treasury bills' return of 7.3 percent.

Table 9-3 shows the asset allocation computer output for five different optimizations. In each case, the computer identifies the optimal portfolio (based on the input variables and any specified constraints) for a client whose volatility tolerance corresponds to a volatility premium of 10 percent. The first optimization is unconstrained in that anywhere from 0 to 100 percent of the portfolio can be committed to any of the nine asset classes. Based on the inputs, the optimal portfolio has over half of its assets committed to real estate, with 41.9 percent and 15.6 percent, respectively, allocated to the real estate separate account and equity REITs. The balance of the portfolio is allocated among international bonds, small company stocks, and the precious metals mutual fund. The portfolio's expected return is 13.0 percent with a standard deviation of 7.6 percent. There is a 96.3 percent probability that this allocation will achieve a positive one-year return.

Does this allocation make good sense? Yes, given the inputs. Although the real estate separate account's expected return is the lowest among the equity asset classes, its standard deviation is extremely low and its cross-correlation with the

TABLE 9-3

Optimization Results and Sensitivity Analysis for a Client Who Specifies a Volatility Premium of 10%*

	1 All 9 Asset Classes	2 8 Asset Classes (Excluding Real Estate Separate Account)	3 Expected Return of Equity REITS Decreased by 1%	4 Standard Deviation of Equity REITS Increased by 1%	5 Equity REITS Perfectly Correlated with Small Company Stocks
Asset Class					
U.S. Treasury bills	0.0%	26.6%	31.3%	29.7%	19.6%
Long-term corporate bonds	0.0	3.0	4.3	3.6	4.2
International bonds	16.8	23.8	25.6	24.7	26.4
Large company stocks	0.0	0.0	0.0	0.0	0.0
Small company stocks	13.6	13.3	20.5	16.7	0.0
International stocks	0.0	0.0	0.0	0.0	0.0
Equity REITS	15.6	21.0	5.9	13.0	37.6
Real estate separate account	41.9	—	—	—	—
Precious metals mutual fund	12.1	12.3	12.4	12.3	12.2
	100.0%	100.0%	100.0%	100.0%	100.0%
Portfolio Characteristics					
Expected return	13.0%	13.2%	12.9%	13.0%	13.1%
Standard deviation	7.6%	8.4%	8.2%	8.3%	8.4%
Probability of achieving a positive one-year return	96.3%	94.8%	94.8%	94.8%	94.8%

*The optimization results shown have been produced using Vestek Systems, Inc., software.

other asset classes is also quite low, thus making it a very attractive building block for the portfolio. It is therefore not surprising that its allocation is so large. Any alteration in the allocation among the nine asset classes would produce a portfolio with less desirable expected return/volatility characteristics for this particular client.

Now, would we recommend this portfolio to our client? Perhaps we would if we had extremely high confidence in all of our data inputs. Is there a basis for such confidence? The real estate separate account is an investment portfolio of nonliquid real estate properties managed by an insurance company. The performance measurement for the real estate separate account relies on a periodic appraisal of the current market values of the real estate properties in the portfolio. There is considerable controversy over whether the appraisal process accurately reflects the actual variability of real estate values. (Just because you can't see the volatility of an investment doesn't mean it isn't there.) My judgment is that the appraisal process understates the magnitude of changes in property values and that the actual variability of returns from real estate investments is much higher than is indicated by the standard deviation statistic. Likewise, although real estate may have a low cross-correlation of returns with some financial asset classes, the appraisal process may result in correlation statistics that overstate the diversification effect to be expected from the inclusion of real estate in the asset mix.

It is also unsettling to note that the cross-correlation statistic of .04 between equity REITs and the real estate separate account indicates that the returns of these two real estate investments are nearly uncorrelated! To the extent to which we lack confidence in our inputs, we should likewise lack confidence in our output. Given the inputs, it is not surprising that the optimal allocation for the client is heavily oriented toward real estate. Rather than concluding from the output that a portfolio heavily oriented toward real estate is best for the client, it may be more appropriate to consider the output as a warning signal not to take the input values too seriously.

Given the strong likelihood that the actual volatility of the real estate separate account is misrepresented by the appraisal-driven standard deviation statistic, we could chose to simply eliminate it as an investment alternative and rely on equity REITs to serve as a proxy for the real estate asset class. Optimization 2 in Table 9–3 does just that by constraining the allocation to the real estate separate account to 0 percent. For the same client, the optimal portfolio now shifts from one that is heavily oriented toward equities to one that slightly favors interest-generating investments. The most significant change is the

addition of a 26.6 percent allocation to Treasury bills. The optimization program introduced Treasury bills to offset the impact
of having eliminated the real estate separate account investment
alternative, which had a very low standard deviation.

This portfolio's expected return of 13.2 percent is actually
higher than the first portfolio's, but the increase in expected
return is accompanied by a higher standard deviation of 8.4 percent.[4] We can be somewhat more comfortable with this portfolio,
because it is better balanced than portfolio 1. But at the same
time it is troubling to see that two major equity asset classes,
large company stocks and international stocks, are completely
unrepresented while the remaining real estate investment alternative, equity REITs, is now the largest equity asset class. Is this
high commitment to equity REITs warranted? Again, it is really
a question of how much confidence we have in the input variables for the various asset classes. Optimizations 1 and 2 estimate that equity REITs have an expected return of 14.40 percent
with a standard deviation of 13.95 percent. This indicates that
chances are approximately two out of three that equity REITs
will give us a return over a one-year horizon of between .45 and
28.35 percent (i.e., 14.40 percent +/− 13.95 percent). Not a very
specific estimate, is it?

Let us engage in some sensitivity analysis. Assume that
our estimate of the standard deviation is perfectly accurate but
that we have slightly overstated the expected return for equity
REITs by 1 percentage point. The "true" typical range of returns
is therefore between −.55 and 27.35 percent (i.e., 13.40 percent
+/− 13.95 percent). For all practical purposes, this is not a significant change in the estimated performance characteristics of
equity REITs. If we revise the input for the expected return
of equity REITs down by 1 percentage point while keeping all
other data inputs constant, what effect will this have on the output? Optimization 3 in Table 9–3 describes the asset allocation
and performance characteristics of the revised optimal portfolio.

---

4. Note that as we hold the volatility-premium input constant at 10 percent, the opti-
    mal portfolio under alternative input assumptions will have varying expected
    return and volatility levels. That is because the optimal portfolio expresses an
    expected return/volatility compromise that changes as the inputs are modified.

Note how this very minor change in one input variable radically alters the allocation among the asset classes. The commitment to equity REITs drops dramatically from 21.0 percent to 5.9 percent! As expected, the portfolio expected return drops, but the portfolio standard deviation is lower as well.

For optimization 4, instead of measuring the impact of using a lower estimate of the expected return for equity REITs, we increase the estimate of the standard deviation for equity REITs by 1 percentage point from 13.95 percent to 14.95 percent. In every other respect, the input variables are identical to those for optimization 2. Again, this very minor revision in one input variable triggers a pronounced redistribution of assets in forming a revised optimal portfolio. The equity REITs commitment drops from 21.0 percent to 13.0 percent. Again, both the expected return and the volatility of this revised portfolio are lower than those of portfolio 2.

There is one more dimension along which we can alter the input data for equity REITs—its cross-correlation relative to other asset classes. By examining the cross-correlation matrix in Table 9–1, we can see that equity REITs have their highest correlation with the small company stocks asset class. For optimization 5, it is assumed that the cross-correlation between equity REITs and small company stocks is one of perfect positive correlation (i.e., no diversification effect between the two asset classes). The cross-correlation of returns between equity REITs and every other asset class therefore will be changed to match the cross-correlation pattern of small company stocks versus the other asset classes. All other input variables are identical to those for optimization 2. This time, the allocation to equity REITs jumps from 21.0 percent to 37.6 percent of the portfolio, accompanied by the complete elimination of small company stocks! As is the case with portfolios 2 through 4, there is no allocation to either large company stocks or international stocks.

The sensitivity analysis we performed with optimizations 3, 4, and 5 should convince anyone that the output is indeed very sensitive to minor changes in the input variables. One reaction to this realization is to attempt to specify the input variables with even greater precision. In my judgment, this is a futile endeavor. Figures 7–5 through 7–7 show the highly variable nature of rolling 60-month (5-year) returns, standard deviations, and the cross-correlation for two asset classes: large company stocks and long-term corporate bonds. These graphs underscore the extreme difficulty in trying to accurately estimate optimization input statistics. This argues for an approach that constrains the propensity for computer optimization programs to make extreme allocations to the various asset classes.

For the final optimization, we will begin by specifying that a core 36 percent of the portfolio will be allocated between corporate bonds and large company stocks—the traditional portfolio building blocks for a U.S. investor. Another constraint is that each asset class must have allocations of not less than 5 percent or more than 25 percent of portfolio assets. This approach blends aspects of a more traditional portfolio design with constrained minimum/maximum allocations for all eight asset classes, thus ensuring breadth of diversification. Table 9–4 shows the range of permissible portfolio commitments to each asset class and the asset allocation for this constrained optimization. By summing the minimum holdings for the asset classes, we see that the constraints operate to prespecify 66 percent of the portfolio. The other 34 percent of assets are optimized subject to the constraints.

If we compare this constrained portfolio to portfolio 2, which uses the same input variables without constraints, we see that the constraints have triggered a loss of .4 percent in the portfolio's expected return, with an increase in the portfolio's standard deviation of .6 percent. But in exchange, we have a much more broadly diversified and well-balanced portfolio with all major asset classes represented. Although this constrained portfolio is mathematically suboptimal relative to the unconstrained portfolio, the benefits of diversification are still largely retained. For example, Table 9–4 indicates that the constrained portfolio has a standard deviation of 9.0 percent based on the historical cross-correlation of returns among the asset classes. If the asset classes were perfectly positively correlated, however, the standard deviation would be 14.2 percent—a volatility level that is over 50 percent higher. Given the difficulties in deriving reliable estimates for each input variable and the sensitivity of computer output to small changes in the input variables, the constrained

TABLE 9–4

Constrained Optimization Results for a Client Who Specifies a
Volatility Premium of 10.0%*

		Permissible Range	
	Constrained Optimal Allocation	Minimum Holding	Maximum Holding
Asset Class			
U.S. Treasury bills	16.2%	5.0%	25.0%
Long-term corporate bonds	16.0%	16.0%	25.0%
International bonds	13.8%	5.0%	25.0%
Large company stocks	20.0%	20.0%	25.0%
Small company stocks	5.0%	5.0%	25.0%
International stocks	5.0%	5.0%	25.0%
Equity REITS	12.1%	5.0%	25.0%
Precious metals mutual fund	11.9%	5.0%	25.0%
	100.0%	66.0%	
Portfolio Characteristics			
Expected return	12.8%		
Standard deviation	9.0%		
Probability of achieving a positive one-year return	92.9%		

*The optimization results shown have been produced using Vestek Systems, Inc., software.

portfolio allocation shown in Table 9–4 is a much more sensible recommendation for the client than the unconstrained portfolio allocation shown in Table 9–3 for optimization 2.

Table 9–5 compares the expected return input values for optimizations 1 and 2 with the subsequent performance of each asset class over the four-year period from 1995 through 1998. Previously, we discussed being uneasy about these two optimizations allocating no funds to large company stocks. Had an investor blindly excluded this asset class from her portfolio, she would have missed the 30.5 percent compound annual return generated by large company stocks over the following four-year period. At that stellar rate of return, a $1000 investment in large company stocks grew to be worth $2900. Concurrently, the optimizer's 12 percent allocation to the precious metals mutual fund was compounding losses at a rate of −17.40 percent. No matter how careful we are in specifying our optimization input values, we cannot eliminate the uncertainty in the markets. This uncertainty cuts both ways, sometimes generating unexpectedly generous gains with one asset class while producing precipitous losses with another.

The constrained optimization in Table 9–4 prespecified minimum and maximum holdings for each asset class, and as a result, this alternative portfolio structure would have participated in the spectacular returns from large company stocks. The only way to have avoided the pain of precious metals' decline over this four-year period would have been to have no money invested there, a stance not recommended by the optimizer. Unfortunately, an optimizer is not a reliable fortune-teller. It models uncertainties; it does not eliminate them.

ADDITIONAL OBSERVATIONS REGARDING OPTIMIZATION

Consider an efficient mix of Treasury bills, bonds, and stocks that has maximized the portfolio expected return subject to a portfolio standard deviation of 9 percent. Now let us permit investment in a fourth asset class, for example, real estate. Depending on the expected return/volatility characteristics of real estate, we may find a new asset allocation using all four asset classes that produces a higher maximum portfolio expected return consistent with a portfolio standard deviation of 9 percent. Assume that the optimal real estate allocation for this four-asset-class portfolio is 30 percent of assets. Do we get the same increase in portfolio expected return from the first half of our optimal 30 percent commitment (as we increase the real estate allocation from 0 percent to 15 percent) that we do with the second half of our commitment (as we continue to increase the real estate allocation from 15 percent to 30 percent)? In other words, does the portfolio expected return increase linearly with an increase in the real estate commitment until the optimal allocation is reached, or does the impact on portfolio expected return change as we incrementally increase the size of the allocation?

T A B L E   9 – 5

Comparison of Optimization Input Values with Subsequent
Performance

		1995 through 1998	
	Expected Return Input Value	Simple Average Return	Compound Annual Return
Asset Class			
U.S. Treasury bills	7.34	5.23	5.23
Long-term corporate bonds	9.57	13.08	12.71
International bonds	11.29	9.29	8.84
Large company stocks	12.09	30.61	30.50
Small company stocks	17.83	16.89	15.83
International stocks	14.95	10.07	9.86
Equity REITS	14.40	13.33	11.53
Real estate separate account	8.78	10.83	10.59
Precious metals mutual fund	23.03	−16.54	−17.40

We can answer this by performing a series of constrained
optimizations that plot the expected returns associated with efficient portfolios with varying real estate commitments. If graphed,
the relationship between portfolio expected return and the percentage real estate commitment might look like that shown in
Figure 9–1. Note that the shape of the curve is steeper as real
estate is first introduced into the asset mix. This indicates that as
real estate diversification begins, the initial impact on the portfolio's expected return is high. As the real estate commitment
increases toward its optimal allocation of 30 percent of assets, the
portfolio's expected return continues to increase, *but it does so at
a diminishing rate.* The curve is relatively flat at and around the
optimal allocation of 30 percent. This indicates that varying the
size of the real estate commitment by a few percentage points on
either side of the optimal 30 percent commitment has a relatively small impact on the portfolio expected return. Beyond 30 percent, an increase in the real estate commitment reduces portfolio
expected return slowly at first and then at a faster rate.

FIGURE 9-1

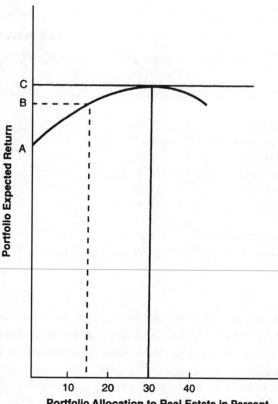

Point A corresponds to the maximum expected return possible for a portfolio with a standard deviation equal to 9 percent
when investment choices are constrained to only Treasury bills,
bonds, and stocks. Point C corresponds to the maximum expected return possible utilizing real estate in addition to the other
three asset classes. The distance AC is therefore the improvement in portfolio expected return made possible by the optimal
allocation of real estate in the asset mix. Point B corresponds to
the maximum expected return possible if the portfolio is constrained to a 15 percent real estate commitment. We can see
that most of the increase in the portfolio expected return is

obtained by changing the allocation from 0 percent to 15 percent, with a smaller increase produced by changing the real estate commitment from 15 percent to 30 percent.

This fact has very important investment implications. First, it removes some of the anxiety of trying to find the exact asset allocation that will maximize the volatility-adjusted portfolio expected return. In utilizing an asset allocation optimization program, we know that we can have only limited confidence in our estimates of expected returns, standard deviations, and cross-correlations used as input variables. Correspondingly, we can have only limited confidence in the optimal asset allocation generated as the output. We also know how even slight changes in the input variables result in rather drastic shifts in the portfolio asset allocation. Although at first this may seem to be somewhat discouraging, there is a bright side. It means that rather significant shifts of assets around the optimal mix may produce surprisingly little change in the portfolio's expected return/volatility characteristics. Thus, there may be a range of alternative asset allocations that produce similar, but not identical, portfolio expected return/volatility characteristics.

For example, in the previous section we performed an unconstrained optimization to identify the best asset allocation for a client who specified a volatility premium of 10 percent. (Refer to optimization 2 in Table 9–3.) Although we knew we had the mathematically correct answer given the inputs, it was uncomfortable to see that two major equity asset classes were completely unrepresented in the recommended asset allocation. Also, one of these asset classes, large company stocks, had extraordinarily high returns over the following four years. By constraining the optimization program to maintain minimum allocations across all asset classes, we derived a different asset allocation that had portfolio expected return/volatility characteristics almost as attractive as the unconstrained alternative. For a passive asset allocation investor, who believes it is impossible to successfully engage in market timing, it is obviously advisable to hold the more broadly diversified portfolio, even though it is not quite mathematically optimal based on the inputs. The justification for choosing the less than optimal asset mix stems from a realistic acknowledgment of the limited confidence we should have in the output.

Although it is true that a variety of asset allocations may have similar portfolio expected return/volatility characteristics, after the fact, the results can vary widely. This variance is expected, and for the passive asset allocation investor it reflects the chance element inherent in investing. For those who want to minimize the impact of chance (which means minimizing the potential impact of both bad luck *and* good luck), the more broadly diversified alternatives are recommended.

The implications are no less important to an active asset allocation investor who wants to engage in market timing. For example, it may be possible to design a portfolio with a restricted range of allocations between two market-timed asset classes. As long as the range is not too wide and is centered near the optimal allocation, the portfolio's expected return/volatility characteristics for the various allocations may be similar along this range. In essence, by maintaining a core diversified portfolio, a market timer may be able to maintain most of the advantages of diversification while still providing an opportunity for limited market timing activities that will (hopefully) produce value-added incremental returns. Although I am not an advocate of market timing, this approach at least eliminates the risk of being entirely out of an advancing market.

Psychologically, it is easy to believe that a precise answer is more certain and therefore deserves a higher level of confidence than does an approximate answer. For example, assume that an investor wants advice concerning what portion of her portfolio to commit to international stocks. For guidance, she decides to consult two different investment advisors. The first advisor recommends exactly 19.3 percent of assets; the second advisor recommends about 20 percent. Even though there is no real difference in the recommended size of the allocation, isn't there a tendency for the investor to have more confidence in the first advisor's recommendation because it is more specific?

Computer optimization programs give asset allocation recommendations that are as precise as those of the first advisor. In addition, optimization programs can specify precise probability estimates of achieving various levels of return over different holding periods and format this information in either tabular or graphic form, with or without color pie charts! All this technology can be seductive to both investment advisors and their clients. Unfortunately, there is also a corresponding opportunity for uninformed or unscrupulous investment advisors to encourage clients to blindly follow the "objective recommendations" generated by the technology. Knowledgeable investment advisors will maintain the proper perspective by keeping in mind that input variables are hard to specify with any degree of confidence and that the output of optimization programs is highly sensitive to small changes in the input variables. Computer programs cannot eliminate the uncertainty inherent in investing. Thoughtful consideration of the output makes this clear. For example, if the standard deviation of an optimized portfolio is 10 percent, what value is there in knowing that the portfolio's expected return is not 12 percent but rather is exactly 12.23 percent?

Despite their limitations, computer asset allocation programs are powerful tools that can be of great value in the money management process if used properly. They quickly and accurately perform very complex mathematical calculations, which are useful in portfolio sensitivity analysis and the comparison of alternative "what if" scenarios. Many commercially available programs have features that also take into consideration such factors as transaction costs and the impact of income taxes. As an additional tool available to investment advisors, optimization programs improve the evaluation and decision-making process by pointing toward alternative asset allocations that may be better suited to the realization of client objectives. They are also of significant educational value in enhancing the client's understanding of the probable performance results associated with alternative strategies.

CHAPTER 10

Know Your Client

The beginning is the most important part of the work.

—*Plato (circa 428–348 B.C.)*
Republic

Money is paper blood.

—*Attributed to Bob Hope*
(1903–   )

We will now turn to a discussion of how to apply the ideas developed thus far to the dynamics of an ongoing client-advisor relationship. Figure 10–1 is a flowchart that describes the steps of the money management process as an interactive loop that continually feeds back into itself. Each of these steps will be discussed in detail in Chapters 10 through 12.

The first two steps—gather client data and identify the client's needs, constraints, and unique circumstances—which we will cover in this chapter, are the foundation of the money management process and are grouped together under the heading *know your client*. The next four steps are grouped under the heading *manage client expectations* and are covered in the next chapter. The positioning of this group of four steps is crucial. They build directly on the foundation of knowing your client and out of necessity *precede* the last four steps, which constitute what we typically consider to be *money management*. The process of managing client expectations is as important to the long-term realization of client objectives as is the process of actually managing the money. Many clients fail to reach their objectives as a result of simply not adhering to a sensible long-term strategy. Often, this can be traced to unrealistic expectations. In essence, it is not enough for an advisor to properly manage a client's portfolio; it is also crucial that the client

FIGURE 10-1

Money Management Process

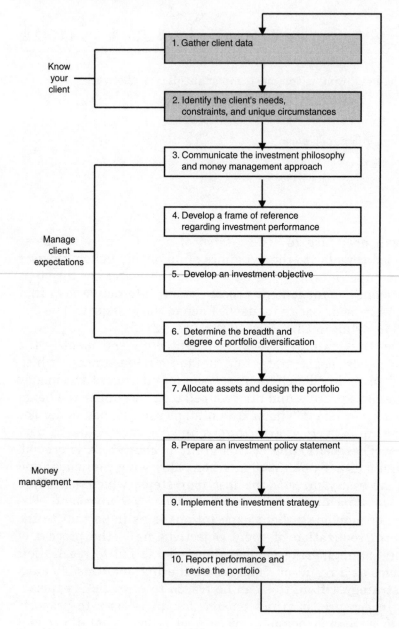

understand that the portfolio is being properly managed. Without that understanding, it is unlikely that a client will be able to adhere to an appropriate, long-term strategy through the pressures of extreme market conditions.

It is interesting to note that money is not actually invested until the next to last step in this flowchart. Unfortunately, many clients view the first six steps of this process as requiring too much time and effort on their part. They prefer to limit their involvement to the initial selection of a money manager who in turn has full responsibility to handle the last four steps of designing the portfolio asset allocation, preparing an investment policy statement, implementing strategy, and providing feedback. Many investment advisors are likewise too quick to shortcut the process and jump immediately to the last four steps. The likelihood of a client reaching his or her objectives, however, is greatly enhanced by resisting the temptation to take shortcuts. Although this 10-step process requires the thoughtful commitment of both advisor and client, it can be effectively and efficiently accomplished within a relatively short period of time.

STEP 1: GATHER CLIENT DATA

The client may be an individual, a couple, or an institutional account such as a trusteed retirement plan, endowment, or foundation. Regardless of the type of client, however, the goal of the data-gathering process is to know the client. Much of the data are factual or quantitative in nature. Beyond this is a realm of more subjective qualitative information that attempts to assess what it is like "inside the client's skin."

Advisors who prefer to delegate the data-gathering process to a support person may be doing themselves and their clients a disservice. It is important for data gathering to be handled by the advisor, with face-to-face interaction with the client. The psychological bonding between client and advisor begins here and helps to establish a sense of comfort that is important given the magnitude of the investment decisions to be made. The client also has the opportunity to begin to understand how the advisor thinks, and certainly the advisor will gain a level of understanding of the client that goes beyond the facts and figures written down in a data questionnaire.

Be alert for clues regarding the client's *present* volatility tolerance. The word *present* is italicized because as we discussed previously, volatility tolerance is subject to modification within a rather broad range, based on providing the client with an informed framework for decision making. Without directly asking for information about volatility tolerance, much can be inferred by the current composition of the portfolio. If the client usually holds 90 percent of his portfolio in money market funds and bank certificates of deposit, it is a strong indication that he may be quite volatility-averse. Another client who holds a disproportionately large portion of her portfolio in gold bullion, rare coins, diamonds, and other hard assets is likewise telling you something about her present investment attitudes. Occasionally, contradictory impressions emerge. For example, a person who describes himself as being very volatility-averse may have a large portfolio commitment to a small company traded over the counter. By eliciting more information, it is learned that the stock was inherited from his mother, who was the company's founder. This information is important because of the psychological/emotional dimension of the decision-making process regarding retention or sale of this stock.

When listing the client's assets and liabilities, it is helpful to organize a balance sheet in a format that supports the investment decision-making process. The following classifications are recommended:

1. Interest-generating investments
2. Equity investments
3. Lifestyle assets
4. Liabilities

As we concluded in Chapter 6, the most important decision a client makes is the balance chosen between interest-generating investments and equity investments. This balance determines the general volatility/return characteristics of the portfolio. By gathering data in the format recommended, the current portfolio balance can be quickly assessed. Lifestyle assets include home and personal property as well as vacation homes. Occasionally, a client objects to the classification of a vacation home as a lifestyle asset, but unless it produces a positive cash flow by generating rental income in excess of the expenses of ownership, it probably is something that consumes rather than generates wealth.

The balance between investment assets and lifestyle assets provides one indication of the client's financial discipline and thrift. More information can be inferred from an analysis of the client's cash flow. How much of her income is absorbed in lifestyle expenditures versus being committed to building investment net worth? Because many investment assets generate taxable income, a client's personal income tax return serves as a useful source of information to double-check that all assets and liabilities have been accounted for.

The data-gathering process also provides a valuable opportunity to assess the client's level of investment knowledge and to begin the educational process. Observations regarding the strengths and weaknesses of her current investment portfolio can be shared, and the client can be encouraged to begin looking at her investment portfolio in the broadest possible terms. Frequently, a client initially seeks investment advice on what she should be doing with a small part of her portfolio, for example, a certificate of deposit that will be maturing soon. Such a client does not realize that the decision optimally should be made within the larger context of her entire portfolio and long-term objectives. Institutional clients must likewise learn to consider investing in a wider context. For example, for a corporate defined-benefit pension plan, broad thinking entails the consideration of the pension plan assets and liabilities within the larger context of the corporation as a whole. After all, it is the corporate pension plan's sponsor that has promised the benefit payments, not the pension plan itself. The risks and rewards of pension plan performance are therefore borne by the corporation, whose financial well-being is intimately tied to the performance of the pension plan assets.

Finally, the data-gathering session gives the advisor an excellent opportunity to communicate the investment philosophy behind the money management approach that will be used in moving toward the realization of the client's financial goals. For all of these reasons, the data-gathering session is an important step in the money management process, which justifies the full involvement of both the client and the advisor.

STEP 2: IDENTIFY THE CLIENT'S NEEDS, CONSTRAINTS, AND UNIQUE CIRCUMSTANCES

Liquidity

Each client's situation should be evaluated in terms of the need for portfolio liquidity. Nonliquid investments, such as direct ownership of investment real estate, should not be made if there is a likelihood that the funds will be needed to meet future expenditures. Even if there is sufficient liquidity elsewhere in the portfolio to meet such expenditures, the size of nonliquid investments must be evaluated with respect to the possible withdrawals from the portfolio.

For example, assume that for a particular client, 15 percent of portfolio assets is an optimal allocation to have in nonliquid real estate investments, with the balance of the portfolio invested in a variety of liquid assets. If within a short period of time thereafter, 25 percent of the portfolio is liquidated to meet various expenditures, the commitment to real estate will rise above the optimal 15 percent allocation to 20 percent of the portfolio. As discussed here, liquidity is an issue separate from a client's yield requirements or income needs.

Portfolio Cash Withdrawal Rate for Anticipated Expenditures

Eventually, all investment portfolios are relied on to support someone's cash needs. The timing and magnitude of required cash withdrawals from an investment portfolio should therefore be quantified and planned for in advance. With the exception of situations involving regulatory or legal yield requirements, investment portfolios generally should not be designed to intentionally produce a certain yield or income stream. The issue of portfolio design is to a large extent *independent* of the question of how to get cash out of the portfolio in order to meet necessary expenditures.

As we discussed in detail previously, the balance chosen between interest-generating investments and equity investments is the primary determinant of an investment portfolio's volatility/return characteristics, and this most important decision is made in reference to the portfolio's time horizon. A portfolio balanced on this basis reflects the best obtainable trade-off between the desire for stability and the need for growth. If the yield on such a properly balanced portfolio is not equivalent to what is needed for required expenditures, this is not a good reason to reallocate the portfolio toward either more or fewer interest-generating investments. Doing so causes a mismatch between the portfolio structure and the time horizon, with the result that the portfolio will be overexposed to either inflation or volatility, depending on the direction of the reallocation.

Provided that the rate of withdrawal from the portfolio is not unnecessarily high, most portfolios can maintain proper balance and broad diversification with more than adequate liquidity for necessary withdrawals. In practice, even passively managed portfolios need to be regularly rebalanced as capital markets move. At these rebalancing points, cash can be set aside in a money market fund and earmarked for the expenditures anticipated until the next scheduled rebalancing. This process is both simple to execute and conceptually sound from an investment management point of view.

Although it is generally true that the question of how to get money out of a portfolio should be considered independently from the determination of proper portfolio design, the two issues become intertwined in cases where the withdrawal rate is unsustainably high relative to the size of the portfolio. For example, a client may have a 25-year investment time horizon over which he intends to rely on his portfolio to meet his cash needs but is withdrawing money so quickly that the portfolio probably will be liquidated within 5 to 10 years. In this situation, the portfolio cash withdrawal rate has triggered a reduction in the investment time horizon, which in turn will influence the portfolio balance decision. Recognize, however, that even in this situation, the portfolio balance decision still is made with reference to the relevant investment time horizon.

Tax Situation

Some institutional clients, such as tax-qualified retirement plans, have been blessed by the tax code and provide for a tax-sheltered environment within which investments can grow. Personal clients are not so fortunate. To properly advise these clients, it is necessary to understand their tax situations. At a minimum, this entails a current-year tax projection that identifies their marginal tax bracket. Preferably, the advisor will also project the client's tax situation for a few years into the future. The most obvious use of this information is in determining the advisability of utilizing federal income tax-free municipal bonds in constructing the interest-generating portion of the portfolio. For example, all other things being equal, it is more advantageous for a 36 percent marginal tax bracket investor to own a tax-free municipal yielding 5 percent than to own a similar quality/maturity taxable bond with a yield of 7 percent, over a third of which is lost to income taxes, leaving the investor with a net yield of 4.5 percent.

Any decision involving the possible sale of an asset needs to be evaluated with respect to its tax impact. The general rule is that investment issues take precedence over tax considerations. In other words, a client should not hold on to an inappropriate investment merely because its liquidation would trigger tax liabilities. But consider the situation where a decision to sell an investment is made near the end of the year, and the client is expected to be in a lower marginal tax bracket the following year. Here, the benefit of selling later in order to save taxes needs to be weighed against the economic risk of continuing to hold the investment in the interim.

These are only a few, simple examples of the implication of understanding the tax dimension of a client's situation. Our current tax code is extremely complex, and there is no end to the variety and subtlety of the tax issues that can arise in the management of a client's investment portfolio. A full discussion of these issues is beyond the scope of this book. If the advisor does not have the requisite tax knowledge to handle such issues, it is wise to enlist the help of other professionals who do.

Regulatory/Legal Constraints

Regulatory and/or legal constraints can take a variety of forms and are more prevalent with institutional clients. For example, the Employee Retirement Income Security Act of 1974 (ERISA) governs many qualified retirement plans and contains provisions concerning such things as the preparation of written investment policy statements, portfolio diversification, and the use of "prudent experts" in the management of plan assets. If a client is an endowment or charitable foundation, there may be minimum distribution rules and/or yield requirements that must be adhered to. If the investment portfolio is a testamentary trust, there may be income beneficiaries who are different from the eventual inheritors of the assets. The potentially adverse interests of these parties need to be considered in designing the portfolio. The trust instrument may give guidance on these issues as well as contain specific language regarding suitability standards for investments.

Personal clients encounter similar constraints with IRAs that have detailed rules regarding contributions and withdrawals. Another example for personal clients is restricted stock that can be sold only under certain, stated conditions. These examples serve to illustrate the kind of regulatory and legal constraints that need to be considered.

Time Horizon

The importance of the time horizon in investment management is attested to by the fact that an entire chapter of this book has been devoted to the subject. It is the crucial variable that underlies the decision on how to allocate portfolio assets between interest-generating investments and equity investments. The two major risks confronting investment portfolios are inflation and volatility of returns. Over long time horizons, inflation is a bigger risk than market volatility. Investment portfolios with long time horizons should accordingly be more heavily weighted in equity investments to secure the long-term capital growth needed to build purchasing power. Over short time horizons, market volatility is more dangerous than inflation. Therefore, portfolios with short time horizons should be more heavily invested in interest-generating investments with more stable principal values.

Clients tend to underestimate their investment time horizons, with the result that portfolios tend to be overexposed to the danger of inflation, due to an underrepresentation of equities. Part of the problem is that many clients assume that their projected retirement dates define their investment time horizons. This leads to the erroneous conventional wisdom that equity investments are appropriate only while building net worth during the pre-retirement years and should be sold at retirement, with the proceeds invested in interest-generating investments that produce the income needed in retirement. The problem with this conventional wisdom is that it ignores the fact that inflation continues to be a threat throughout the retirement years, while the portfolio is being relied on to meet necessary expenditures. For a typical husband and wife, the time horizon extends beyond the survivor's life expectancy.[1] This can be quite long, and hence the need for capital growth remains. The same argument holds true for institutional portfolios, such as endowment funds and corporate qualified retirement plans, some of which expect to have perpetual existences.

Psychological and Emotional Factors

I would prefer that the investment decision-making process be a series of logical steps that systematically build to a conceptually sound, rational portfolio strategy. However, there are numerous psychological and emotional factors that can impact the decision-making process, and it is therefore important to be aware of them. Most clients evaluating investment alternatives have pre-existing preferences. Attempts should be made to

---

1. By definition, a person has a 50 percent likelihood of living beyond his or her life expectancy. A conservative posture therefore requires an investment-planning horizon beyond life expectancy.

accommodate reasonable preferences in order to maximize the client's comfort with the portfolio. But if a client's preferences are based on misconceptions or result from a lack of investment knowledge, it is important to take the time to educate the client. Ultimately, it is the client's money, and there may be limits to the extent to which a client will endorse a recommended strategy. With a good understanding of a client's psychological and emotional factors, an advisor will be better able to present new ideas in a way that facilitates their acceptance.

The Decision-Making Dynamic

Institutional clients often have investment decision-making authority vested in a committee of trustees. The time horizons for these portfolios are often quite long, and trustees must assume the responsibility for making long-term investment decisions even though their terms of office may be of limited duration. Given the many interested parties who may engage in second-guessing investment decisions, the temptation is always present for a committee of trustees to manage the money for safe, short-term results. This tendency is aggravated by the practice of measuring institutional portfolio performance on a quarterly basis. Trustees need courage and confidence to do their job, and they deserve support and recognition for making tough decisions that have the potential for looking bad in the short run but are nevertheless wise in the long run. By contrast, with an individual as a client, there is more continuity to decision making. The money is the client's own, and he or she can make decisions with greater flexibility and freedom.

CHAPTER 11

Managing Client Expectations

There is no free lunch.

—*Anonymous*

Nothing astonishes men so much as common sense and plain dealing.

—*Ralph Waldo Emerson (1803–1882)*
Art, 1841

Human wants are never satisfied.

—*J. Willard Marriott, Jr. (1932–   )*
Marriott

In this chapter we will cover steps 3 through 6 of the money management process outlined in Figure 11–1. Note that the steps involved in managing client expectations follow the first two, which deal with knowing your client, and of necessity precede the last four, which deal with what is more commonly thought of as money management. This order is very important: First get to know your client, next manage the client's expectations, and only then manage the client's money.

STEP 3: COMMUNICATE THE INVESTMENT PHILOSOPHY AND MONEY MANAGEMENT APPROACH

A sure prescription for trouble is a client who has an investment worldview different from that of his or her investment advisor. For example, an investment advisor may believe it is impossible

FIGURE 11-1

Money Management Process

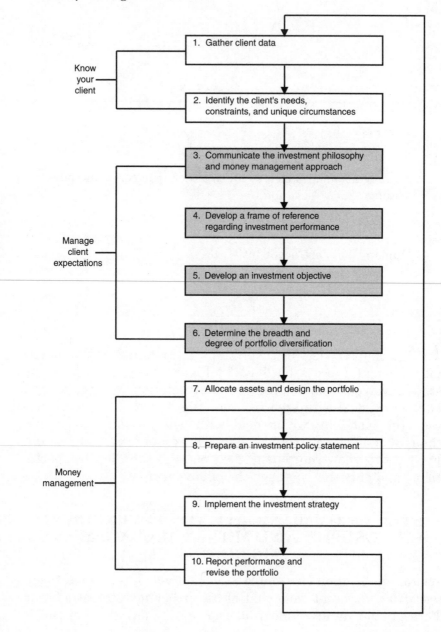

to successfully engage in market timing and therefore makes no attempt to do so. But if a client believes that it is part of the investment advisor's job to protect him or her from bad markets, it is only a matter of time until adverse market conditions will strain and perhaps end the advisory relationship. Clients' expectations tend to err in an optimistic direction; they believe that higher returns are possible with less volatility than may actually be the case in the long run. There are important advantages to both advisor and client in managing client expectations prior to, and then throughout, the money management process. When the client and the advisor share a common investment worldview, they will be in agreement regarding the nature of the risks involved with and the potential rewards of alternative strategies.

Worldview Determines Money Management Approach

Before beginning the process of managing client expectations, it is important to know where you stand. Every money management approach has an investment philosophy behind it that is built on a particular investment worldview. In my judgment, the two most important worldview questions are:

1. Is successful market timing possible?
2. Is superior security selection possible?

Depending on how these two questions are answered, a 2 by 2 matrix of worldview possibilities exists, as shown in Figure 11–2. Although not all investors can be pigeonholed neatly into one of these quadrants, for our discussion we will assume that we have four different investors, each standing squarely in a different quadrant. The purpose of this discussion is to:

1. Illustrate the close tie between investment worldview and money management approach.
2. Emphasize the importance of a shared worldview between clients and their advisors.

Quadrant 1 Worldview

The first investor answers "yes" to both of these questions and therefore has a quadrant 1 worldview. She believes that it is pos-

FIGURE 11-2

Worldview Determines Money Management Approach

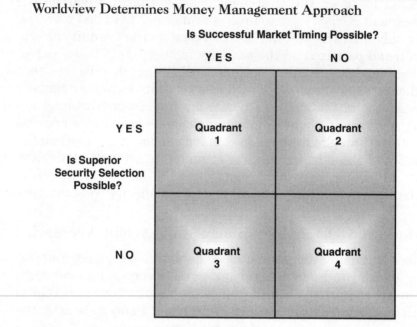

Is Successful Market Timing Possible?

	YES	NO
YES Is Superior Security Selection Possible?	Quadrant 1	Quadrant 2
NO	Quadrant 3	Quadrant 4

Source: ©Roger C. Gibson, 1995.

sible to both profitably predict the short-run movements of different asset classes and choose securities within each asset class that will outperform the asset class as a whole. What money management approach is consistent with this worldview? If successful market timing is possible, she will want to concentrate her entire investment portfolio in whichever asset class will now generate the highest returns. When a different asset class is poised to generate the highest returns, investments in the first asset class are sold and the proceeds are repositioned in the next winning asset class, and so on. If it simultaneously is possible to engage in superior security selection, she will invest only in those securities that will outperform the asset class as a whole. If her investment strategy succeeds with this worldview, she has it made. She does not need to worry about portfolio losses since successful market timing will sidestep market declines. Simultaneously, returns will be maximized by investing in the best-performing securities within the best-performing asset class.

Many unsophisticated investors hold this worldview and bring it to the investment advisory relationship. They expect the investment advisor to know which asset class will deliver the best returns and to choose the best-performing securities within that asset class. That is why they hired a professional. If the investment advisor shares that worldview, he is accountable for it, and his performance should be evaluated accordingly. Managing client expectations will not be the problem; delivering results that are consistent with that worldview is the challenge. The first time an advisor places a client's money in an underperforming asset class, he has failed. If the advisor chooses a portfolio of securities that underperforms the asset class, again he has failed. This worldview is easy to sell but very hard, if not impossible, to deliver. In my judgment, any investor or advisor who holds this worldview is setting himself or herself up for failure.

Quadrant 2 Worldview

The second investor has a quadrant 2 worldview and therefore believes it is impossible to predict which asset class will outperform the others in the short run. He believes, however, that it is possible to choose securities within an asset class that will outperform the asset class as a whole. This investor will diversify his portfolio across multiple asset classes in order to mitigate the risks of markets that are unknowable in the short run. The good news with this approach is that regardless of which major asset class generates the highest returns, the investor will participate by having a portion of his portfolio invested there. The bad news is that regardless of which major asset class has the worst performance, he will have a portion of his portfolio invested there as well! Because he believes superior security selection is possible, he will limit his investments in each asset class to those securities that will outperform the asset class as a whole. The majority of professional money managers and investment advisors have a quadrant 2 worldview.

Quadrant 3 Worldview

The third investor stands in quadrant 3. She believes that the relative short-run performance of different asset classes can be predicted but does not believe that superior security selection is possible. Her money management approach concentrates her portfolio in one asset class and then another, based on her forecast of which asset class will generate the highest returns. Because she does not believe in superior security selection, she uses low-cost index funds to implement her strategy. An index fund is a passively managed, diversified portfolio of securities designed to mimic the performance of a specific market index. By using index funds, she minimizes the costs associated with active security selection and eliminates the possibility of significantly underperforming the asset class in which she is invested. This particular worldview has the fewest proponents. It is reserved for the real market timing purists.

Quadrant 4 Worldview

The last investor stands in quadrant 4. He believes that markets are efficient. This means that the current prices of securities reflect the relevant, publicly available information concerning them. This information includes factual data as well as consensus expectations about any uncertainties that are important in determining the prices of the securities. If this worldview is true, what moves security prices and markets in the short run? Basically, surprises that people do not foresee. Modern portfolio theory and much of the academic investment research undertaken in the past 50 years support this worldview. The quadrant 4 investor follows a broadly diversified, multiple-asset-class investment strategy, using index funds as the building blocks. It is important to note that this money management approach is not a simple "buy and hold" strategy. As the markets move, the portfolio will stray from the allocation targeted for each of the asset classes. This triggers a need to rebalance the portfolio back to its long-term, strategic asset allocation commitments.

With a quadrant 4 worldview, there are three big issues. The first is proper asset allocation, because diversification is the primary means of mitigating investment risks. The second is cost minimization as the necessary prerequisite of obtaining performance that approaches the upper limit of what is achievable—that is, market returns. This can be accomplished by utilizing low-cost index funds as portfolio building blocks. The third is management of clients' expectations, since there is no reasonable hope of outperforming the markets in which they are invested. Whereas quadrant 1 is "easy to sell, hard to deliver," quadrant 4 is "hard to sell, easy to deliver."

Comparing Alternative Worldviews

Quadrant 1, 2, and 3 worldviews share one thing in common: the notion that skill has a significant impact on investment performance. With any of these worldviews, the investor does not have to settle for the underlying growth path of the market. The investor can beat the market in either one of two ways:

1. By moving in and out of a market as it gyrates on either side of its long-term growth path, that is, through successful market timing.

2. By taking advantage of the divergent movement of securities within the market through superior security selection.

By contrast, a quadrant 4 investor does not believe that skill can add value, and therefore "beating the market" is not a realistic investment objective. In other words, a quadrant 4 investor must accept the underlying long-term growth path of an asset class as the best outcome achievable from it.

Where Are We Going?

Even though intelligent investors may disagree about which of these four competing worldviews most accurately represents reality, we should find more of a consensus on where things are heading—and that is toward a quadrant 4 worldview. The more strongly investors adhere to a quadrant 1, 2, or 3 worldview, the more strenuously they will attempt to beat the market through superior skill. This creates a fierce field of competition that provides generous rewards to the winners. It is not surprising that many talented, hard-working, intelligent people are drawn to professional money management. It is this same pool of money management talent, however, that makes it so difficult for any person to consistently beat everyone else. The professionals are not competing with unsophisticated investors. They are competing against one another for the brass ring. If one money manager discovers a strategy that leads to superior results, his or her competitive advantage lasts only as long as others do not imitate that approach. Success, however, tends to encourage competitors to discover and replicate the strategy. As this occurs, the rewards of the approach simultaneously begin to trend downward. In essence, the more vigorous the competition among money managers, the more quickly quadrant 4 becomes reality.

Implications of a Quadrant 4 Worldview

If quadrant 4 is the most accurate worldview or if we are indeed inexorably heading in that direction, it is important to consider the implications. First, a quadrant 4 worldview undercuts to a large degree the reason for the existence of the money management profession. If skill cannot be relied on to add value, why pay fees and incur transaction costs in a futile attempt to beat the market? First consider an efficient market where, hypothetically, there are no transaction costs or fees. In this world, trading securities is a zero-sum game with an expected risk-adjusted net present value of zero. It is a zero-sum game in that one investor's wins are always exactly offset by another's losses. It has a risk-adjusted net present value of zero since you can only expect to get what you pay for. Security prices in equilibrium equal risk-adjusted net present value.

Now consider a more realistic world—an efficient market with transaction costs and fees. In this world, trading securities is not a zero-sum game; it is a negative-sum game. In a negative-sum game, the participants expect to lose money by the mere act of playing it. A Las Vegas slot machine is an example of a negative-sum game. Even though you may get lucky and win more money than you put into the slot machine, on average, the flow of money is from the players toward the casino owner. (There is a good reason why slot machines are called "one-arm bandits.")

We have evidence that the capital markets can be described as a negative-sum game. On average, most managers underperform the markets in which they invest. This occurs because, before fees, the expected outcome is to match the market. Therefore, after fees, the average participant will lag the market. The way to win a negative-sum game is not to play it. Those who adhere to a quadrant 4 worldview strategically expect to win the investment game by not playing it. They accept the return of an asset class as their upside and attempt to get as close to it as possible by minimizing their costs. Hence, index funds, which are designed to replicate the performance of an asset class while minimizing the associated costs, are the preferred building blocks for their portfolios.

Whereas with quadrants 1, 2, and 3 an investor *fights* the forces of the markets through the exercise of skill, a quadrant 4 investor *uses* the forces of the market with the humble acknowledgment that the attempt to exercise skill will, in the long run, be a detriment to performance. If we think of the trend line of an asset class's growth path as the signal and the random fluctuations of security prices around that growth path as the noise, quadrant 1, 2, and 3 investors believe the key to investment success lies in the noise, whereas quadrant 4 investors believe it lies in the signal. The quadrant 4 investor's money management approach can best be summarized by a quote from R. Buckminster Fuller: "Don't fight forces; use them."

As we increasingly move toward a quadrant 4 worldview, the importance of the skill factor declines while the importance of decision factors increases. The decision factors concern the choice of asset classes and the relative weighting of funds across those asset classes. This in turn shifts the focus of energy from the investment professional, previously looked to for the exercise of skill, to the client, who is the locus of investment decision making. Once again we are back to the importance of realistically managing client expectations. In a world where skill cannot protect you from bad outcomes, investors need both to make informed decisions *and* to live with the consequences, with discipline, through both good and bad times.

There are also important business implications for investment professionals. In a world where skill drives results, a successful money management firm separates the money management function from the marketing and client service functions. Since investment genius is a rare commodity, the talented money manager's time and energy should be focused on the clients' portfolios of securities. It would be a mistake to distract the money manager with responsibilities for maintaining client relationships or developing new business. Those duties are better handled by sales and account representatives whose job it is to bring new clients to the firm and then hold their hands while the talented money manager beats the market through his or her superior skill. In this business model, the focus of attention is on the portfolio manager's skill.

By contrast, a quadrant 4 worldview spawns a different kind of investment organization. If the asset allocation decisions drive investment performance, the client/advisor relationship becomes central, given the importance of the decisions that the client must make regarding the structure of his or her portfolio and the necessity for the client to live with results that are market-driven. With this business model, *the investment professional must be in a relationship with the client,* because the client is the focus of attention. The client's perception of investment risks, as well as his volatility tolerance, financial goals, asset allocation decisions, and interpretation of investment results are the crucial variables determining investment success.

A Conspiracy Against a Quadrant 4 Worldview

There is one final observation pertinent to this discussion, and it impacts both the long-term viability of the investment advisory profession and the topic of managing client expectations. There is a conspiracy against a quadrant 4 worldview with three interlocking conspirators:

1. Investors
2. The money management profession
3. The financial press

Investors do not want to accept a quadrant 4 worldview because it means that there is no way for them to fully protect themselves from the sometimes harsh realities of the capital markets. If the quadrant 4 worldview is true, skill cannot be relied on to come to the rescue during a bad market. Successful investing will require the investor to knowledgeably make difficult decisions concerning expected return and volatility and then adhere to those decisions with discipline and courage. It is little wonder that investors prefer to embrace a different worldview. The money management profession rejects the quadrant 4 worldview, since its very existence is threatened by it. Finally, the financial press thrives on writing articles that in one way or another feed the notion that there are ways to beat the market. If members of the financial press fully embraced a quadrant 4 worldview, they would have *much* less to write about. It is fascinating to me how these three co-conspirators have strong, mutually aligned interests in rejecting the evidence that supports a quadrant 4 worldview. To quote a passage from Ecclesiastes: "A cord of three strands is not easily broken."

Summary

Many problems that occur in client/advisor relationships arise because the client stands in one quadrant while his or her advisor stands in a different quadrant. Most investors want to stand in quadrant 1, the majority of professional money managers stand in quadrant 2, staunch market timers stand in quadrant 3, and the proponents of modern portfolio theory stand in quadrant 4. Radically different investment approaches are associated with these different worldviews, and a successful long-term client/advisor relationship, at a minimum, requires that both parties be in agreement concerning what is realistically achievable in the management of the client's portfolio. Both parties should firmly and consciously acknowledge this agreement *before* money is invested. Without such an agreement, the advisor and client should not work together.

This book is based on the worldview that in the long run, it is not possible to successfully engage in market timing. Most of the academic research work done on this subject reaches that conclusion, and as Charles D. Ellis states in his book *Investment Policy,* "The evidence on investment managers' success with market timing is impressive—and overwhelmingly negative."

Step 4, "Develop a frame of reference regarding investment performance," is important precisely because it is not possible to successfully predict short-run market performance. The jury is divided regarding whether superior security selection is possible. Many academicians maintain that superior security selection is not possible. The vast majority of professional money managers and investors believe otherwise, but it may only be their belief, not the reality. A full resolution of the issue is not required for our purposes. Money can be managed within a strategic asset allocation framework with or without active security selection.

STEP 4: DEVELOP A FRAME OF REFERENCE REGARDING INVESTMENT PERFORMANCE

On any given day, an investor can look up the value of her securities in *The Wall Street Journal* and know exactly how much her portfolio is worth. Both the losses and the gains stand out in sharp relief. In a world where investors are exposed to the twin dangers of market volatility on the one hand and inflation on the other, there is no completely safe place to stand. The risks inherent in investing one's money are unavoidable. The pain of that realization is the motivation for investors to learn about capital market behavior and the principles of successful investing.

An investment advisor who spends time educating his or her clients about the nature of the capital markets empowers those clients to make wise decisions with greater equanimity. This educational process begins with a review of the long-term historical performance of Treasury bills, government bonds, corporate bonds, common stocks, and inflation, as we did in Chapters 2 and 3. The simple models of security returns that we developed provide the client with a sense of the comparative performance and relative payoff for assuming various forms of risk. By gaining an appreciation of all of the types of risk confronting them, clients will understand that there is no ideal investment that is liquid, has a stable principal value, and generates returns sufficient to stay ahead of the combined impact of inflation and income taxes.

Once the fantasy of the ideal investment is dissolved, clients will understand the necessity of compromise in building an investment portfolio. It is possible to get stable, predictable returns from some investments, but the stability is purchased at the price of lower returns. Other investments will provide the expectation of long-term growth of capital but necessarily entail the assumption of volatility. With all of the uncertainty inherent in money management, clients understandably look for some reliable constants. One constant is that people will continue to prefer stable returns over unpredictable returns. For this reason, clients can be confident that the buying and selling activities of investors will price volatile investments, such as common stocks, to have higher expected returns than investments with stable principal values, such as Treasury bills. Without the uncertainty and volatility of common stock returns, there would be no incremental payoff from equity investing.

Guiding clients through the concept of the time horizon, developed in Chapter 5, teaches them that although the passage of time may not, in equilibrium, change the expected returns of investment asset classes, it does significantly alter the magnitude of the possible penalty associated with volatility. The longer the time horizon, the more opportunities there are for good and bad years to offset one another, producing an average return that converges toward the long-term growth path of the asset class. Time thereby transforms the short-run enemy of volatility into a long-run friend that fuels the higher expected returns of equity investments.

Cultivating realistic expectations lays the foundation for developing realistic investment objectives. A client's volatility tolerance can shift within a rather broad range based on a proper understanding of the investment time horizon and a greater familiarity with capital market behavior. As a result, the client more likely will choose an investment portfolio structure appropriate for the realization of his or her financial goals. The goal of this process is to enable the client to make an informed decision regarding the proper portfolio balance between interest-generating investments and equity investments. The resulting portfolio will reflect the most satisfactory compromise between the desire for stability and the need for long-term capital growth.

STEP 5: DEVELOP AN INVESTMENT OBJECTIVE

When a client is asked to list his financial goals, his response may be something like: "A vacation home in an exclusive resort, eight years of fully funded college and postgraduate expenses at the best private institutions for each of three children, and early retirement at age 55 with an annual income of $100,000 after taxes." With a few quick calculations, it becomes clear that to achieve these goals, a very large investment portfolio will be needed. Given reasonable capital market assumptions, most clients have portfolios that are simply too small to achieve all of their desired goals, regardless of how their portfolios are structured. Human desires tend to surpass the resources available for their fulfillment.

Structuring a portfolio capable of generating the return necessary to meet the client's financial goals may require the assumption of an unacceptable level of portfolio volatility. For this reason, it is generally more appropriate to focus on a client's volatility tolerance than on his or her return requirement. Once a client's volatility tolerance is determined, the upper limit on the portfolio's long-term expected return is defined. If this return is inadequate, it is necessary for the client to prioritize his or her financial goals and make the necessary compromises. If the return associated with the client's maximum volatility tolerance is greater than that necessary to reach his or her goals, it is easy to move down the volatility scale and structure a more stable portfolio, if that is the client's preference.

Chapter 6 describes the series of steps that enable an advisor to infer a client's volatility tolerance, based on the client's preferred portfolio allocation between two investment alternatives: Treasury bills and large company stocks. The choice of a broad portfolio balance is an investment policy decision that requires the active involvement of the client. Without the guidance of a skilled investment advisor, few clients are equipped to make the best choice for themselves. This is why it is so important to provide clients with a good frame of reference regarding investment performance and the importance of the time horizon in money management.

The beauty of the process described in Chapter 6 is that it forces the client to acknowledge and realistically deal with the return/volatility trade-off inherent in the money management process. It also fosters the formation of realistic investment performance expectations. A client generally should be encouraged to choose a portfolio balance that places her near the upper end of her volatility-tolerance range while simultaneously making sure that she can remain committed to her portfolio balance decision through market extremes. The goal is to maximize the portfolio's expected return, subject to the client's need to sleep well at night.

Once a broad portfolio balance has been chosen, the next step is to develop a qualitative statement of the corresponding investment objective. I do not use traditional investment objectives, such as "aggressive growth," "growth and current income," or "income." Rather, I prefer to word the objective in a way that acknowledges the return/volatility trade-off. For example, based on my investment worldview, it is impossible to have an objective of "long-term growth of capital with stability of principal value." Examples of suitable investment objectives are:

1. Low portfolio volatility with low total return.
2. Medium total return with medium portfolio volatility.
3. High total return with high portfolio volatility.

The first investment objective, "low portfolio volatility with low total return," would be appropriate for a client who chooses portfolio 2 in Table 6–2. A client who chooses portfolio 3 would have an objective of "medium total return with medium portfolio volatility," and a client choosing either portfolio 4 or portfolio 5 would have an objective of "high total return with high portfolio volatility."

STEP 6: DETERMINE THE BREADTH AND DEGREE OF PORTFOLIO DIVERSIFICATION

Once the client chooses a broad portfolio balance between interest-generating and equity investments and formulates the corresponding investment objective, the next step is to determine the breadth and degree of portfolio diversification. The *breadth* of portfolio diversification refers to the choice of asset classes to be used to construct the portfolio. The *degree* of portfolio diversification refers to the relative allocation of money across those asset classes.

Based on the discussion we had in Chapter 7, we concluded that the volatility of a diversified portfolio is *less than* the weighted average of the volatility levels of the investments composing the portfolio. The difference is due to the diversification effect of partially offsetting patterns of return among the investments. In Chapter 8, we reviewed the significant rewards of multiple-asset-class investing both in reducing portfolio volatility and in potentially increasing long-term returns. The rewards of a multiple-asset-class investment approach, however, come with a price: a pattern of returns that is different from a U.S. capital market frame of reference. There are significant challenges involved in dealing with this "frame-of-reference risk," and so it is important that clients understand the trade-off involved with this issue and actively participate in the decisions made.

Figure 8–5 and the associated Table 8–3 are wonderful for illustrating the surprisingly powerful benefits of portfolio diversification. Unfortunately, they do not convey any sense of what it is like to live with each of these equity portfolios on a year-to-year basis. A U.S.-based investor will typically have a U.S. stock market index such as the S&P 500 as his or her frame of reference for evaluating investment performance. Figure 8–5 from Chapter 8 is reproduced here as Figure 11–3. Note how the equally weighted equity portfolio ABCD had a long-term compound annual return nearly equivalent to that of portfolio A (S&P 500), but with much less volatility.[1] Based on this graph, portfolio ABCD obviously delivered better volatility-adjusted returns than portfolio A. This is confirmed by portfolio ABCD's

---

1. Portfolio ABCD is an annually rebalanced, equally allocated portfolio of four equity asset classes, each represented by an index:
      A. U.S. stocks: S&P 500 Composite Index
      B. International stocks: EAFE Index (Europe, Australia, and Far East)
      C. Real estate equity securities: NAREIT Equity Index (National Association of Real Estate Investment Trusts)
      D. Commodities: GSCI (Goldman Sachs Commodity Index)

F I G U R E   1 1 – 3

The Rewards of Multiple-Asset-Class Investing (1972–1998)

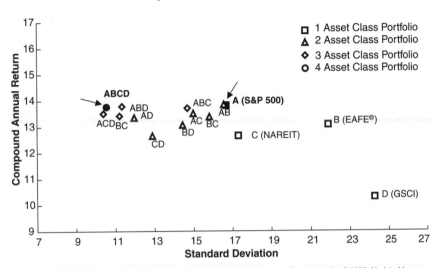

Source: ©Roger C. Gibson, "Asset Allocation and the Rewards of Multiple-Asset-Class Investing," 1998. Updated by author, Roger C. Gibson; Standard & Poor's; Morgan Stanley Capital International; Copyright © 1998 by National Association of Real Estate Investment Trusts®. NAREIT® data is reprinted with permission. Statements, calculations, or charts made by the author which use NAREIT® data have not been approved, verified, or endorsed by NAREIT®; *GSCI® performance data used with permission of Goldman, Sachs & Co.*

Sharpe ratio of .66 compared to portfolio A's Sharpe ratio of .48. But what was it like living with portfolio ABCD?

Figure 11–4A compares the patterns of return of the equally weighted equity allocation (portfolio ABCD) with that of the S&P 500 (portfolio A). It is clear that the equally weighted equity allocation has given the investor a smoother ride through time and has not been as susceptible to major losses. For example, during the particularly painful bear market in 1973–74, the S&P 500 suffered losses of −14.66 percent and −26.47 percent, respectively, while the equally weighted equity allocation had returns of 7.65 percent and −7.63 percent. During periods when the S&P 500 excelled, however, the equally weighted equity allocation understandably generated returns that lagged those of large company U.S. stocks as a result of the diversification into asset classes with lower rates of return. For example, note the last four years on the graph from 1995 through 1998. Despite the fact that

FIGURE 11-4

Equally Weighted Equity Allocation versus S&P 500
A. Pattern of Annual Returns

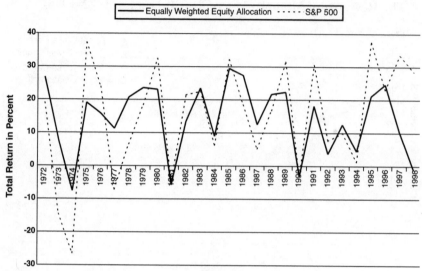

B. Growth of $1

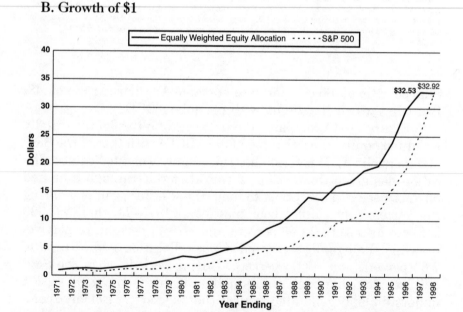

Source: ©Roger C. Gibson, "Asset Allocation and the Rewards of Multiple-Asset-Class Investing," 1998. Updated by author, Roger C. Gibson; Standard & Poor's; Morgan Stanley Capital International; Copyright © (1998) by National Association of Real Estate Investment Trusts®. NAREIT® data is reprinted with permission. Statements, calculations, or charts made by the author which use NAREIT® data have not been approved, verified, or endorsed by NAREIT®; *GSCI® performance data used with permission of Goldman, Sachs & Co.*

the equally weighted equity allocation generated superior volatility-adjusted returns when considering the entire 27-year time period, an investor with a U.S. stock market frame of reference would have felt considerable pain living with this allocation from 1995 through 1998.

Figure 11-4B compares the growth of a $1 investment in the equally weighted equity allocation and the S&P 500. The equally weighted equity allocation had actually built up a significant lead over the S&P 500 and then lost it during the last year of the analysis, due to the sharply negative returns in 1998 from real estate securities and commodities. Over any given investment horizon, though, each year's portfolio return is as important as any other year's.[2] Investors, however, psychologically attach more significance and meaning to recent investment experience. As a result, many U.S. investors found it increasingly difficult to follow the discipline of a multiple-asset-class investment approach during the multiple-year period of S&P 500 dominance at the end of the 27-year period.

I have used the blindfolded exercise in Table 11–1 as a way to encourage clients to give more equal psychological weight to each year's portfolio return. This is accomplished by masking the identity of all five equity portfolios and then presenting their annual returns ranked from low to high. This format permits an easy comparison of the range of results for each portfolio, as well as the frequency and severity of negative returns. The client is told that over the last 27 years, each of the five portfolios generated each of the returns listed for it, but in an order different from the one shown.[3] When asked which portfolio they would prefer to own, clients almost always choose portfolio E because:

1. It generated the best volatility-adjusted returns as evidenced by its Sharpe ratio.
2. It has the least severe and fewest number of negative return years.

2. For the purposes of this discussion, we will assume there are no contributions to or withdrawals from the portfolio.
3. The compound annual return associated with a series of numbers is the same regardless of the order in which the numbers are multiplied.

TABLE 11-1

Five Equity Portfolios: Annual Returns Ranked from Low to High

Year	Portfolio A	Portfolio B	Portfolio C	Portfolio D	Portfolio E
1	−26.47	−23.19	−21.40	−35.75	−7.63
2	−14.66	−22.15	−17.50	−23.01	−5.74
3	−7.18	−14.17	−15.52	−17.22	−3.16
4	−4.91	−11.85	−15.35	−14.07	−1.08
5	−3.17	−1.03	−3.64	−12.33	3.71
6	1.31.	−0.86	3.17	−11.92	4.46
7	5.23	2.05	6.00	−6.13	7.65
8	6.27	3.74	8.01	1.05	9.03
9	6.56	6.18	8.84	2.04	10.40
10	7.67	6.34	10.34	4.42	11.26
11	9.99	7.86	13.49	5.29	12.56
12	16.81	8.06	14.59	10.01	12.57
13	18.44	10.80	15.27	10.37	13.43
14	18.47	11.55	19.10	11.08	15.81
15	18.98	12.49	19.16	11.56	18.15
16	21.41	19.42	19.30	16.26	19.09
17	22.51	20.33	19.65	20.33	20.70
18	23.07	24.43	20.26	23.77	21.15

19	23.84	24.61	20.93	27.93	21.71
20	28.58	24.93	21.60	29.08	22.35
21	30.55	28.59	22.42	31.61	23.08
22	31.49	32.94	24.37	33.81	23.50
23	32.16	34.30	30.64	33.92	23.57
24	32.42	37.10	35.27	38.28	24.65
25	33.36	37.60	35.70	39.51	26.75
26	37.20	56.72	35.86	42.43	27.40
27	37.43	69.94	47.59	74.96	29.50
Number of negative years	5	6	5	7	4
Number of 20+% years	12	11	10	11	11
Standard deviation	16.69	21.90	17.31	24.25	10.55
Simple average return	15.09	15.06	14.01	12.86	14.25
Compound annual return	13.82	13.08	12.65	10.30	13.77
Sharpe ratio	0.48	0.36	0.41	0.25	0.66

3. Its volatility level is by far the lowest, as evidenced by its standard deviation statistic.

4. Its compound annual return is within 5 basis points of the highest among the five portfolios.

By intentionally avoiding a chronological presentation of annual return data, the client cannot attach greater significance to more recent experience. Now we remove the blindfold and place the returns for each portfolio back into chronological order in Table 11–2. Portfolios A, B, C, D, and E are, respectively, the Standard & Poor's 500 Stock Composite Index (U.S. large company stocks), the EAFE Index (international stocks), the NAREIT Equity Index (real estate equity securities), the GSCI (Goldman Sachs Commodity Index), and finally an annually rebalanced, equally weighted allocation of all four indices. Despite a clear vote in favor of the equally weighted equity portfolio E, clients tend to recoil from their choice when they compare the returns of this portfolio with those of the S&P 500 over the most recent period from 1995 through 1998.

Investors evaluate their investment results against some backdrop or frame of reference, and for investors in the United States, that backdrop is the U.S. stock market. Frame of reference is reinforced every time an investor picks up a newspaper or listens to the evening news. Most of what he or she hears is oriented toward the U.S. economy and capital markets. The stock market report will talk about the Dow Jones Industrial Average, not the performance of a globally diversified portfolio. Frame of reference is also reinforced in the conversations investors have with their friends at cocktail parties or during a round of golf. For investors who have a more traditional portfolio composed of U.S. stocks and bonds, there is a close correspondence between what they hear on the evening news and the performance of their portfolios. The broadly diversified, multiple-asset-class investor, however, is still in the minority. His portfolio will not behave in the same way as the portfolios of his golfing buddies who do not follow a strategy with the same breadth and degree of diversification. If the multiple-asset-class investor knows that the U.S. stock market has been rising sharply over the last year but his portfolio has not kept up due to diversification into other asset classes with lower rates of return, there is a painful dissonance between his investment experience and what he hears going on around him. This is frame-of-reference risk. The distress it causes investors should not be underestimated.

Of course, there are times when the multiple-asset-class investor is ahead of the game, but there is not as much pleasure in being ahead as there is pain in being behind. It is worth repeating a comment made to me by a client: "I would rather follow an inferior strategy that wins when my friends are winning and loses when my friends are losing than follow a superior long-term strategy that at times results in my losing when my friends are winning." Over the 1995 through 1998 period of S&P 500 dominance, a Japanese investor following a globally diversified, multiple-asset-class investment strategy would have been delighted with the same investment results that a U.S. based investor found so difficult to live with. Same results, same time period—different frame of reference!

As we discussed in Chapter 8, the equally weighted equity allocation is a teaching illustration. I do not recommend it to my clients. Instead, I suggest that the domestic common stock asset class be the most heavily weighted, with decreasing allocations to international stocks, real estate investments, and commodities. Table 11–3 shows the allocations for three new equity portfolio structures, all of which have this pattern of decreasing weights across the four asset classes. The "greater equity diversification" has the greatest degree of diversification across the four asset classes, with 38 percent allocated to the S&P 500 and the remaining 62 percent allocated across the other three asset classes. By comparison, the "limited equity diversification" has the least degree of diversification, with 70 percent of the portfolio concentrated in the S&P 500 and the balance diversified across the other three asset classes.

Figures 11–5 through 11–7 show the year-by-year patterns of returns and growth of a $1 investment for each of these three portfolios compared with the S&P 500. It should come as no surprise that as the percentage commitment to the S&P 500 increases, the corresponding patterns of returns approach that of the S&P 500. This movement reduces frame-of-reference risk,

TABLE 11–2

Five Equity Portfolios: Annual Returns in Chronological Order

Year	Portfolio A S&P 500*	Portfolio B EAFE†	Portfolio C NAREIT‡	Portfolio D GSCI§	Portfolio E Equal Allocation of ABCD
1972	18.98	37.60	8.01	42.43	26.75
1973	–14.66	–14.17	–15.52	74.96	7.65
1974	–26.47	–22.15	–21.40	39.51	–7.63
1975	37.20	37.10	19.30	–17.22	19.09
1976	23.84	3.74	47.59	–11.92	15.81
1977	–7.18	19.42	22.42	10.37	11.26
1978	6.56	34.30	10.34	31.61	20.70
1979	18.44	6.18	35.86	33.81	23.57
1980	32.42	24.43	24.37	11.08	23.08
1981	–4.91	–1.03	6.00	–23.01	–5.74
1982	21.41	–0.86	21.60	11.56	13.43
1983	22.51	24.61	30.64	16.26	23.50
1984	6.27	7.86	20.93	1.05	9.03
1985	32.16	56.72	19.10	10.01	29.50
1986	18.47	69.94	19.16	2.04	27.40
1987	5.23	24.93	–3.64	23.77	12.57
1988	16.81	28.59	13.49	27.93	21.71
1989	31.49	10.80	8.84	38.28	22.35

1990	-3.17	-23.19	-15.35	**29.08**	-3.16
1991	30.55	12.49	**35.70**	-6.13	18.15
1992	7.67	-11.85	**14.59**	4.42	3.71
1993	9.99	**32.94**	19.65	-12.33	12.56
1994	1.31	**8.06**	3.17	5.29	4.46
1995	**37.43**	11.55	15.27	20.33	21.15
1996	23.07	6.34	**35.27**	33.92	24.65
1997	**33.36**	2.05	20.26	-14.07	10.40
1998	**28.58**	20.33	-17.50	-35.75	-1.08
Number of negative years	5	6	5	7	4
Number of 20+% years	12	11	10	11	11
Standard deviation	16.69	21.90	17.31	24.25	10.55
Simple average return	15.09	15.06	14.01	12.86	14.25
Compound annual return	13.82	13.08	12.65	10.30	13.77
Sharpe ratio	0.48	0.36	0.41	0.25	0.66
Future value of $1	$32.92	$27.61	$24.92	$14.10	$32.53
Highest annual return frequency	5	7	10	5	0

(Highest annual return is in boldface)

*Domestic stocks: Standard & Poor's 500 Index.
†International stocks: Europe, Australia, Far East Index.
‡Equity REITS: National Association of Real Estate Investment Trust, Inc.
§Goldman Sachs Commodity Index.

Source: ©Roger C. Gibson, 1998; Standard & Poor's; Morgan Stanley Capital International; Copyright © 1998 by National Association of Real Estate Investment Trusts®. NAREIT® data is reprinted with permission. Statements, calculations, or charts made by the author which use NAREIT® data have not been approved, verified, or endorsed by NAREIT®; GSCI® performance data used with permission of Goldman, Sachs & Co.

TABLE 11–3

Equity Asset Allocations

Equity Asset Classes	Equally Weighted Equity Allocation	Greater Equity Diversification*	Moderate Equity Diversification*	Limited Equity Diversification*	S&P 500
S&P 500: Domestic stocks	25%	38%	52%	70%	100%
EAFE: International stocks	25%	30%	30%	19%	0
NAREIT: Real estate securities	25%	19%	11%	7%	0
GSCI: Commodities	25%	13%	7%	4%	0
Totals	100%	100%	100%	100%	100%

*Rounded to the nearest percentage point.

Source: ©Roger C. Gibson, 1999.

FIGURE 11–5

Greater Equity Diversification versus S&P 500
A. Pattern of Annual Returns

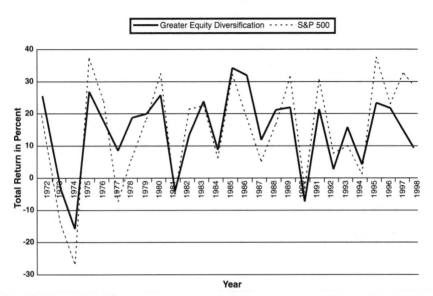

B. Growth of $1

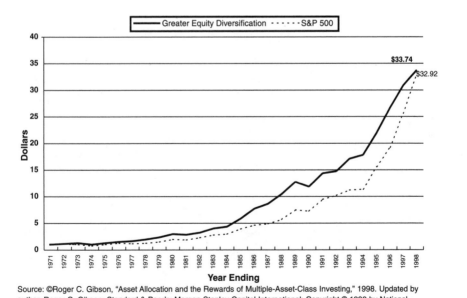

Source: ©Roger C. Gibson, "Asset Allocation and the Rewards of Multiple-Asset-Class Investing," 1998. Updated by author, Roger C. Gibson; Standard & Poor's; Morgan Stanley Capital International; Copyright © 1998 by National Association of Real Estate Investment Trusts®. NAREIT® data is reprinted with permission. Statements, calculations, or charts made by the author which use NAREIT® data have not been approved, verified, or endorsed by NAREIT®; GSCI® performance data used with permission of Goldman, Sachs & Co.

Moderate Equity Diversification versus S&P 500
A. Pattern of Annual Returns

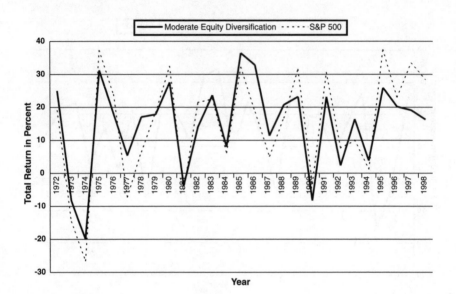

B. Growth of $1

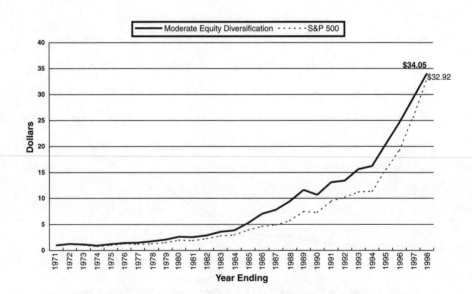

Source: ©Roger C. Gibson, "Asset Allocation and the Rewards of Multiple-Asset-Class Investing," 1998. Updated by author, Roger C. Gibson; Standard & Poor's; Morgan Stanley Capital International; Copyright © 1998 by National Association of Real Estate Investment Trusts®. NAREIT® data is reprinted with permission. Statements, calculations, or charts made by the author which use NAREIT® data have not been approved, verified, or endorsed by NAREIT®; *GSCI® performance data used with permission of Goldman, Sachs & Co.*

FIGURE 11-7

Limited Equity Diversification versus S&P 500
A. Pattern of Annual Returns

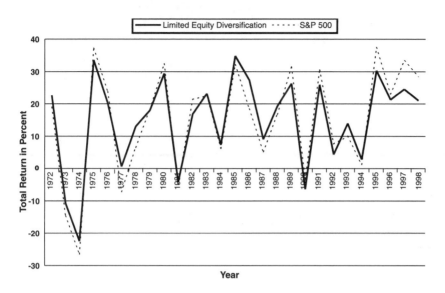

B. Growth of $1

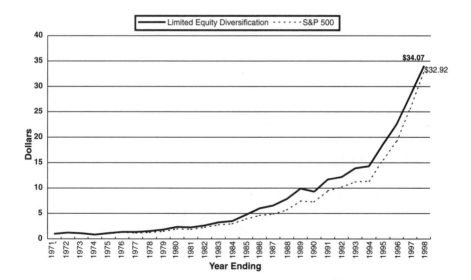

Source: ©Roger C. Gibson, "Asset Allocation and the Rewards of Multiple-Asset-Class Investing," 1998. Updated by author, Roger C. Gibson; Standard & Poor's; Morgan Stanley Capital International; Copyright © 1998 by National Association of Real Estate Investment Trusts®. NAREIT® data is reprinted with permission. Statements, calculations, or charts made by the author which use NAREIT® data have not been approved, verified, or endorsed by NAREIT®; *GSCI® performance data used with permission of Goldman, Sachs & Co.*

but it is simultaneously accompanied by a deterioration in port-folio risk-adjusted returns as a result of the lesser degree of diversification. Clients must deal with this trade-off: How much pain of dissimilarity in pattern of returns can they bear in exchange for an expected improvement in long-term volatility-adjusted returns?

Table 11–4 provides performance statistics for each of the portfolios described in Table 11–3. Note that as we move from the equally weighted equity allocation on the left to the S&P 500 on the right, the Sharpe ratios steadily decline, indicating the deterioration in volatility-adjusted returns. This is due primarily to the increasing level of portfolio volatility as indicated by the standard deviation statistics. Table 11–5 shows the total returns of each of the diversified portfolio structures relative to the S&P 500. The standard deviation statistic at the bottom of each column measures the degree of dissimilarity in patterns of return for each portfolio relative to the S&P 500. As such, this standard deviation statistic is a measure of the degree of frame-of-reference risk inherent in each diversified portfolio. The greater the degree of diversification, the greater the frame-of-reference risk. By comparing the relative returns for each port-folio structure over the time period 1995 through 1998, we can see the greater degree of pain experienced by the investor in an equally weighted equity allocation. That pain is the price paid for a pattern of returns that is on average much less volatile and that also offered the greatest protection against severe domestic stock market losses such as those that occurred in 1973–74.

There are no right or wrong answers here. There is a trade-off: Better volatility-adjusted expected returns are accompanied by more frame-of-reference risk. The advisor's job is to educate the client regarding the trade-off and provide a menu of portfolio structures with varying degrees of diversification. It is up to the client to then make an informed choice. If the client chooses a broadly diversified, multiple-asset-class structure, she or he needs to simultaneously adopt a broadly diversified frame of reference.

Congratulations! If you have guided the client successfully to this point, you have accomplished much. You and the client have a common frame of reference. You agree about how and why the capital markets behave as they do. The client has developed realistic investment expectations and a reasonable invest-ment objective based on a broad portfolio allocation between interest-generating investments and equity investments that is consistent with his or her time horizon and capacity to tolerate volatility. The client understands the benefits of diversification and has determined the breadth and degree of his or her portfo-lio's diversification. Although this is a significant job, it does not require an extraordinary time commitment on the part of the client. We are now ready to design the final portfolio structure.

TABLE 11–4

Performance Statistics

Year	Equally Weighted Equity Allocation	Greater Equity Diversification	Moderate Equity Diversification	Limited Equity Diversification	S&P 500
1972	26.75	25.53	24.98	22.67	18.98
1973	7.65	-3.20	-8.25	-10.78	-14.66
1974	-7.63	-15.79	-19.91	-22.47	-26.47
1975	19.09	26.87	31.27	33.57	37.20
1976	15.81	17.65	17.98	20.25	23.84
1977	11.26	8.55	5.42	0.62	-7.18
1978	20.70	18.79	17.09	13.07	6.56
1979	23.57	19.97	17.84	18.06	18.44
1980	23.08	25.79	27.59	29.44	32.42
1981	-5.74	-4.03	-3.79	-4.19	-4.91
1982	13.43	13.50	14.05	16.86	21.41
1983	23.50	23.85	23.62	23.21	22.51
1984	9.03	8.81	8.05	7.38	6.27
1985	29.50	34.26	36.47	34.85	32.16
1986	27.40	31.94	32.82	27.39	18.47
1987	12.57	11.86	11.45	9.06	5.23
1988	21.71	21.15	20.76	19.24	16.81

1989	22.35	21.94	23.18	26.33	31.49
1990	−3.16	−7.31	−8.27	−6.37	−3.17
1991	18.15	21.39	23.11	25.98	30.55
1992	3.71	2.69	2.37	4.39	7.67
1993	12.56	15.82	16.39	13.98	9.99
1994	4.46	4.19	3.83	2.87	1.31
1995	21.15	23.36	25.93	30.31	37.43
1996	24.65	21.71	20.21	21.29	23.07
1997	10.40	15.46	19.11	24.57	33.36
1998	−1.08	9.30	16.29	21.01	28.58
Simple average return	14.25	14.59	14.80	14.91	15.09
Standard deviation	10.55	12.28	13.62	14.40	16.69
Compound annual return	13.77	13.92	13.96	13.96	13.82
Future value of $1	$32.53	$33.74	$34.05	$34.07	$32.92
Sharpe ratio	0.66	0.60	0.55	0.53	0.48

Source: ©Roger C. Gibson, 1999.

TABLE 11-5

Total Returns Relative to S&P 500

Year	Equally Weighted Equity Allocation Minus S&P 500	Greater Equity Diversification Minus S&P 500	Moderate Equity Diversification Minus S&P 500	Limited Equity Diversification Minus S&P 500
1972	7.77	6.55	6.00	3.69
1973	22.31	11.46	6.41	3.88
1974	18.84	10.68	6.56	4.00
1975	-18.11	-10.33	-5.93	-3.63
1976	-8.03	-6.19	-5.86	-3.59
1977	18.44	15.73	12.60	7.80
1978	14.14	12.23	10.53	6.51
1979	5.13	1.53	-0.60	-0.38
1980	-9.34	-6.63	-4.83	-2.98
1981	-0.83	0.88	1.12	0.72
1982	-7.98	-7.91	-7.36	-4.55
1983	0.99	1.34	1.11	0.70
1984	2.76	2.54	1.78	1.11
1985	-2.66	2.10	4.31	2.69
1986	8.93	13.47	14.35	8.92
1987	7.34	6.63	6.22	3.83
1988	4.90	4.34	3.95	2.43

1989	−9.14	−9.55	−8.31	−5.16
1990	0.01	−4.14	−5.10	−3.20
1991	−12.40	−9.16	−7.44	−4.57
1992	−3.96	−4.98	−5.30	−3.28
1993	2.57	5.83	6.40	3.99
1994	3.15	2.88	2.52	1.56
1995	−16.28	−14.07	−11.50	−7.12
1996	1.58	−1.36	−2.86	−1.78
1997	−22.96	−17.90	−14.25	−8.79
1998	−29.66	−19.28	−12.29	−7.57
Standard deviation	12.59	9.49	7.70	4.76

Source: ©Roger C. Gibson, 1999.

CHAPTER 12

Money Management

Don't fight forces; use them.

—*R. Buckminster Fuller (1895–1983)*
Shelter, 1932

Clients love to make money and hate to lose it. The most important conclusion of this book is that broad portfolio diversification among multiple asset classes will in the long run deliver better volatility-adjusted returns than will traditional approaches that utilize fewer asset classes. Look once again at the distribution of the world's investable capital as shown in Figure 1–1. If all clients restructured their portfolios to have a meaningful allocation in each of the major asset classes shown, the expected return/volatility characteristics of their portfolios would be substantially improved and the likelihood of their experiencing major portfolio losses would drop significantly.

The tendency for most money managers to underperform the market underscores the value of the performance advantages gained from a more broadly diversified approach. The remarkable aspect of this is that much of the improvement in portfolio performance flows from the simple *decision* to utilize a broader array of asset classes. This is contrasted with improvements in portfolio performance that require the exercise of superior management *skill*. Although they are undoubtedly more rare than most people realize, money managers with truly superior skill may exist, and their contributions to improved portfolio performance may be significant. Due to the inherent difficulty in conclusively identifying these managers, however, superior skill should not be relied on as the driving force behind investment strategy. Rather, strategy should be grounded in realistic capital market performance expectations and implemented within a disciplined asset allocation framework. Should superior skill in security selection add value within an asset class, this becomes the "icing on the cake."

We will now cover steps 7 through 10 of the money management process outlined in Figure 12–1. Step 7 describes a *process* for making asset allocation decisions and selecting specific investment positions. Alternatives at each level of decision making are described in order to provide an overview of the issues that need to be considered. The example portfolios provide concrete illustrations of my methods in addressing these issues.

STEP 7: ALLOCATE ASSETS AND DESIGN THE PORTFOLIO

Once the broad portfolio balance has been determined, the advisor is ready to develop a detailed allocation strategy using multiple asset classes. Figure 12–2 shows a format for progressing from the current cash value of the client's total investment portfolio to a detailed, recommended portfolio structure. Starting from the left, the advisor begins by entering the current cash value of the client's total investment portfolio. Based on the client's broad portfolio balance decision, the advisor enters the percentage and dollar commitment to short-term debt investments, longer-term bonds, and equity investments. Once these percentages are set, they generally remain fixed unless there is a meaningful change in the client's volatility tolerance, time horizon, or financial circumstances.

Subject to the broad portfolio balance, the client and advisor then determine an appropriate asset allocation among seven asset classes:

1. Short-term debt investments
2. Domestic bonds
3. International bonds
4. Domestic stocks
5. International stocks
6. Real estate investments
7. Investment hedges

FIGURE 12-1

Money Management Process

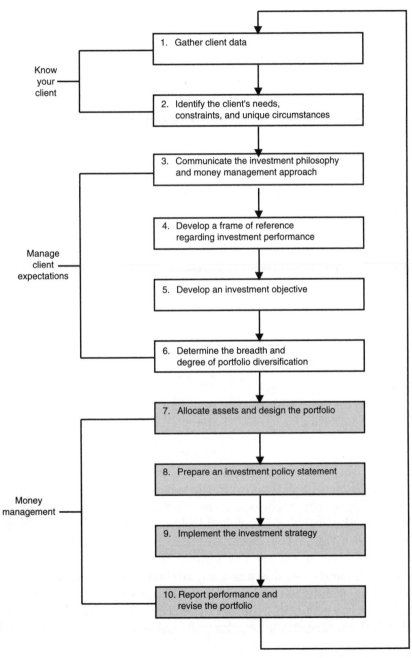

FIGURE 12-2

Investment Portfolio Design Format

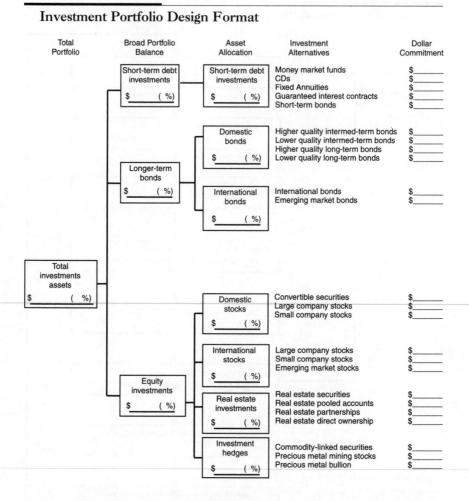

One approach for determining the recommended asset allocation among these asset classes is to consider their relative proportions in the world market capitalization. For example, Figure 1–1 shows that as of December 31, 1998, international bonds accounted for a larger percentage of world wealth than did domestic bonds. On this basis, an advisor may recommend giving a heavier weight to the international bonds than to the domestic bonds in the portfolio. Similarly, the relative weightings of domestic versus international stocks and real estate versus other equities can be used as a basis for determining the recommended allocation to these asset classes. Although there is a theoretical argument for this method of determining asset class weightings, such an allocation would be quite unusual for a U.S. investor and the perceptual "frame-of-reference" risk would be high.

Other approaches rely on economic scenario forecasting and sophisticated projections regarding the expected returns, standard deviations, and cross-correlations among the various asset classes. Here, a computer optimization program can be useful as an additional tool to help determine the percentage commitments to the various asset classes; however, because the output from optimization programs is quite sensitive to the input variables, which are very difficult to specify with confidence, such programs should be used with caution. Regardless of the approach used to determine the recommended asset allocation, it is advisable to establish minimum percentage commitments for each of the asset classes in order to ensure a good breadth of diversification.

A number of investment alternatives are listed beside the *short-term debt investments* asset class. The investment alternatives in this asset class have little or no interest rate risk. The list is not exhaustive but provides a sample menu of possible choices. The investments are listed in order of increasing maturity. In this manner, investments with no interest rate risk are listed first, followed by those with low interest rate risk, such as short-term bonds.

The next asset class is *domestic bonds.* The investment choices are differentiated along two dimensions: quality and maturity. An advisor may choose to vary the allocation between intermediate-term and long-term bonds based on the slope of the yield curve or on the basis of anticipated changes in interest rates. Similarly, the allocation between high-quality and low-quality bonds may be varied depending on the economic outlook. I do not have confidence, however, that these kinds of active decisions will materially improve investment results.

Just a few years ago, alternatives for investing in *international bonds* were limited for all but the very large investor. Fortunately, there are now a significant number of international bond mutual funds that provide an efficient, low-cost means for any investor to gain access to this diversification alternative.

Domestic stocks include the full range of U.S. common stock alternatives. As a hybrid investment with both debt and equity characteristics, convertible securities are classified here in order to emphasize their equity risk characteristics. (Alternatively, they could be classified under the domestic bonds asset class, but clients might underestimate their risk with this classification.) For simplicity, the remaining domestic stock investments are classified into large company and small company stock categories. Diversification among investment management styles and approaches can also be considered. At times, for example, growth managers outperform value managers, and at other times the reverse is true. By having multiple approaches represented in the portfolio, the risk of relying on only one approach is eliminated.

International stocks provide an important diversification alternative to domestic stocks. This form of diversification has been more widely used than international bond diversification. Thus, the number of alternatives available to investors is correspondingly greater. As with the domestic stocks asset class, both large company and small company international stocks are listed as investment alternatives. In addition, emerging market stocks are shown in recognition of the increasing importance of rapidly growing third world economies. Mutual funds that are composed exclusively of non-U.S. stocks should be utilized because the balance between domestic and international stocks is handled at the asset allocation level of decision making.

Real estate investments can be held in a variety of forms, and several alternatives are listed. Historically, real estate investments often have had significant tax benefits. Although the Tax Reform Act of 1986 largely eliminated these benefits, real estate is nevertheless an important building block for an investment portfolio. For many client situations, equity REITs and mutual funds that invest in REITs are effective choices for real estate diversification. Personal residences and vacation homes usually are not held primarily for investment purposes, and accordingly they are not listed here. Instead, they are carried on the client's balance sheet under the heading of "Lifestyle Assets."

Investment hedges such as commodity-linked securities and precious metal investments are positions that historically have had patterns of returns decidedly different from those of other asset classes. The percentage commitment to them is small, and the hope is that they may perform well during adverse economic conditions, when other parts of the portfolio may be losing ground. In this context, commodity-linked securities are probably the best example of an investment hedge. Commodities are negatively correlated to many financial asset classes and are therefore powerful portfolio diversifiers (refer to Figure 8–6).

Until recently, commodities diversification was generally available only within partnership structures that typically had incentive-based management fees. A mutual fund is now available, the Oppenheimer Real Asset Fund, that is designed to closely replicate the performance of the Goldman Sachs Commodity Index. Although at the time of this writing it is one of a kind, hopefully other funds with lower cost structures will become available to compete with this fund in providing commodities diversification.

A precious metals investment may be in gold or silver. Less frequently, platinum is used. If precious metals are owned in physical form, bullion coins such as the one-ounce South African Krugerrand and the Canadian Gold Maple Leaf are preferred over bullion bars. Bullion coins are readily identifiable in regard to their gold content and are therefore much easier to buy and sell. Precious metal mining stocks provide an alternative to physical bullion ownership. Unlike bullion, precious metal mining stocks are often income-producing, and the long-term investment performance usually has been better. Geographic diversification is recommended among the three major gold mining regions of South Africa, North America, and Australia.

The most general level of decision making concerns the broad portfolio balance. Once those decisions are made, decision making proceeds to the asset allocation level. Here choices are made regarding which asset classes will be represented in the portfolio and the relative commitment of funds across the asset classes. It is important to have the client tackle the issue regarding the degree of portfolio diversification. As we discussed in Chapters 8 and 11, although more broadly diversified portfolios have better expected return/volatility characteristics, those advantages come with a price—a pattern of returns that is different from one's customary frame of reference. It is only after the asset allocation decisions have been made that specific investment alternatives are chosen. As the decisions proceed from the most general level to the more detailed levels of decision making, the impact of the decisions on long-term portfolio performance declines.

I am a strong advocate of client involvement at each of these levels of portfolio design. Indeed, many of these decisions are the nondelegable responsibility of the client. The advisor's role is to point the client in the right direction and provide a frame of reference for improving the quality of the client's decisions.

Figures 12–3, 12–4, and 12–5 show example asset allocations that correspond to the broad portfolio balance choices numbered 2, 3, and 4 in Table 6–2. For example, Figure 12–3, shows the recommended asset allocation for a client who chooses a portfolio balance of 70 percent Treasury bills/30 percent large company stocks with a "moderate" degree of portfolio diversification (refer to Chapter 11, Step 6: Determine the breadth and degree of portfolio diversification). Table 12–1 shows the alternative asset allocations for either "limited" or "greater" degrees of portfolio diversification (refer to Table 11–3).

We will assume that these examples are for institutional clients such as qualified retirement plans or endowment funds. Accordingly, preference has been given to choosing investment alternatives that are liquid and easy to value. Notice that the same building blocks are used for each portfolio. By changing the allocation of assets among short-term debt investments, longer-term bonds, and equity investments, the volatility profile of each portfolio is controlled at the *broad portfolio balance* level of decision making.

Some investment advisors alternatively prefer to use the same asset allocation for *all* clients and accommodate differences in client volatility tolerance at the level of investment position selection. For example, all clients may have 25 percent in short-term debt investments, 20 percent in longer-term bonds, and 55 percent in equity investments. Clients with a lower volatility tolerance, though, will build their portfolios with high-quality bonds; more conservative, lower beta large company stocks; and unleveraged real estate, whereas clients with a

FIGURE 12-3

Lower-Volatility Portfolio Asset Allocation

Investment objective: Low portfolio volatility with low total return*
Degree of portfolio diversification: Moderate**

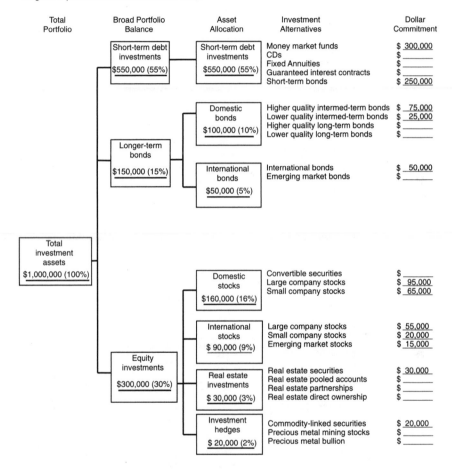

Total Portfolio	Broad Portfolio Balance	Asset Allocation	Investment Alternatives	Dollar Commitment
	Short-term debt investments $550,000 (55%)	Short-term debt investments $550,000 (55%)	Money market funds CDs Fixed Annuities Guaranteed interest contracts Short-term bonds	$ 300,000 $ _____ $ _____ $ _____ $ 250,000
	Longer-term bonds $150,000 (15%)	Domestic bonds $100,000 (10%)	Higher quality intermed-term bonds Lower quality intermed-term bonds Higher quality long-term bonds Lower quality long-term bonds	$ 75,000 $ 25,000 $ _____ $ _____
		International bonds $50,000 (5%)	International bonds Emerging market bonds	$ 50,000 $ _____
Total investment assets $1,000,000 (100%)	Equity investments $300,000 (30%)	Domestic stocks $160,000 (16%)	Convertible securities Large company stocks Small company stocks	$ _____ $ 95,000 $ 65,000
		International stocks $ 90,000 (9%)	Large company stocks Small company stocks Emerging market stocks	$ 55,000 $ 20,000 $ 15,000
		Real estate investments $ 30,000 (3%)	Real estate securities Real estate pooled accounts Real estate partnerships Real estate direct ownership	$ 30,000 $ _____ $ _____ $ _____
		Investment hedges $ 20,000 (2%)	Commodity-linked securities Precious metal mining stocks Precious metal bullion	$ 20,000 $ _____ $ _____

*Refer to example portfolio choice # 2 in Table 6-2.
**Refer to Chapter 11, Step 6: Determine the breadth and degree of portfolio diversification.

FIGURE 12-4

Medium-Volatility Portfolio Asset Allocation

Investment objective: Medium total return with medium portfolio volatility*
Degree of portfolio diversification: Moderate**

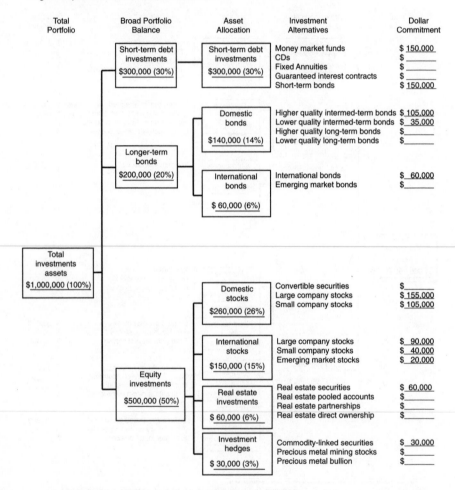

Total Portfolio	Broad Portfolio Balance	Asset Allocation	Investment Alternatives	Dollar Commitment
	Short-term debt investments $300,000 (30%)	Short-term debt investments $300,000 (30%)	Money market funds CDs Fixed Annuities Guaranteed interest contracts Short-term bonds	$ 150,000 $ _____ $ _____ $ _____ $ 150,000
	Longer-term bonds $200,000 (20%)	Domestic bonds $140,000 (14%)	Higher quality intermed-term bonds Lower quality intermed-term bonds Higher quality long-term bonds Lower quality long-term bonds	$ 105,000 $ 35,000 $ _____ $ _____
		International bonds $ 60,000 (6%)	International bonds Emerging market bonds	$ 60,000 $ _____
Total investments assets $1,000,000 (100%)	Equity investments $500,000 (50%)	Domestic stocks $260,000 (26%)	Convertible securities Large company stocks Small company stocks	$ _____ $ 155,000 $ 105,000
		International stocks $150,000 (15%)	Large company stocks Small company stocks Emerging market stocks	$ 90,000 $ 40,000 $ 20,000
		Real estate investments $ 60,000 (6%)	Real estate securities Real estate pooled accounts Real estate partnerships Real estate direct ownership	$ 60,000 $ _____ $ _____ $ _____
		Investment hedges $ 30,000 (3%)	Commodity-linked securities Precious metal mining stocks Precious metal bullion	$ 30,000 $ _____ $ _____

*Refer to example portfolio choice # 3 in Table 6-2.
**Refer to Chapter 11, Step 6: Determine the breadth and degree of portfolio diversification.

F I G U R E   1 2 – 5

Higher-Volatility Portfolio Asset Allocation

Investment objective: High total return with high portfolio volatility*
Degree of portfolio diversification: Moderate**

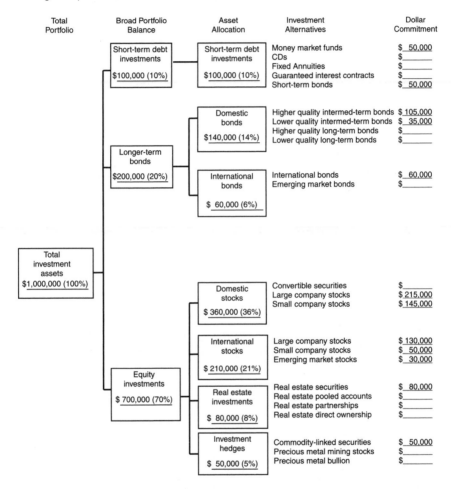

Total Portfolio	Broad Portfolio Balance	Asset Allocation	Investment Alternatives	Dollar Commitment
	Short-term debt investments $100,000 (10%)	Short-term debt investments $100,000 (10%)	Money market funds	$ 50,000
			CDs	$_____
			Fixed Annuities	$_____
			Guaranteed interest contracts	$_____
			Short-term bonds	$ 50,000
	Longer-term bonds $200,000 (20%)	Domestic bonds $140,000 (14%)	Higher quality intermed-term bonds	$ 105,000
			Lower quality intermed-term bonds	$ 35,000
			Higher quality long-term bonds	$_____
			Lower quality long-term bonds	$_____
		International bonds $ 60,000 (6%)	International bonds	$ 60,000
			Emerging market bonds	$_____
Total investment assets $1,000,000 (100%)	Equity investments $ 700,000 (70%)	Domestic stocks $ 360,000 (36%)	Convertible securities	$_____
			Large company stocks	$ 215,000
			Small company stocks	$ 145,000
		International stocks $ 210,000 (21%)	Large company stocks	$ 130,000
			Small company stocks	$ 50,000
			Emerging market stocks	$ 30,000
		Real estate investments $ 80,000 (8%)	Real estate securities	$ 80,000
			Real estate pooled accounts	$_____
			Real estate partnerships	$_____
			Real estate direct ownership	$_____
		Investment hedges $ 50,000 (5%)	Commodity-linked securities	$ 50,000
			Precious metal mining stocks	$_____
			Precious metal bullion	$_____

*Refer to example portfolio choice # 4 in Table 6-2.
**Refer to Chapter 11, Step 6: Determine the breadth and degree of portfolio diversification.

TABLE 12-1

Portfolio Structures for Limited, Moderate, and Greater Degrees of Diversification

PORTFOLIO STRUCTURE

Asset Allocation	LOWER VOLATILITY Diversification Degree			MEDIUM VOLATILITY Diversification Degree			HIGHER VOLATILITY Diversification Degree		
	Limited	Moderate	Greater	Limited	Moderate	Greater	Limited	Moderate	Greater
	%	%	%	%	%	%	%	%	%
Short-Term Debt Investments	55.0	55.0	55.0	30.0	30.0	30.0	10.0	10.0	10.0
Longer-Term Bonds									
Domestic bonds	12.0	10.0	9.0	16.0	14.0	12.0	16.0	14.0	12.0
International bonds	3.0	5.0	6.0	4.0	6.0	8.0	4.0	6.0	8.0
Equity Investments									
Domestic stocks	21.0	16.0	11.0	35.0	26.0	19.0	49.0	36.0	27.0
International stocks	6.0	9.0	9.0	10.0	15.0	15.0	13.0	21.0	21.0
Real estate investments	2.0	3.0	6.0	3.0	6.0	9.0	5.0	8.0	13.0
Investment hedges	1.0	2.0	4.0	2.0	3.0	7.0	3.0	5.0	9.0
	%	%	%	%	%	%	%	%	%
Total	100.0	100.0	100.0	100.0	100.0	100.0	100.0	100.0	100.0

PORTFOLIO STRUCTURE

Investment Alternatives	LOWER VOLATILITY Diversification Degree			MEDIUM VOLATILITY Diversification Degree			HIGHER VOLATILITY Diversification Degree		
	Limited	Moderate	Greater	Limited	Moderate	Greater	Limited	Moderate	Greater
	%	%	%	%	%	%	%	%	%
Short-Term Debt Investments									
Money market	30.0	30.0	30.0	15.0	15.0	15.0	5.0	5.0	5.0
Short-term bonds	25.0	25.0	25.0	15.0	15.0	15.0	5.0	5.0	5.0

	%	%	%	%	%	%	%	%	%
Longer-Term Bonds									
Domestic Bonds									
High quality/intermediate	9.0	7.5	6.5	12.0	10.5	9.0	12.0	10.5	9.0
Low-quality/intermediate	3.0	2.5	2.5	4.0	3.5	3.0	4.0	3.5	3.0
International Bonds									
International bonds	3.0	5.0	6.0	4.0	6.0	7.0	4.0	6.0	7.0
Emerging market bonds	—	—	—	—	—	1.0	—	—	1.0
Equity Investments									
Domestic Stocks									
Large company stocks	12.5	9.5	8.5	21.0	15.5	14.0	29.5	21.5	20.0
Small company stocks	8.5	6.5	2.5	14.0	10.5	5.0	19.5	14.5	7.0
International Stocks									
Large company stocks	3.5	5.5	5.5	6.0	9.0	9.0	8.0	13.0	12.5
Small company stocks	1.5	2.0	2.0	2.5	4.0	4.0	3.0	5.0	5.5
Emerging market stocks	1.0	1.5	1.5	1.5	2.0	2.0	2.0	3.0	3.0
Real Estate Investments									
Real estate securities	2.0	3.0	6.0	3.0	6.0	9.0	5.0	8.0	13.0
Investment Hedges									
Commodity-linked securities	1.0	2.0	4.0	2.0	3.0	7.0	3.0	5.0	9.0
Total	100.0	100.0	100.0	100.0	100.0	100.0	100.0	100.0	100.0

259

higher volatility tolerance will have portfolios composed of low-quality bonds; more aggressive, higher beta small company stocks; and leveraged real estate.

I prefer to handle portfolio tailoring for volatility tolerance differences at the broad portfolio balance level for several reasons. First, it builds directly from the model described in Chapter 6 for determining the broad portfolio balance. Second, it is easy for clients to understand, and this enhances their comfort level. Third, it facilitates the design of portfolios to accommodate clients with either unusually high or unusually low capacities for tolerating volatility. Last, and most important, it permits a broader diversification of the portfolio for all clients regardless of volatility tolerance. That is, by handling the volatility tolerance issue at the level of broad portfolio balance, all clients can benefit from diversification with *both* high- and low-quality bonds, large company and small company stocks, and so on.

Occasionally, the issue is raised of using stock options and/or futures to modify the volatility characteristics of a portfolio. If the need is felt to modify the volatility characteristics of the portfolio, one of two things is often true. First, the portfolio's asset allocation may have strayed from its targets, and rebalancing will restore it to its appropriate volatility level. The other possibility is that the portfolio's asset allocation is not matched to the client's volatility tolerance, in which case the broad portfolio balance or the breadth and degree of portfolio diversification should be reworked. In either case, options or futures are usually not the preferred solution.

Figure 12–2 shows several stages of decision making that link the broad portfolio balance decision to the final detailed target portfolio. Each of these steps can be characterized along an active/passive dimension. Ultimately, it is the responsibility of both investment advisors and their clients to evaluate the likely gains and potential risks inherent in pursuing active strategies. For example, at the broad portfolio balance level of decision making, a passive approach requires a systematic rebalancing of the portfolio to the target percentage allocations that have been endorsed by the client and the advisor. A more active approach would specify a range of percentage allocations for each of the three broad investment classifications. (Refer to

Table 12–2.) Within these ranges, an active advisor would engage in a restricted form of market timing among short-term debt investments, longer-term bonds, and equity investments. In the example shown in Table 12–2, the minimum allocations guarantee that at least 65 percent of the assets will be committed to a "core portfolio" consisting of 25 percent short-term debt investments, 10 percent longer-term bonds, and 30 percent equity investments.

Figure 12–2 shows seven asset classes at the asset allocation level of decision making. This, too, can be handled in either an active or a passive way. More active approaches presume exploitable inefficiencies among the various asset classes. By maintaining minimum and maximum percentage allocations for each asset class, the risk of errors in judgment can be kept within limits while the attempt is made to add value. The passive alternative is to simply periodically rebalance the portfolio back to the target percentages established for each asset class.

Other active decisions may be made, for example, in the choice of balance among quality or maturity sectors in the bond markets. For example, long-term bonds have not been used in any of the three example portfolios shown. At first, this may appear to be a very active decision by an investment advisor who is of a relatively passive persuasion. The rationale for excluding them was based on a relatively flat yield curve at the time the example portfolio allocations were developed. That is, beyond intermediate-term maturities, there was very little incremental yield available from longer-term bonds. This

TABLE 12-2

Medium-Volatility Portfolio

Broad Investment Classification	Passive Management Fixed Percentage	Active Management Percentage Range
Short-term debt investments	35%	25–45%
Longer-term bonds	20	10–30
Equity investments	45	30–60
Total investments	100%	65% core portfolio

resulted in a situation where there was insufficient compensation for the increased interest rate risk associated with longer-maturity bonds. In my judgment, the assumption of that risk is justified only if one is confident that interest rates will decline and wants to bet accordingly.[1] Because the approach endorsed here is not based on forecasts of interest rate movements, it becomes a risk not worth taking. In this case, the uncertainties inherent in the capital markets argued for the exclusion of long-term bonds.

In choosing investment alternatives within each of the seven asset classes, more possibilities present themselves. At one extreme, passively managed, low-cost index funds can be used as portfolio building blocks. Alternatively, actively managed alternatives can be used with the hope that superior security selection will add value.

An index fund seeks to replicate the performance of a specified market index by owning all or substantially all of the securities within the index. There is no attempt to outperform the market through superior security selection. The argument in favor of using index funds rests on a simple and irrefutable premise: Investors as a group *are* the market and therefore cannot outperform the market. Further, the attempt to beat the market through superior security selection comes with a price tag: higher expenses in the form of advisory fees, operating expenses, and portfolio transaction costs that result in a direct reduction of realized returns for the active investor. This would not be a problem if there were a reliable way to identify which money managers will outperform the markets, net of their expenses. But the majority of research studies suggest that markets operate relatively efficiently and that the identification of tomorrow's superior money managers is a very difficult undertaking.

By contrast, an index fund, which minimizes costs and portfolio turnover, locks in an automatic performance advantage that may be small in the short run but becomes increasingly powerful over time. As John C. Bogle, the founder of the Vanguard family of mutual funds, eloquently observed:

---

1. In implementing an immunization strategy, investment in longer-term bonds may
   also be justified even though the yield curve is relatively flat.

The fact is that indexers always win. That is, in any financial market—and any segment of any financial market—indexers owning all of the securities in that market at low cost *must* provide better returns than the other investors in the market in the aggregate, simply because the costs incurred by active investors—commissions, fees, taxes—are substantially higher.[2]

If actively managed mutual funds or separate accounts are used to build the portfolio, a rigorous due diligence process should be followed in evaluating money managers. An example of such a due diligence methodology is contained in the *money manager selection* section of the sample investment policy statement contained in the Appendix to this chapter.[3]

STEP 8: PREPARE AN INVESTMENT POLICY STATEMENT

We are almost ready to implement the strategy—almost, but not quite. It is time to document our investment decisions and the parameters within which the portfolio is to be managed over time. If the portfolio is for a pension plan, foundation, or trust, there is likely to be legislation or regulations that either require or strongly recommend the formulation of a written investment policy statement (IPS). Even in the absence of specific legal requirements, an IPS is highly recommended. In addition to providing all interested parties with documentation regarding investment policies and procedures, the preparation of a well-written IPS has several advantages:

- It supports a disciplined, consistent execution of the portfolio's investment strategy. This is particularly important during extremely good or bad capital market environments.

---

2. Excerpt from an address given by John C. Bogle at the Fourth Annual Superbowl of Indexing conference.
3. The due diligence criteria described were developed by Donald B. Trone of the Investment Management Council and are taught at the Center for Fiduciary Studies in association with the Katz Graduate School of Business at the University of Pittsburgh. The Center for Fiduciary Studies is a research and training organization supporting trustees of pension plans, foundations, and private trusts as well as professionals who render investment advice.

- For institutional portfolios managed by investment committees, an IPS can provide for continuity in investment approach as new committee members replace those who are stepping down.

- An IPS provides a defense against "Monday morning quarterbacking" where prior investment decisions may be second-guessed.

- An IPS also provides evidence of investment stewardship and the fulfillment of fiduciary duties in properly overseeing the money management process.

The Appendix to this chapter contains a sample IPS for an individual. The first section is an *executive summary* containing information concerning the type of client, the size of the portfolio, the investment time horizon, the portfolio's return characteristics, and its asset allocation. A *background and purpose* section and the *statement of investment objective and parameters* follow. Here the client's financial goals are itemized and linked to a qualitative investment objective that acknowledges the return/volatility trade-off. Information is also itemized regarding the client's asset class preferences, investment time horizon, modeled portfolio return, and portfolio rebalancing policy. The *duties and responsibilities* of the investment advisor, money managers, and custodian are described in the next section. The *money manager selection* section describes the due diligence criteria for selecting money managers. The *control procedures* are then documented for monitoring money manger performance, measuring costs, and reviewing the IPS on an annual basis. Finally, the appendix to the IPS contains modeled return, standard deviation, and correlation statistics for the asset classes used to diversify the portfolio.

The IPS is the most important document in the fiduciary process. It ensures that all the relevant aspects of the money management process have been addressed, that roles are clearly defined, and that a proper frame of reference exists for evaluating the portfolio strategy over time. The litmus test for a well-written IPS is whether there is sufficient detail and clarity for the portfolio strategy to be implemented by an investment advisor who is unfamiliar with the client.

STEP 9: IMPLEMENT THE INVESTMENT STRATEGY

After the client approves the blueprint for the portfolio and the investment policy statement has been written, it is time to implement the strategy. If the client's current portfolio balance is different from that of the recommended target portfolio, the question arises as to the timetable for moving the portfolio to its target. For example, assume that a client currently has a short-term debt investments/longer-term bonds/equity investments portfolio balance of 70 percent/10 percent/20 percent. His target portfolio, however, is 35 percent/20 percent/45 percent. On the one hand, if his current balance is not appropriate given his investment objective and volatility tolerance, there is an argument for moving the portfolio quickly to its target. On the other hand, there are offsetting economic and psychological benefits to be gained by using a dollar-cost averaging strategy to gradually move the portfolio to its target.

Dollar-cost averaging is a simple technique that requires equal dollar investments to be made in an investment at regular time intervals. For example, if we want to invest $180,000 in common stocks, this could be accomplished by investing $10,000 per month for 18 months. When placing money in investments with variable principal values, such as common stocks, ideally you want to buy when prices are low. By following a dollar-cost averaging strategy, more shares are purchased when prices are low and fewer shares are purchased when prices are high. At the completion of the strategy, the average cost per share will be less than the average price paid for the shares. We know that in the short run, the returns from volatile investments can be very different from average long-term expectations. By establishing an investment position with equal dollar commitments at regular intervals, the probability increases that the client's investment experience will more closely resemble longer-term expectations.

There are psychological advantages as well. A target portfolio may have volatility/return characteristics that are decidedly different from the client's current portfolio. By moving to the target mix gradually, the client has a greater opportunity to

become familiar with and therefore more comfortable with the
new strategy. With greater comfort comes an increased likelihood that the client will remain committed to the strategy
through good and bad market conditions.

The time frame chosen for establishing the target portfolio
will be a compromise between the conflicting goals of establishing
the target portfolio quickly and taking more time to mitigate the
effects of possible adverse short-run market movements. In our
example above, 35 percent of the client's short-term debt investments will be moved to longer-term bonds and equity investments.
The more volatile the investment alternative to which you are
adding money, the longer the time period during which the investments should be dollar-cost averaged. Because stocks are more
volatile than bonds, it may be advisable to take 12 to 24 months
to move the portfolio to its target common stock commitment but
only 6 to 12 months to reach the target allocation for bonds.

Situations will arise where a client's current portfolio is
already at or near the ideal allocation among short-term debt
investments, longer-term bonds, and equity investments, but a
different mix of investment positions is advisable. In this case,
the new strategy can be implemented much more rapidly, provided the client is comfortable with the pace of implementation
and appropriate consideration has been given to the tax issues
involved.

Some unique planning considerations are involved with
clients who have a portion of their total investment portfolio
committed to tax-qualified retirement plans and IRAs.[4] We will
first consider the situation where the client has discretion over
how these funds are invested. Conventional wisdom says IRAs
are long-term investment vehicles and therefore should be funded
with long-term investments, such as common stocks. In this
case, however, conventional wisdom may not lead to the optimal
outcome. An IRA provides valuable tax-sheltering capability. To
derive maximum advantage from this tax deferral, it is important to use IRAs to shelter those portfolio investments that on
average generate the most annual taxable income per dollar of

---

4. Throughout this discussion we will refer to IRAs, but the logic applies equally to
   tax-qualified retirement plans and other tax-deferral vehicles.

value. These are not necessarily the common stock investment positions. To facilitate the correct decision regarding IRA investments, a two-step process is recommended. First, design the target investment portfolio without regard to the fact that an IRA will shelter part of the portfolio. Second, determine which one of the investment positions in the target portfolio generates the highest level of average annual taxable income per dollar invested. This is the investment that should be positioned inside the IRA. If there is room in the IRA for more investments, select the investment that generates the next highest level of taxable income from those investments remaining outside the IRA. By proceeding in this manner until the IRA is fully invested, the client will be assured of making the best use of the tax deferral available from the IRA.

For example, let us consider a client with a $400,000 investment portfolio, as shown in Table 12–3. Half of her portfolio is to be positioned outside of her IRA, with the other half positioned within her IRA. For this illustration, we will assume that the long-term capital gains are preferentially taxed with a 50 percent capital gain exclusion. Both of the common stock funds are expected to have pre-tax total returns of 12 percent. The S&P 500 Common Stock Index Fund, however, has a very significant portion of its total return in the form of unrealized capital appreciation. It is anticipated that the client will retain this position for the long term. Thus, this unrealized appreciation is in itself a valuable form of tax deferral. We can see under column (G) in Table 12–3 that the average annual taxable income generated by the position is only $2,500. By contrast, the Actively Traded Common Stock Fund has a high portfolio turnover, which constantly churns out most of its total return in the form of short-term and long-term capital gain distributions, leaving a smaller component of average unrealized capital appreciation.

By examining column (G), we see that the Actively Traded Common Stock Fund generates the highest level of average taxable income per dollar invested, followed by the Long-Term Corporate Bond Fund, the total return of which is almost entirely currently taxable ordinary income. Accordingly, the IRA should be funded with these two investment positions,

TABLE 12-3

Comparison of Investment Alternatives for an Individual Retirement Account

Investment Position	Amount Invested	(A) Taxable Interest or Dividend Income	(B) Average Short-Term Capital Gain Distribution	(C) Average Long-Term Capital Gain Distribution	(D)=.5(C) Capital Gain Exclusion	(E) Average Unrealized Capital Appreciation	(F)=(A)+(B)+(C)+(E) Pretax Total Return	(G)=(F)−(D)−(E) Average Taxable Income Generated
Short-Term Corporate Bond Fund	$100,000	$5,500	$ 200	$ 100	$ 50	$ 0	$ 5,800	$5,750
Long-Term Corporate Bond Fund	100,000	6,500	200	200	100	0	6,900	6,800
S&P 500 Common Index Fund Stock	100,000	2,000	0	1,000	500	9,000	12,000	2,500
Actively Traded Stock Fund Common	100,000	2,000	4,000	2,000	1,000	4,000	12,000	7,000

with the Short-Term Corporate Bond Fund and the S&P 500 Common Stock Index Fund held personally outside of the IRA.

Often, clients do not have discretion over the investment of money in their pension and profit-sharing plans. Investment advisors sometimes ignore these assets because there are no decisions to be made concerning them. This practice invites the creation of a less than optimal asset mix. Consider a client who has a $1 million investment portfolio, $400,000 of which is in an employer-sponsored retirement plan. Assume that the appropriate broad portfolio balance for the client is 45 percent short-term debt investments/15 percent longer-term bonds/40 percent equity investments. Table 12–4(A) shows the investment portfolio balance for the $600,000 that is under the client's control, if no consideration is given to the other $400,000 in the retirement plan.

Perhaps, however, the $400,000 in the employer-sponsored retirement plan is entirely invested in short-term debt investments. From the broader point of view of the client's entire $1 million portfolio, the actual balance is skewed heavily toward short-term debt investments, with a short-term debt investments/longer-term bonds/equity investments allocation of 67 percent/9 percent/24 percent, as shown in Table 12–4(B)(1). Alternatively, if the $400,000 in the retirement plan is invested in common stocks, the actual portfolio balance for the client is a short-term debt investments/longer-term bonds/equity investments balance of 27 percent/9 percent/64 percent, as shown in Table 12–4(B)(2). Table 12–4(C)(1) and (2) show the allocation of funds outside of the retirement plan required in order to achieve the proper balance for the portfolio as a whole. This example underscores the importance of always making portfolio decisions from a holistic point of view.

A subtler example of the same issue involves paying careful attention to the composition of the assets *within* an employer-sponsored tax qualified plan. It is not enough to simply make sure that the broad portfolio balance among short-term debt investments/longer-term bonds/equity investments is correct from the point of view of the total portfolio. If a significant portion of the client's equity investments is inside the employer-sponsored retirement plan and heavily oriented toward domestic large company stocks, it may be advisable for the client to invest his personally controlled equity money heavily toward international stocks, real estate investments, and small company stocks.

These issues become most pronounced in client situations that are heavily constrained. This occurred in the example in Table 12–4 where a significant percentage of the client's portfolio was under the control of the trustees of an employer-sponsored retirement plan. Similar constraints may occur where a large percentage of the client's portfolio is committed to nonliquid investments. The best way to handle these situations is to nevertheless go through the exercise of developing the ideal target portfolio as if the investment process could start from an all-cash position with no constraints. A comparison between the client's current, constrained portfolio and the ideal target will immediately clarify which modifications are most important and the order in which they should be implemented. The portfolio can then be moved toward the ideal target as the constraints permit.

At times, this will lead to what may appear to be strange investment advice. Consider an extremely constrained situation where only 10 percent of a $1 million portfolio can be repositioned. Perhaps the client has at least modest diversification across all major asset classes except international bonds and commodity-linked securities. The advisor's recommendation

T A B L E   1 2 – 4

Portfolio Balance Where a Client Lacks Investment Discretion over a Portion of the Portfolio

Facts			
$ 600,000	Fully discretionary investment funds		
400,000	Employer-sponsored retirement plan (no discretion)		
$1,000,000	Total portfolio		

(A) *45%/15%/40% Portfolio Balance If Considering Only Discretionary Funds*

Short-term debt investments	$270,000	45%
Longer-term bonds	90,000	15
Equity investments	240,000	40
Discretionary funds	$600,000	100%

T A B L E   1 2 - 4   (*Concluded*)

(B)(1) *Total Portfolio Balance If the Retirement Plan Is Invested in Short-Term Debt Investments*

	Discretionary Funds	Retirement Plan	Total	
Short-term debt investments	$270,000	$400,000	$ 670,000	67%
Longer-term bonds	90,000	0	90,000	9
Equity investments	240,000	0	240,000	24
Total portfolio	$600,000	$400,000	$1,000,000	100%

(B)(2) *Total Portfolio Balance If the Retirement Plan Is Invested in Equity Investments*

	Discretionary Funds	Retirement Plan	Total	
Short-term debt investments	$270,000	$ 0	$ 270,000	27%
Longer-term bonds	90,000	0	90,000	9
Equity investments	240,000	400,000	640,000	64
Total portfolio	$600,000	$400,000	$1,000,000	100%

(C)(1) *Required Positioning of Discretionary Funds to Maintain Proper Portfolio Balance If the Retirement Plan Is Invested in Short-Term Debt Investments*

	Discretionary Funds	Retirement Plan	Total	
Short-term debt investments	$ 50,000	$400,000	$ 450,000	45%
Longer-term bonds	150,000	0	150,000	15
Equity investments	400,000	0	400,000	40
Total portfolio	$600,000	$400,000	$1,000,000	100%

(C)(2) *Required Positioning of Discretionary Funds to Maintain Proper Portfolio Balance If the Retirement Plan Is Invested in Equity Investments*

	Discretionary Funds	Retirement Plan	Total	
Short-term debt investments	$450,000	$ 0	$ 450,000	45%
Longer-term bonds	150,000	0	150,000	15
Equity investments	0	400,000	400,000	40
Total portfolio	$600,000	$400,000	$1,000,000	100%

may be to invest $60,000 in international bonds and $40,000 in commodity-linked securities. Considered in isolation from the point of view of the $100,000 available for investment, this is indeed strange advice, but it is nevertheless entirely appropriate from the point of view of the total portfolio. This presents some obvious problems regarding the measurement of the investment advisor's performance results. It is thus essential that clients understand the context within which such recommendations are made.

Comprehensive portfolio management in today's world requires two separate levels of decision making. Each level can add value for the client if done properly, and each level therefore justifies appropriate compensation. The first level, which is the more important of the two, involves the development of realistic investment objectives and asset allocation strategies. This requires that investment advisors have an in-depth knowledge of and close working relationships with their clients. The second level of decision making involves the selection of individual investments within each of the asset classes. We have already commented on the difficulties inherent in trying to "beat the market" through superior investment skill. Those who are capable of doing so usually specialize in one particular segment of the world's capital markets, and their continued success necessitates their full-time organizational commitment to their specialty. A successful domestic small company stock manager, for example, is not likely to become a leader in real estate investing. Similarly, managers who specialize in security selection for a particular market segment will not have the means for developing the kind of relationship needed with a client in order to tackle issues at the asset allocation level of decision making.

The days of a client giving his investment portfolio to a single, balanced manager are over. Today money management requires the different skills and organizational commitments that correspond to the two levels of investment decision making just described. Mutual funds provide an excellent means of obtaining the desired breadth of diversification for an investment portfolio. This, of course, raises the issue of two layers of management fees. The two layers of fees are justified, provided that value is being added at each level of decision making. In the long run, the asset allocation decisions are more important with respect to their impact on long-term portfolio results than is the selection of individual investments within each asset class. These tasks accordingly deserve compensation if done well. If they are not done well, the advisory relationship should be terminated. Similarly, at the level of individual security selection, the money management specialist should be paid for work well done. If a specialist does not perform adequately, a replacement should be found who will be worthy of the compensation. Alternatively, index funds can be used as portfolio building blocks.

In Chapters 10 through 12, we have completed all but the last step of the money management process outlined in Figure 12–1. Figure 12–6 shows a sample investment policy decision-making agenda, which guides the client through the steps to develop an individually tailored investment strategy consistent with his or her volatility tolerance and financial goals. At times, clients may express impatience with the time and energy commitment that this investment decision-making process demands. I strongly recommend, however, that the process not be rushed to a conclusion. A client who takes the time required to thoughtfully participate in the design of his or portfolio will be a better investor who is more likely to reach his or her financial goals.

STEP 10: REPORT PERFORMANCE AND REVISE THE PORTFOLIO

Performance Reporting

Performance measurement is a particularly troublesome issue for both investment advisors and their clients. One difficulty arises from the fact that the performance measurement interval, usually a calendar quarter, is much too short relative to the typical investment time horizon. The broad portfolio balance decision-making model in Table 6–2 emphasizes this fact by placing the modeled return in the context of its associated typical range of results. The investment policy statement should also contain information regarding the range and likelihood of

FIGURE 12-6

Investment Policy Decision-Making Agenda

I.   Determinants of Portfolio Performance –*Figure 1-2*

II.   Historical Review of Capital Market Investment Performance –*Figure 2-1* and
        Table 3-1

III.   Two Major Risks All Investors Face
        A.   Inflation – *Table 2-1*
        B.   Volatility – *Figure 6-1*

IV.   Time Horizon –*Table 5-1, Figures 5-1* and *5-2*

V.   The Broad Portfolio Balance Decision –*Tables 6-1 and 6-2, Figures 6-2* through *6-6*

VI.   Multiple-Asset-Class Investing
        A.   The Diversification Effect – *Figure 7-3*
        B.   International Diversification of a Bond Portfolio – *Figure 8-1*
        C.   International Diversification of a Stock Portfolio – *Figure 8-2*
        D.   The Rewards of Multiple-Asset-Class Investing – *Figure 8-5, Tables 8-3 and 8-4*
        E.   Frame of Reference Risk – *Figure 11-4, Tables 11-1 and 11-2*

VII.   Asset Allocation Decisions
        A.   World Capital Market Pie Chart –*Figure 1-1*
        B.   Investment Portfolio Design Format –*Figure 12-2*
                1. First: Broad Portfolio Balance Decision
                2. Second: Choice of Asset Classes
                            Short-term debt investments
                            Domestic bonds
                            International bonds
                            Domestic stocks
                            International stocks
                            Real estate investments
                            Investment hedges
                3. Third: Allocation Across the Asset Classes to Determine the Degree of
                    Diversification –*Table 11-3, Figures 11-5* through *11-7, Tables 11-4* and 11-5

VIII.   Portfolio Modeling
        A.   Modeling the Performance Characteristics of the Asset Allocation Design
                1. Are the return characteristics consistent with the financial goals?
                2. Is the downside risk acceptable?
        B.   Confirmation or Modification of the Asset Allocation Design

IX.   Final Portfolio Design
        A. Choice of Investment Positions for Strategy Implementation
        B. Logistics and Time Frame for Implementing the Investment Strategy

X.   Preparation of the Investment Policy Statement

possible portfolio returns. (See the sample investment policy statement in the Appendix to this chapter.)

An additional performance measurement challenge arises from the dissimilarities between the returns of a broadly diversified portfolio compared with those of a more traditional mix of U.S. stocks, bonds, and cash equivalents. This is the frame-of-reference risk issue we discussed at length in Chapter 11. The S&P 500 is simply not a suitable benchmark for a broadly diversified portfolio. A more appropriate evaluation benchmark can be constructed by taking a weighted average of the portfolio's asset class index returns. This evaluation benchmark methodology is illustrated in the executive summary section of the sample investment policy statement contained in the appendix. Given the volatility inherent in the capital markets and the issue of frame-of-reference risk, clients should not attach too much significance to their short-term investment experience. The effectiveness and value of an asset allocation strategy can be measured only over longer periods of time.

For an investment advisor pursuing an active asset allocation approach, the actual results can be compared with the results that would have been achieved had the normal asset mix been maintained. Finally, the returns for the various specific investment positions should be compared to appropriate benchmarks. For example, the performance of a large company stock manager can be measured against the Standard & Poor's 500 Stock Composite Index (S&P 500) and an intermediate-term, high-quality bond manager's results can be compared with the Lehman Brothers Intermediate Government/Corporate Bond Index.

In the long run, the goal of money management is the successful fulfillment of the client's objectives. In this context, less attention should be focused on "beating the market" and more attention should be given to evaluating the portfolio's performance in terms of its progress toward the realization of the client's financial goals.

Portfolio Revision

A client's asset allocation decisions define a "normal asset mix." We will refer to this normal asset mix as the *strategic asset allocation*. The normal asset mix is, by definition, the most appropriate portfolio balance to maintain on average over time, given the client's investment objective and volatility tolerance. For an advisor advocating a passive asset allocation approach, the normal asset mix is the target percentage allocations to be closely maintained in managing the portfolio. A passive approach assumes that markets are efficient and that gains from market timing are unlikely.

A passive approach is not synonymous with a buy and hold strategy. With a buy and hold strategy, there is no portfolio rebalancing. As a result, the relative proportions of the asset classes will vary over time as the capital markets move. This will produce an undesirable variation in the portfolio's volatility level. In the short run, it will also result in always being wrong at every major market turn. For example, with a buy and hold strategy, the portfolio's equity commitment, and hence its volatility exposure, reaches its maximum as a bull market ends and a bear market begins. Conversely, the equity commitment will be at its minimum at the end of a bear market, as the next bull market gets under way. In the long run, a buy and hold strategy will result in an increasingly greater percentage of the portfolio being committed to equities, due to their higher returns. This produces an undesirable trend of increasing volatility exposure coupled with a shortening time horizon.

By contrast, a passive rebalancing of the portfolio back to its target percentages has several advantages:

- It is easy to understand and implement.

- A more constant portfolio volatility level is maintained for the client.

- A balanced diversification of portfolio assets is preserved.
- It provides strict discipline that prevents the portfolio from becoming overweighted in equities at market tops and underweighted in equities at market bottoms.

In order to rebalance the portfolio to the normal asset mix, money is continually reallocated from the most recent better-performing investments to the relative underperformers. For example, during a bull stock market, the portfolio's equity commitment will become larger than its target allocation. Returning to the target allocation thus necessitates selling stocks during a bull market. Conversely, to maintain portfolio balance during a bear market, stocks must be bought. The passive asset allocation approach is inherently "buy low, sell high" and is also contrarian in nature.

Active asset allocation can take a variety of forms. *Dynamic asset allocation* alters the asset mix in an attempt to gain downside protection. As stock prices decline, stocks are sold, thus making the portfolio less susceptible to further losses. As stock prices advance, stocks are bought in an attempt to increase the equity participation on the upside. This approach can be characterized as "sell low, buy high."

Tactical asset allocation approaches engage in market timing in an attempt to "beat the market." These approaches attempt to "buy low, sell high." To accomplish this, deviations from the normal asset mix are intentionally made in response to perceived changing market opportunities. Of course, tactical asset allocation approaches presume the existence of exploitable market inefficiencies and the requisite skill to capitalize on them. Advisors engaged in tactical asset allocation use a variety of methods, many of which rely on business cycle analysis involving multiple economic scenario forecasting. For example, an advisor may describe the future state of the economy according to four possibilities: depression, stagflation, favorable conditions, or high inflation. Probabilities are then assigned to each of the four possible states of the economy. To do this, projections are made for a wide variety of economic factors, such as GNP growth, interest rate outlook, corporate profitability, government fiscal and monetary policy, inflation outlook, level and growth rate of private versus public debt, international balance of trade, consumer spending and savings rates, currency exchange rates, and so on. Next, return estimates are made for each asset class under each of the four scenarios. Finally, the estimated return for each asset class is determined by taking the weighted average of each asset class's return estimates for the four scenarios, using the probabilities of the scenarios as weights. Table 12–5 shows an example of these calculations. Based on a comparison of the asset classes' estimated returns, opportunities are identified that (hopefully) can be translated into advantageous deviations from the normal asset mix. To the extent to which the approach produces exploitable, unique insights different from consensus market expectations, there may be an opportunity to add value.

Another tactical asset allocation approach involves the use of a dividend discount model to project the estimated return

TABLE 12-5

Calculation of Expected Returns Based on Economic Scenario Forecasting

(A)	(B)	(C)	(D)	(E)	(F)=(B)×(C)	(G)=(B)×(D)	(H)=(B)×(E)
		Scenario-Based Estimated Return			Expected Return Calculation		
Economic Scenario	Probability	Treasury Bills	Bonds	Stocks	Treasury Bills	Bonds	Stocks
Depression	.1	3%	25%	–20%	.3%	2.5%	–2.0%
Stagflation	.4	7%	8%	12%	2.8%	3.2%	4.8%
Favorable conditions	.3	5%	12%	25%	1.5%	3.6%	7.5%
High inflation	.2	10%	–10%	10%	2.0%	–2.0%	2.0%
Expected return =					6.6%	7.3%	12.3%

from stocks. This tactical approach rests on the notion that there are normal relationships between the returns available from cash equivalents, bonds, and stocks. The return for a Treasury bill or bond is easily estimated by simply calculating the security's yield to maturity. To estimate the return for a stock, however, requires a different approach. For example, to estimate IBM's return, projections would be made of IBM's future stream of dividend payments. The estimated return for IBM is simply the discount rate that equates the present value of the future stream of dividend payments to the current market value of IBM. By proceeding in this manner for all other common stocks, an estimated return for the stock market as a whole can be built from the bottom up.

If the spread between Treasury bill yields and the estimated return on the stock market is narrow relative to normal relationships, the portfolio will be tilted toward short-term debt investments due to the less than normal payoff anticipated from owning stocks. Conversely, if the spread is unusually wide, stocks may be undervalued and the portfolio will accordingly be tilted toward a heavier stock commitment. Although this approach has produced some good results in the past, as more investors utilize the approach, the efficiency of the market will increase along this dimension and the corresponding rewards from following the strategy will trend toward zero.

With less than truly superior predictive ability, it is quite easy for an active asset allocation strategy to provide returns inferior to those available with passive asset allocation approaches. For this reason, if active asset allocation strategies are employed, it is wise to establish minimum and maximum allocation limits for each asset class. This will ensure some minimum level of portfolio diversification and limit the potential for problems associated with an overcommitment to any single asset class.

APPENDIX: Investment Policy Statement

INVESTMENT POLICY STATEMENT

for

Mary Smith

Approved on December 31, 1998

It is intended that this investment policy statement be reviewed and updated at least annually. Any change to this investment policy statement should be communicated in writing on a timely basis to all interested parties.

The Center for Fiduciary Studies has prepared this Investment Policy Statement (IPS). It is intended to serve as an example of the type of information that would be included in a comprehensive IPS. Clients are advised to have legal counsel review their IPS before it is approved.

TABLE OF CONTENTS

EXECUTIVE SUMMARY

Type of Client: Taxable, Individual

Current Portfolio Assets: $1,000,000

Time Horizon: Greater than 15 years

Modeled Return: 10.7% (6.7% over CPI)

Modeled Distribution of Returns:

The table below describes the modeled range of probable returns from the portfolio. It also describes the likelihood of these returns. For example, there is a 10% likelihood that the portfolio will have a 1-year return below –3.3%.

Year	Modeled Downside Volatility 1st%	10th%	25th%	50th%	75th%	90th%	99th%
1	-13.5	-3.3	3.1	10.7	18.9	26.8	41.7
3	-4.0	2.4	6.3	10.7	15.4	19.8	27.7
5	-0.8	4.2	7.2	10.7	14.3	17.7	23.6
10	2.4	6.1	8.3	10.7	13.3	15.6	19.7
15	3.9	6.9	8.7	10.7	12.8	14.7	18.0
25	5.4	7.8	9.2	10.7	12.3	13.8	16.3

Projected Returns Across Time Horizon

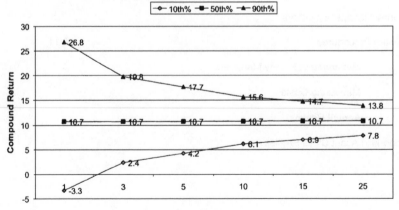

EXECUTIVE SUMMARY – CONTINUED

Broad Portfolio Balance:

Interest-Generating Investments	30%
Equity Investments	70%
Total Portfolio	100%

Asset Allocation:

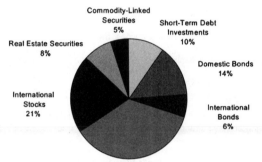

	Lower Limit	**Strategic Allocation**	Upper Limit
Short-Term Debt Investments	8%	**10%**	12%
Domestic Bonds	12%	**14%**	16%
International Bonds	5%	**6%**	7%
Domestic Stocks	31%	**36%**	41%
International Stocks	17%	**21%**	25%
Real Estate Securities	6%	**8%**	10%
Commodity-Linked Securities	4%	**5%**	6%

Evaluation Benchmark: Weighted average of the asset class index returns.

BACKGROUND and PURPOSE

This Investment Policy Statement (IPS) has been prepared for Mary Smith ("Client"), a taxable entity. The assets covered by this IPS currently total approximately $1,000,000 in market value and the Client's net worth is estimated to be $1,350,000. Assets not covered by this IPS include a home and tangible personal property valued at $350,000.

Key Information:

SSN:	123-45-6789
Investment Advisor:	ABC Investment Group, Inc.
Custodian:	XYZ Custodial Services, Inc.
Accountant:	John Smith, CPA
Attorney:	Jane Doe, Esq.

The purpose of this IPS is to assist the Client and Investment Advisor (Advisor) in effectively supervising, monitoring and evaluating the management of the Client's assets. The Client's investment program is defined in the various sections of this IPS by:

1. Stating in a written document the Client's attitudes, expectations, objectives and guidelines in the management of her assets.

2. Setting forth an investment structure for managing the Client's assets. This structure diversifies the Client's portfolio across various asset classes and investment management styles in accordance with specified strategic allocation targets and acceptable lower/upper limits for the asset class commitments. In designing the structure, consideration has been given to the Client's investment time horizon, volatility tolerance, tax status and investment objective.

3. Encouraging effective communications between the Client and the Advisor.

4. Establishing formal criteria to select, monitor, evaluate and compare the performance of money managers on a regular basis.

STATEMENT of INVESTMENT OBJECTIVE and PARAMETERS

This IPS describes the prudent investment process that the Advisor deems appropriate for the Client's situation. The Client desires to maximize returns within prudent levels of volatility and to meet the following stated financial goals and investment objective:

Financial Goals:

1. Retire in December, 2007—The Client wants to maintain her current lifestyle during retirement by withdrawing an annual inflation-adjusted, after-tax cash flow of $50,000 (1998 dollars) from her portfolio to supplement her pension and social security benefits.

2. Provide $60,000 of educational funds for her grandson who will be entering college in September, 1999.

Investment Objective: High total return with high portfolio volatility

Volatility Tolerance

The Client recognizes and acknowledges that volatility must be assumed in order to achieve the investment objective, and that there are risks and uncertainties associated with the investment markets.

In determining the investment objective, the Client's ability to withstand short and intermediate term portfolio volatility was considered. The Client's current financial condition, prospects for the future, and other factors suggest that interim fluctuations in portfolio market value and rates of return can be tolerated in seeking to achieve the investment objective.

Asset Class Preferences

The Advisor and Client believe that investment performance is determined largely by the portfolio's asset allocation. The Client has reviewed the long-term performance characteristics of different asset classes in order to understand the various kinds of investment risks and the expected rewards associated with bearing those risks.

Historically, interest-generating investments, such as Treasury bills, have had the advantage of relative stability of principal value, but they provide little opportunity for real long-term capital growth due to their susceptibility to inflation. On the other hand, equity investments, such as common stocks, have a significantly higher expected return but have the disadvantage of much greater volatility of principal value. From an investment decision-making point of view, this volatility is worth bearing, provided the time horizon for the portfolio is sufficiently long. The longer the investment time horizon, the more likely it is that equity investments will outperform interest-generating investments.

In order to have a sound frame of reference for making the asset allocation decisions, the Client has reviewed research concerning the advantages, disadvantages, as well as the "frame of reference" risk, associated with multiple-asset-class investing. The Client and Advisor have agreed to follow a policy of diversification across multiple asset classes in order to mitigate the risks associated with the investment objective.

The following asset classes were selected:
- Short-Term Debt Investments
- Domestic Bonds
- International Bonds
- Domestic Stocks
- International Stocks
- Real Estate Securities
- Commodity-Linked Securities

The performance characteristics (modeled returns, standard deviations and correlations) for the asset classes are contained in Appendix A.

Investment Time Horizon

The investment guidelines are based upon an investment horizon of greater than 15 years. Therefore, interim portfolio volatility should be viewed with an appropriate perspective. Short-term liquidity requirements are anticipated to be minimal.

Modeled Return

The Client understands that, as of the date of this IPS, the portfolio has a modeled return of 10.7% with an equal likelihood of either outperforming or under-performing that return. The portfolio's downside risk for a 1-year horizon is modeled as follows:

- 50% likelihood of a return less than 10.7%
- 25% likelihood of a return less than 3.1%
- 10% likelihood of a return less than −3.3%

Over the Client's 15-year investment time horizon, the portfolio's downside risk is modeled as follows:

- 50% likelihood of a compound return less than 10.7%
- 25% likelihood of a compound return less than 8.7%
- 10% likelihood of a compound return less than 6.9%

Rebalancing of Strategic Asset Allocation

The percentage allocation to each asset class will be reviewed at least quarterly and will be permitted to vary within the range specified in the Executive Summary. Cash inflows and outflows will be deployed in a manner consistent with the strategic asset allocation of the portfolio. If there are no cash flows, or if the cash flows are insufficient to bring the portfolio within the specified asset allocation range, the Advisor will confer with the Client regarding the transactions necessary to restore the appropriate portfolio allocation.

DUTIES AND RESPONSIBILITIES

Investment Advisor

The Client has retained an objective, third-party Advisor to assist in managing the investments. The Advisor will be responsible for guiding the Client through a disciplined and rigorous investment process. As a fiduciary to the Client, the primary responsibilities of the Advisor are to:

1. Prepare and maintain an investment policy statement.

2. Provide sufficient asset classes with different expected return/volatility profiles so that the Client can prudently diversify the portfolio.

3. Prudently select investment options for the Client's consideration.

4. Control and account for all investment expenses.

5. Monitor and supervise all service vendors and investment options.

6. Monitor the portfolio's asset allocation and rebalance the portfolio in accordance with the Client's instructions.

7. Avoid prohibited transactions and conflicts of interest.

Money Managers

As distinguished from the Advisor, who is responsible for managing the investment process, money managers are co-fiduciaries responsible for security selection and price decisions. The specific duties and responsibilities of each money manager are to:

1. Manage the assets under their supervision in accordance with the guidelines and objectives outlined in their respective Prospectus, Trust Agreement, or Contract.

2. Exercise full investment discretion with respect to buying, managing, and selling securities held in the portfolios.

3. Vote promptly all proxies and related actions in a consistent manner. The money manager shall keep detailed records of the voting of proxies and related actions and will comply with all applicable regulatory obligations.

4. Use the same care, skill, prudence, and due diligence under the circumstances then prevailing that experienced investment professionals, acting in a like capacity and fully familiar with such matters, would use in similar activities for like Clients with like aims in accordance and compliance with all applicable laws, rules, and regulations.

Custodian

Custodians are co-fiduciaries responsible for safe keeping of the Client's assets. The specific duties and responsibilities of the custodian are to:

1. Maintain separate accounts by legal registration (individual, joint, in trust).

2. Hold title to the assets on behalf of the Client.

3. Value the assets.

4. Collect all income owed to the Client and make payments on behalf of the Client that are related to the assets held for the Client.

5. Settle transactions on behalf of the Client. The Advisor or Money Manager places a buy or sell order with a broker and communicates the details of the open order to the custodian. The broker contacts the custodian to deliver the asset and receive payment or to make payment and receive the asset. The Advisor or Money Manager never has possession of the Client's assets.

6. Report to the Client on a regular basis a detailed list of transactions, cash activity, and assets owned including the number of units held, the unit price and total value.

MONEY MANAGER SELECTION

The Advisor and Client will apply the following due diligence criteria in selecting each individual investment option.

1. *Regulatory oversight:* Each money manager must be subject to regulatory oversight as either a mutual fund, a bank, an insurance company, or a registered investment advisor.

2. *Correlation to style or peer group:* The manager's investment product should be highly correlated to an appropriate index and/or peer group. This is one of the most critical parts of the analysis, since most of the remaining due diligence involves comparisons of the manager to the appropriate peer group.

3. *Performance relative to a peer group:* The product's performance should be above median for the peer group for annual and cumulative periods (1, 3, and 5-year returns).

4. *Performance relative to assumed risk:* The product should have above median risk-adjusted performance when measured against the manager's peer group as reflected by the fund's Alpha statistic, Sharpe ratio, and/or other risk-adjusted performance measures.

5. *Minimum track record:* The product's inception date should be greater than three years, and the same portfolio management team should have been in place for at least two years.

6. *Assets under management:* The manager should have at least $75 million under management within the screened product.

7. *Holdings consistent with style:* The screened product should have no more than 20% of the portfolio invested in "unrelated" asset class securities. For example, a U.S. large cap stock fund should not hold more than 20% of its portfolio in non-U.S. stock investments such as cash equivalents, bonds or international securities.

8. *Expense ratios/fees:* The screened product should not be in the top quartile (most expensive) of its peer group.

9. *Stability of the organization:* There should be no perceived organizational problems. Examples include personnel turnover, regulatory issues, assets coming in faster than the manager can handle, or problems in obtaining "best price and execution" in trading.

Low cost, passively managed index funds that track asset class indices are viable investment options when available.

CONTROL PROCEDURES

Monitoring of Money Managers

The Client acknowledges that fluctuating rates of return characterize the securities markets, particularly in the short run. Recognizing that short-term market volatility will cause variations in performance, the Client intends to evaluate manager performance from a longer-term perspective.

On a timely basis, but not less than quarterly, the Advisor will provide the Client with a review as to whether each manager continues to conform to the search criteria outlined in the previous section; specifically:

- The manager's adherence to the investment guidelines;
- Material changes in the manager's organization, investment philosophy and/or personnel; and,
- Any legal, SEC and/or other regulatory agency proceedings affecting the firm of which the Advisor is aware.

The Advisor has specified performance benchmarks for each investment manager. Manager performance will be evaluated relative to an appropriate market index and the relevant peer group. For example, an international stock manager's performance will be compared to the MSCI EAFE Index, as well as the Foreign Stock mutual fund universe.

Asset Class	Index	Peer Group Universe
Short-Term Debt Investments		
Cash Equivalents	90 Day T-Bills	Money Market Database
Short-Term Bonds	Lehman Brothers 1-3 Year Government	Short-Term Bond
Domestic Bonds		
Intermediate-Term	Lehman Brothers Intermediate Government/Corporate	Intermediate-Term Bond
Long-Term	Lehman Brothers Long-Term Government/Corporate	Long-Term Bond
International Bonds	Salomon Brothers Non-U.S.-Dollar World Government	International Bond
Domestic Stocks		
Large Company	S&P 500	Large Cap Blend
Mid Company	S&P 400	Mid Cap Blend
Small Company	Russell 2000	Small Cap Blend
International Stocks		
Major Markets	MSCI EAFE	Foreign Stock
Emerging Markets	MSCI Emerging Markets	Diversified Emerging Markets
Real Estate Securities	NAREIT Equity	Specialty Real Estate
Commodity-Linked Securities	Goldman Sachs Commodity Index	N/A

The Client is aware that the ongoing review and analysis of a money manager is just as important as the due diligence implemented during the manager selection process. A manager evaluation may be initiated if a significant event occurs that could interfere with the manager's ability to fulfill its role in the future. Examples of such events include:

- Change in investment professionals
- Significant account losses
- Significant growth of new business
- Change in ownership

A manager evaluation may also be initiated for investment performance reasons, such as:

- A manager performs in the bottom quartile (75th percentile) of the peer group over two or more quarters.
- A manager performs below the median (50th percentile) of the peer group over three or more years.

- A manager's 3-year risk-adjusted return falls below that of the median manager within the peer group.

The manager evaluation may include:

- An analysis of recent transactions, holdings and portfolio characteristics to determine the cause for under performance or to verify a change in style.
- A review of correspondence from the manager or reports from research firms on the manager's performance.

The gathered information is evaluated to provide a basis for a decision to either:

- Retain the manager in a normal capacity;
- Retain subject to a "watchlist" status; or
- Terminate.

Ultimately the decision to retain or terminate a manager cannot be made by a formula. It is a judgment based on the Advisor's and Client's confidence of the manager's ability to perform in the future.

Measuring Costs

The Advisor will review, at least annually, all costs associated with the management of the Client's investment program, including:

- Expense ratios, or investment fees, of each investment option against the appropriate peer group.
- Custody fees: The holding of the assets, collection of the income and disbursement of payments.

Annual Review

The Client will review this IPS at least annually to determine whether stated investment objectives are still relevant. The Advisor will review the IPS at least annually to determine the continued feasibility of achieving the Client's investment objectives. It is not expected that the IPS will change frequently. In particular, short-term changes in the financial markets should not require adjustments to the IPS.

Prepared: Approved:

December 31, 1998   December 31, 1998

ABC Investment Group, Inc.   Client

Appendix: Asset Class Profiles

Modeled Performance Statistics

Asset Class	Simple Average Return	Standard Deviation	Compound Annual Return
	%	%	%
Short-Term Debt Investments	5	3	5
Domestic Bonds	6	8	6
International Bonds	7	12	6
Domestic Stocks	14	20	12
International Stocks	15	22	13
Real Estate Securities	12	18	10
Commodity-Linked Securities	9	24	6

The simple average return is approximately equal to the compound return plus one-half of the variance. For example, Domestic Stocks have a modeled simple average return of 14 percent, a modeled compound annual return of 12 percent, and a standard deviation of 20 percent. The simple average return of 14 percent is approximately equal to the compound annual return of 12 percent plus one-half of the variance (standard deviation squared):

$$14 \text{ percent} = .14 \approx .12 + .5(.20)^2 = .14 = 14 \text{ percent}$$

The simple average return (not the compound annual return) should be used as the expected return input to a portfolio optimization program.

Modeled Correlations

Asset Class	(1)	(2)	(3)	(4)	(5)	(6)	(7)
(1) Short-Term Debt Investments	1.00						
(2) Domestic Bonds	.03	1.00					
(3) International Bonds	-.45	.17	1.00				
(4) Domestic Stocks	-.02	.42	.13	1.00			
(5) International Stocks	-.20	.16	.58	.55	1.00		
(6) Real Estate Securities	-.06	.28	.04	.70	.40	1.00	
(7) Commodity-Linked Securities	.03	-.31	-.03	-.35	-.12	-.19	1.00

CHAPTER 13

Resolving Problems Encountered During Implementation

There is nothing more profitable for a man than to take good counsel with himself; for even if the event turns out contrary to one's hope, still one's decision was right, even though fortune has made it of no effect: whereas if a man acts contrary to good counsel, although by luck he gets what he had no right to expect, his decision was not any the less foolish.

—Herodotus (c. 485–425 B.C.)
Histories

CLIENT INERTIA

Recommendations to sell old familiar investments in order to buy new unfamiliar investments can generate client anxiety even though the changes may substantially improve the risk/return characteristics of a portfolio. This is complicated by the fact that clients tend to psychologically equate familiarity and comfort with safety. This can result in inertia. Although the recommended target portfolio looks good, it is difficult for the client to begin implementing the strategy. More than once I have had the following kind of conversation with a client:

> *Advisor:* "You have a very large percentage of your total portfolio committed to XYZ stock."
>
> *Client:* "Yes, it has really done well. I bought it a few years ago for $10 per share, and now it is worth $85 per share."

> *Advisor:* "That is great performance, but I'm concerned about the diversifiable volatility you retain by continuing to hold such a large position. The marketplace does not provide any compensation for volatility that can be eliminated through broad diversification."
>
> *Client:* "Yes, but I really like XYZ stock."
>
> *Advisor:* "The target portfolio we have designed can accommodate a position in the stock if you prefer, but we recommend that you substantially reduce the commitment. We have considered the tax implications of our recommendation and suggest that at least one third of your position be sold this year, with another one third sold next year. The remainder can be retained."
>
> *Client:* "I understand what you are saying, but why should I get off a winning horse?"
>
> *Advisor:* "Assume for a moment that you do not own the stock but have a sum of cash equal in value to your current stock commitment. Would you buy that much XYZ stock at today's price of $85 per share?"
>
> *Client:* "No. I would never purchase a position that big if I had to buy it at today's price!"

The conversation is followed by a long pause while the client ponders his response.

There is a tendency for clients to view appreciated assets as bargains, because they think of them in terms of their low purchase prices. Of course, historical cost has nothing to do with whether the stock will continue to perform well from its current market value of $85 per share. By being asked whether he would purchase the stock today if he did not already own it, the client will be liberated from his preoccupation with his low historical cost. This is sometimes sufficient to resolve the issue in favor of reducing the commitment. If an inappropriately high position in the stock is retained, the client should understand that he is assuming diversifiable volatility for which there is no expected compensation.

The tax issues involved with the sale of an appreciated investment often complicate the decision, however. Unless a client expects to hold the appreciated investment until he or she dies, the income taxes due on the gain will have to be paid sooner or later. Although it is true that the taxes will not be paid until the investment is sold, the government's claim on its share of the appreciation nevertheless exists. For this reason, it may be advisable to carry the investment on the client's balance sheet at a lower value that adjusts for the anticipated taxes due upon sale. This accomplishes two things. First, it generates client awareness that the investment should not be retained merely because its sale will trigger the payment of income taxes. Second, it avoids the perception of a decrease in net worth as a result of the sale.

Another complicating factor is added when the appreciated asset has a good income yield. Although the government has a claim on the unrealized appreciation, the client nevertheless gets the entire income stream from the investment. Consider a stock with a $10 per share tax basis, now selling for $60 per share. If it pays $3.60 per year in dividends, its current income yield is 6 percent. Assume that upon sale, 30 percent of the realized gain will be lost to income taxes. This leaves after-tax sale proceeds of $45 available for repositioning. In order to generate the same $3.60 per share in income, we need to find a stock with an 8 percent yield ($45.00 × .08 = $3.60). This factor needs to be carefully weighed in the retention/disposition decision.

A client's age and health also need to be considered when evaluating the disposition of an appreciated asset. Our current income tax code provides for a "stepped-up tax basis" for appreciated assets upon the investor's death. If the investor in the above example was terminally ill, retention of this stock would probably be advisable. Upon his death, his survivors would inherit the stock with a tax basis stepped up to the current market value. This sidesteps the $15 per share that would otherwise be lost to income taxes had the investor sold the stock prior to his death.

Sometimes the advisor recommends that an investment be sold that has an unusually large unrealized capital loss. Here, the advisor/client conversation may sound like this:

Advisor: "We recommend that your position in ABC Company be liquidated because it is not a preferred investment for the recommended target portfolio we designed together."

Client: "Yes, that stock has been rotten. I bought it for $50 per share, and now it's worth only $8 per share. But if I sell it now, I'll lose money." (Note the subtle implication that if it is not sold, no money is lost!)

Advisor: "You have already lost the money."

Client: "No, I haven't. It's just a paper loss." (The comment presumes paper losses have no economic significance.)

Advisor: "Assume for a moment that you do not own the stock but have a sum of cash equal to your current commitment. Would you buy it today at $8 per share?"

Client: "No way. I can't wait to sell it, and as soon as it gets back to $50 per share, I'm dumping it!"

The psychology underlying the "paper loss syndrome" is the conviction that no money is lost unless the position is sold and that paper losses have no economic substance. Again, apart from tax considerations, historical cost should have nothing to do with the retention/sale decision. What the client is really resisting is the admission of having made an investment that did not work out well. Once it is sold for a loss, the verdict is unavoidably apparent. But if the investment is held, there is still hope that some day the investment will break even.

These problems can often be overcome by the recommended exercise of having the client hypothetically assume that his or her entire portfolio has been converted to cash before designing the new target portfolio. This frees the client from past decisions, with the result that new recommendations are no longer pitted against the sale of old and familiar positions. The entire range of investment options, including those positions the client currently owns, are available for consideration as building blocks for the target portfolio. With this approach, a client may still decide to have some of the old familiar investments retained, but the likelihood is that the chosen percentage allocation for these investments will be more reasonable.

Investment decisions should be active. Traditionally, investment recommendations have been classified as *buy, hold,* or *sell*. I think "hold" recommendations often evade the responsibility for making active decisions and that the sell rule and the buy rule should be one and the same. The general rule stated simply is: Hold in your portfolio only those investments that you would actively repurchase if you did not already own them. Sell everything else.

BIG DOLLAR DECISIONS

Investing large sums of money is an anxiety-producing situation for many clients. This is particularly true for unsophisticated clients who may have suddenly won the lottery or received a large inheritance. For the first time in their lives they may be facing the need to make major investment decisions. Encouraging the client to think holistically regarding the entire portfolio and expressing investment recommendations as a percentage of the total portfolio can alleviate part of the anxiety. For example, a recommendation to invest 3 percent of a $1 million portfolio in commodity-linked securities sounds much less dramatic than investing $30,000 in the same position.

RESISTANCE TO SPECIFIC INVESTMENT RECOMMENDATIONS

It is the client's money, and it is appropriate that the client have veto power over any investment recommendation. Occasionally, however, a client rejects a specific investment for the wrong reasons. For example, a client may reject a recommended position in an international stock mutual fund. As you dig deeper, it becomes apparent that she is not objecting to the specific investment recommendation. Rather, she is uncomfortable with international stocks as an asset class. When this occurs, it indicates that a prior, more general level of decision making was not firmed up properly before proceeding to the next step.

The portfolio design process should proceed from the broad portfolio balance level to the more delineated asset allocation level and then finally to the specific investment positions. Each level of decision making should be firmly established before proceeding to the next. If done properly, this will generate a positive momentum in the decision-making process and avoid the situation where a client objects to a specific investment for reasons that should have been addressed at a more general level of decision making. It is fine for a client to object to a specific investment as long as the objection relates to that level of decision making. If it does not, it is important to withdraw the recommendation and move back to the more general level of decision making that involves the source of the objection. The resolution may require a modification of either the broad portfolio balance decision or the asset allocation strategy, which in turn will necessitate a redesigned target portfolio.

OBTAINING CASH FROM THE PORTFOLIO FOR THE CLIENT'S EXPENDITURES

Advisor: "Here is the recommended target portfolio. It is broadly diversified among multiple asset classes and will maximize the portfolio's expected return subject to your volatility tolerance and time horizon."

Client: "Nice portfolio, but I couldn't possibly live on that yield. Why don't we cut down on the stock investments and reposition the proceeds in bonds until the portfolio yield matches my income needs?"

Table 13–1 shows the components of return for three asset mixes of bonds and stocks. Assume that a particular client should have an asset mix of 50 percent bonds and 50 percent stocks, given her investment time horizon and volatility tolerance. This portfolio has an expected total return of 9 percent, composed of a 4 percent current yield plus a 5 percent average rate of capital appreciation. If the client has a $1 million portfolio, this mix will generate an income yield of $40,000. But what if she needs $60,000 per year to live on? This would require the invasion of principal. Most clients have had it drilled into them to "never spend your principal." Although this is good advice in spirit, too literal an interpretation of the warning can result in poor investment decisions. A properly balanced portfolio maximizes the total return for a client subject to his or her volatility tolerance. If the income yield on the portfolio is less than what is needed for current expenditures, the client's first impulse is often to boost the portfolio yield by selling appreciation-oriented equity investments in order to buy more interest-generating investments. In our example, the client would have to move to a portfolio composed entirely of bonds in order to generate a current income yield sufficient for her needs. Ironically, if the client does this, she will subject herself to the very danger she was trying to avoid by not spending her principal. That is, the action to increase her income yield from 4 percent to 6 percent will be accompanied by a 3 percent reduction in total return, thereby increasing her exposure to purchasing power erosion!

The solution is to educate the client to think in terms of total return (yield plus capital appreciation) rather than income yield. Within a total return framework, clients gain an appreciation that it is better to spend a little principal to supplement the lower income yield from a portfolio with a higher total return than to choose a portfolio with a higher income yield but a lower total return.

TABLE 13-1

Components of Return

	Asset Mix 1	Asset Mix 2	Asset Mix 3
Bonds	100%	50%	0%
Stocks	0%	50%	100%
Total	100%	100%	100%
Asset mix yield	6%	4%	2%
Capital appreciation	0	5%	10%
Asset mix total return	6%	9%	12%

SUSTAINABLE PORTFOLIO WITHDRAWAL RATES

In Chapter 2 we discussed the plight of a 50-year old widow with $1 million invested in certificates of deposit. In a world with even modest levels of persistent inflation, the purchasing power of a portfolio can erode significantly over time if too much of its average total return is used to meet expenditures. Sometimes, clients respond by saying that they do not want to leave a huge portfolio to their survivors, and so periodic invasions of principal are acceptable to them. The problem with this is that even an intentional full liquidation of principal may not materially increase the cash available for meeting expenditures. For example, the widow with $1 million invested in certificates of deposit at 5 percent has an interest income of $50,000 per year. If instead of spending only the interest she systematically liquidates the principal over her 30-year life expectancy, her annual cash flow will increase only to approximately $65,000. This is of little help in an inflationary environment that will more than triple the cost of living over her remaining life expectancy.

Ideally, it would be advisable to maintain the purchasing power of the investment portfolio by limiting the portfolio withdrawals to a rate equal to the difference between the average total expected return and the average inflation rate. Table 13–2 shows the sustainable withdrawal rates for the three asset mixes of bonds and stocks previously discussed. These with-

TABLE 13–2

Sustainable Real Portfolio Withdrawal Rates

	Asset Mix 1	Asset Mix 2	Asset Mix 3
Bonds	100%	50%	0%
Stocks	0%	50%	100%
Total	100%	100%	100%
Asset mix total return	6%	9%	12%
(Inflation adjustment)	(4)	(4)	(4)
Withdrawal rate	2%	5%	8%

drawal rates are obviously quite modest in relation to the size of the portfolio, but they have one important characteristic: As the portfolio maintains its purchasing power by growing at a rate sufficient to offset inflation, the cash withdrawals from the portfolio can also be increased over time to keep pace with inflation.

In practice, many clients will be unable to limit their withdrawals to the level necessary to maintain portfolio purchasing power. But even a small portion of the total return left untouched to partially offset inflation will enhance the client's long-term financial security.

Conclusion

That's enough, Charlie. Don't show me any more figures; I've got the smell of the thing now.

—*Henry Ford (1863–1947)*
To Charles Sorenson, his lieutenant

Certainty generally is illusion, and repose is not the destiny of man.

—*Oliver Wendell Holmes, Jr. (1841–1935)*
The Path of the Law

The greatest gift is the power to estimate correctly the value of things.

—*Francois, Duc de La Rochefoucauld (1613–1680)*
Maximes, 1664

Money management is simple but not easy. It is simple because the principles of successful investing are relatively few in number and are easy to understand. Although all clients face a variety of risks in the management of their money, the two most important are inflation and volatility of returns. To the extent to which a portfolio is structured to avoid one of these risks, it unfortunately becomes exposed to the other. For this reason, clients must determine which risk is more dangerous to them. Time horizon is the relevant dimension along which this judgment is made. For short time horizons, volatility is a bigger risk than inflation, and such portfolios should accordingly follow an asset allocation strategy that gives greater weight to interest-generating investments with stable principal values. For long time horizons, inflation is the more significant danger, and these portfolios should therefore have larger allocations to equity investments. Regardless of the time horizon, however, the risk-mitigating benefits of broad diversification argue for the utilization of multiple asset classes for all clients regardless of volatility tolerance.

Because money management is simple, it is within the capacity of all clients to be meaningfully involved with the investment decision-making process. It is neither necessary nor advisable for a client to leave major investment decisions to the sole discretion of the investment advisor. It is the client's money, and he or she will have to live with the results. As a client becomes better educated regarding the money management process, his or her volatility tolerance will change toward that which is most appropriate given the facts of the situation. With greater understanding, better decisions will be made and the client will also benefit by having a realistic frame of reference for evaluating the results. This leads to greater equanimity and staying power, both of which are extremely important to the realization of investment objectives.

Although money management is simple, it is not easy. There are uncertainties inherent in the money management process that cannot be avoided, and these uncertainties are hard for clients to live with. It is natural to fear the unknown and want to reduce or eliminate uncertainty whenever possible. But as the past Federal Reserve Chairman Paul A. Volcker said at an Institute of Chartered Financial Analysts' conference: "You cannot hedge the world."

I toured Japan many years ago. Several people in our group wanted to see majestic Mount Fuji, and so a day trip by bus was organized. We were warned before we left that there was probably no better than a 50/50 chance of actually seeing the mountain peak due to poor visibility conditions typical during that time of year. When we arrived, Mount Fuji was nowhere in sight. Heavy fog and clouds blanketed the entire valley and mountain range. Having invested four hours by bus to get there, several people decided to take pictures anyway. Despite how carefully they focused their cameras, however, the fog would not go away. All they could do was get a sharper picture of the fog. So it is with money management. Clients often believe that as professional advisors, we should have some method to eliminate the uncertainties that are so difficult for them to live with. As we focus on the uncertainties inherent in money management, however, all we can hope to accomplish is to get a better picture of the uncertainties—we cannot eliminate them. As a friend of mine who is an economist once said: "The window to the future is opaque."

As difficult as it is to live with, uncertainty is not necessarily bad. For the client with a long time horizon, volatility is rewarded by the higher expected returns of equity investing. If we can teach our clients to understand this, they can use it to their advantage. There is a difference, though, between intellectually understanding something and living with the results on a day-to-day basis. Successful investing therefore will always be as much of a psychological process as it is a money management endeavor.

Money management is not easy, because without a very firm commitment to long-term investment policies within an asset allocation framework, it is easy for clients to be distracted by investment schemes that promise high returns with little or no risk. Those who depart from long-term strategy in order to pursue these investments will in the end build portfolios in the same way they collect shells at the beach, picking up whatever catches their eye at the moment. The bottom line is that there is no safe, quick, and easy way to build wealth. As an old saying reminds us: "If wishes were horses, beggars would ride."

Imagine that you are standing in the middle of a large group of slot machines at a Las Vegas casino. All around you, you can hear the sound of people winning as the jackpots from lucky pulls of the handle drop coins noisily into metal trays. Although it is always true that at any point in time there are those who are ahead of the game (and these people always stand out from the crowd), on average the flow of money is from the pockets of those who play the game to the casino that owns the machines. Objectively we know this, but in the midst of the magic of a casino, our excitement can override better judgment as we win just often enough to make us believe that we can get ahead by continuing to play. Fueling our hope for beating this system is the evidence of our senses, which tells us that other people are indeed winning—if only we can find a "hot" slot machine.

The messages our clients receive from the day-to-day investment environment can be as distracting and misleading as the sounds of intermittently winning slot machines. Whether it be a new market-timing guru or an investment idea that seems to promise better results than a well-diversified portfolio, there will always be temptations that encourage clients to depart from a well-conceived, long-term strategy. At times, adherence to long-term asset allocation decisions can seem dangerous, as we urge our clients during a bear market to allocate more money to common stocks in order to restore the proper balance in their portfolios. At other times, the equity commitment may become too great as a result of a market rise. To persuade clients to rebalance their portfolios back to target asset allocations in the midst of a bull market can sound like a parent telling a child that he has to leave a party just when everybody really starts to have fun. These difficulties are another reason why money management is not easy.

Historically, the money manager's job has been to enhance return and minimize risk by exercising superior skill in security selection and/or market timing. Success has been measured in terms of whether the manager has "beaten the market." The engine driving portfolio performance was presumed to be the superior talent of the manager; little attention was paid to the asset allocation decisions. Today, the capital markets are highly efficient and it is dangerous to presume that superior skill can be safely relied on as the primary determinant of a portfolio's performance. If future performance results will be determined primarily by the asset allocation decisions made in the management of the portfolios, it should be at the asset allocation level of decision making that investment advisors and their clients address issues of risk and return. This implies that investment portfolio design and performance expectations should be based primarily on the risk/return characteristics of the capital markets themselves rather than on the often elusive positive impact of active management. We would do well to follow the advice of R. Buckminster Fuller, creator of the Geodesic Dome, who said: "Use forces; don't fight them."

If money management is simple but not easy, what are the implications of this for the investment advisory profession? Because it is simple, advisors have a tremendous opportunity to add value for clients by properly educating them. Knowledgeable clients will more likely choose and remain committed to those strategies that are most appropriate for realizing their objectives. In addition to being educators, we must also be architects and general contractors, designing and implementing broadly diversified investment strategies that we create in collaboration with our clients. Because money management is not easy, we will have important work to do on an ongoing basis. As the capital markets move, our services will be needed to provide perspective to our clients regarding their investment experience. Particularly during extreme market conditions, clients may need the discipline and assurance of a steady hand that urges them to remain committed to their long-term strategies. We have witnessed many changes in the world capital markets over the past several decades. More changes will undoubtedly occur in the future. In this evolving investment environment, clients do not need sporadic investment suggestions. They need and will value the comprehensive management of their portfolios by knowledgeable investment professionals committed to their financial well-being.

INDEX

Note: The *n.* after a page number refers to a note.

Active approach (broad portfolio balance level of decision making), 260–262
Active asset allocation, 277–279
Active security selection, 11
Advisors:
  advisor-client mismatch, 19–20, 221
  client expectations, 199
  computer optimization programs, 197
  fees, 272–273
  gather client data, 201–204
  identify client needs/constraints, 204–209
  money management process (*see* Money management process)
  pension/profit-sharing plans, 269
  role, 306–307
  same allocation for all clients, 254
  (*See also* Money managers)
Anwar-i-Suhaili, 73
Appreciated assets, 294–295
Arbitrage pricing theory, 150
Aristotle, 80
Arithmetic difference, 66
Arithmetic mean, 55, 65
Asset allocation:
  active approach, 277–279
  bad allocation, 177
  changing views of, 5–6
  efficient frontier, and, 134
  good allocation, 177
  importance, 12
  interest-generating investments vs. equity investments, 108
  market timing, 11–12, 14
  minimum percentage commitments, 251
  optimization program (*see* Portfolio optimization)
  passive approach, 275–276
  process, 247–263, 298

Asset class mispricing, 11
Asset classes, 10, 248

Bear market, 34, 75–76, 79
Benchmarks, 275
Beta, 148
Bogle, John C., 262–263
Bond duration, 49–51
Bonds:
  corporate (*see* Long-term corporate bonds)
  coupon rate, 28
  creditworthiness, 31
  current yield, 29
  domestic, 259
  duration, 49–51
  government (*see* Intermediate-term government bonds, Long-term government bonds)
  interest rate risk, 28
  interest-rate-risk sensitivity, 29–31, 49
  international, 152–154, 251
  market price, 28
  par value (face value), 28
  tax status, 31
  yield to maturity, 29
Breadth/degree of portfolio diversification, 225–245
Broad portfolio diversification (*see* Multiple-asset-class investing)
Bull market, 75–76, 79
Bullion coins, 253
Business cycle analysis, 277
Buy and hold strategy, 11, 276
Buy low, sell high, 276–277

Canadian Gold Maple Leaf, 253
Capital appreciation index, 32

ABOUT THE AUTHOR

Roger C. Gibson, CFA, CFP, is a nationally recognized expert in asset allocations and investment portfolio design. The president of Gibson Capital Management, a leading provider of money management services for high net worth individuals, he was named by both *Money* and *Worth* as one of America's top financial advisors. Gibson is a member of the editorial board of the *Journal of Financial Planning* and is frequently interviewed by publications including *The Wall Street Journal, Forbes, Money, Fortune, The New York Times,* and *U.S. News &x World Report.* He is also codirector and founder of the Center for Fiduciary Studies, a research and training organization that operates in association with the Katz Graduate School of Business at the University of Pittsburgh.